teapotONE

"LIVE YOUR LIFE"

[signature]

BRUCESMART

ISBN 978-0-9932901-0-7

© Copyright 2015 Bruce Smart. Published by Bruce Smart. All text, images and layout by Bruce Smart. All rights reserved.

Many thanks to Christine Watts, Martin McDonald, & Nikki Bradford for proof reading.

See www.teapotone.com for more information on this trip and YouTube channel 'teapotonevids' for the accompanying video series.

DVD "LIVE your life" also available, see website for details.

All rights reserved. No part of this publication may be reproduced, stored in a retrieval system, or transmitted in any form or by any means, electronic, mechanical, photocopying, recording or otherwise, without the prior permission of the copyright owner.

ACKNOWLEDGEMENTS

The following companies all supported the trip, either financially or through kit donation. I can't thank you enough for your support.

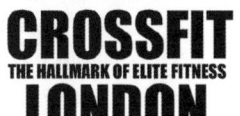

Simon Wheatcroft AKA 'Black Rider'

The following individuals kept the dream alive by keeping my fuel tank full, pre-ordering copies of this book and accompanying DVD, or buying t-shirts, wristbands and lanyards. Folks your support meant the world, allowing me to complete the journey and keep a promise. I'll never be able to repay any of you, but I hope you enjoy reading this book and reliving the memories of our journey. Thank you to each and every one of you.

Bruce.

123web.ca
Adam Ellis
Adam Pugh
Adam Shaw
Adam Thomas
Aiveen McManus
Alan Beeden
Alan Pattison
Alex Shelton
Alistair Scott
Amelie Ryan
Andrew Geer
Andrew Scobie
Andrew Wilkinson
Andy & Caroline Wood
Andy Buckley
Andy Chalmers
Andy Reynolds
Andy Wilson
Anonymous
Ashley Davies
Ashley Kean
Boastie
Bonnie Scholz
Bonome Ben
Brian Jones
Brian Mair
Brian McConnell
BritKit LLC
Bryan O'lynn
Cameron Sutherland
Carl Bradbury

Charles Audenaert
Chris & Jessie Blackhall
Christopher Forster
Chris Johnson
Chris Sandison
Chris Warburton
Claude Abegglen
Colin Burrows
Colin Edwards (Snr)
Colin Menniss
Colin Williams
Connor Robertson
Craig Johnson
Craig McCarthy
Craig Stratford
Craig Wilson
Cynthia Reed
Daan de Jong
Damien Knight
Dan Phillips
Daniel Houlton
Dave Carrick
Dave Newbold
Dave Spooner
Dave Thomson
Dave Varela
Dave Watret
David Laudermilch
David McClure
David Waite
Dillan Perras
Dominic Simmons

Doug Gunn
Doug Smart
Duncan Askew
Duncan Fenwick
Duncan Hutchison
Eddie Wilson
Edgars Barons
Edgaras Kitkovskis
Emil Bang Larsen
Emma Spooner
Faye Cartwright
Fergus Campbell
Frank Teeuwen
Gary Sankey
Geoff Grimmett
Gerald Flood
Gillian Kerr
Glenn Bridgeman
Graeme Hood
Graeme Shnnie
Graham Key
Giulio Leone
Harry Smart
Hector Smart
Hugh Patience
Ian Blaiklock
Ian Cockburn
Ian Lindsay
Ian Maley
Ian Turner
James Buntjer
James Molineux

James Palmer
James Nesbitt
Jamie Bassett
Janet Bradford
Jarek Malonowski
Joanne Bartholomew
Joanne Hourcastagne
Jody Carson
Joe Baker
Johnathan Hofstra
Jonathan Burns
Jonny Mickleboro
Josh Hoole
Justin Joyce
Kathryn Murchison
Kelvin Prevett
Ken Dickson
Kevin Burr
Kevin McShane
Kevin Rushforth
Laura Edwards
Laura Smart
Leanne Banks
Lee Shaw
Lee Weaver
Leigh Brownsmith
Leigh Burch
Liam Smith
Lim Wei Liang
Linda McFarlane
Lolly Smart
Luc Van Parys
Lyle Cairns
Maggie Smart
Mal Bone
Margaret Chilton
Mark 'Laptop' Vosper
Mark & Petrina Turner
Mark Stead
Mark Stewart
Mark Walsh
Martin McDonald
Martina Swainson
Masie Burley
Mat Watkin
Matt Carter
Matt Chaters
Michelle Pryal
Mike Harrison
Miklos Nagy
Nathan Rowe
Neil Pow
Nicholas Helsby
Nick Munt
Nikki Bradford
Norman Easter
Paddy Munro
Pamela Logan
Patricia Masters
Patrick Kraus
Paul Harbour
Paul Jones
Paul Stein
Paul Wardle-Millar
Peter Piegl
Phil Krix
Philip Cope
Philip Wilde
Rebecca Kennedy
Ricci Giff
Rich Vines
Richard Farquharson
Richard Harper
Richard Harris
Richard Kingston
Richard Loveys
Rob Brookes
Rob Loveys
Robbie Banks
Robert Dean
Robert Macaulay
Robin Carr
Robin Mansell
Rodney Scott
Roman Damaschin
Roy Thain
Samantha McCaig
Sarah Jacob
Scott Haliburton
Scott Halman
Sean Crosby
Sean May
Shane Jasprizza
Shaun Venner
Shirlee McCourty
Shona Corner
Simon Brown
Simon Cooper
Simon Godden
Simon Holt
Simon Kennedy
Simon Wood
Stefan Berendijk
Stefan Meckelburg
Stephen Henning
Stephen Hepple
Stephen Rutter
Steve Hamilton
Steve Harries
Steve Middleton Solutions
Stoklosa Sebastian
Stuart Dobson
Stuart McCourty
Sunnyside Productions
Tam Reid
Terry Scroggie
Terry Unwin
The Cruickshanks
The Fennellys

The Muir Clan
The Pickups
The Turners
The Wades
The Wandering Waltons
The Watts
Thomas Hailand
Thomasina Smoor
Tiga-Rose Nercessian

Tim Hull
Tim Poat
Tim Watson
Tim Wilcox
Tom Kurvits
Tom Rayner Larsen
Tony Galbraith
Trevor Seaton
Walshy & Lou

White Rose Armoury
Wilks Clan
William Baxter
William Smart
Wim Cleys
www.2wtt.org

For Mum, Nikki & Ellis.

FOREWORD

Stories of achievers sometimes provide a roadmap for others' personal quests. The story of Bruce Smart may do just that for you.

Bruce was inspired by his late mother to fulfill his dream to ride a motorbike around the world. Following 3 years of hard work and preparation, he left London in October 2012 on his Suzuki sports bike to travel 100,000 miles, through more than 80 countries, on an extraordinary journey which was planned to take 18 months. In doing so, he collected money for worthy charities along the way. Before the end of that year, after travelling 9,000 grueling miles through 14 countries, the project came to an abrupt end after crossing the Sahara Desert.

Lessons were learned, and 2012 was spent reassessing, reorganising and encouraging others to support his ambition. A new route was planned and additional sponsors were engaged. Undeterred by the considerable obstacles that he faced, Bruce set off from London once again in May 2013, and reached his goal 14 months later.

This story chronicles Bruce's adventures on his epic journey, during which the kindness of others enabled him to overcome great hardship. The overwhelming legacy of the journey is the friendship of the people whom he met along the way.

I am proud to have been asked to contribute this foreword and for our company to have been a sponsor of Teapot One. Bruce Smart is an achiever in the true sense of the word.

Bob Iles
CEO
Delta Energy Services

'LIVE YOUR LIFE'... the story of TeapotOne
INTRODUCTION

Lying in the hot Sahara sand, the urge to just close my eyes and drift away was overpowering. The bike's back was broken, I'd been robbed umpteen times already that day, my food and water gone. I was in no pain, but my ears screamed into my brain, my body gagging for hydration. As I shut my eyes I saw my Nikki and my son Ellis, then the words of my dear old mum popped right to the forefront of my mind.

"Look after those you love, but LIVE your life."

Whose bloody idea was this then…..?

www.teapotone.com

**54 countries
442 days
74,000 miles**

Contents

1	Inception	19
2	**Preparation**	23
2.1	The Bike	24
2.2	The Personal Life	25
2.3	My Patron	26
2.4	Sponsorship	28
2.5	All Wrapped Up & Ready To Go	31
2.5.1	The Bike Wrap	31
2.5.2	The Lid	32
2.6	The Carnet	32
2.7	The Kit	35
3	**The Trip: Launch Day & We're Off!!**	41
4	**France & Into Europe**	45
5	**Italy & Beyond**	61
6	**Spain & The N260**	69
7	**Portugal**	73
8	**Jerez & The Road of Bones**	75
9	**Gibraltar the Frontier**	79
10	**Africa**	83
10.1	The Atlas Mountains	86
10.2	Ait Benhaddou to Agadir	86
11	**From Dream to Nightmare**	91
12	**Mauritania**	99
13	**We're Off Again**	119
14	**UK to the Arctic Circle**	129
15	**Norway**	133
16	**Transfagarasan Highway & On To Russia**	151
17	**Russia**	163
18	**South Korea & Japan**	201

19	**Thailand, Malaysia & Laos**	233
19.1	- Day 135: The Myanmar Border	236
19.2	- Day 156: motoGP at Sepang, Malaysia	242
19.3	- Day 160: Back to Thailand	244
19.4	- Day 170: Plain of Jars, Laos	254
19.5	- Day 179: Return to Malaysia	262
20	**Indonesia & East Timor**	267
20.1	- Day 185: Medan, Indonesia	267
20.2	- Days 194-197: Jakarta	274
20.3	Java	276
20.4	- Days 201-205: Bali	278
20.5	The Journey Through the Isles	280
20.6	- Day 211: Aimere, Ferry to Kupang, Flores	285
21	**Australia**	293
21.1	- Day 225: Quarantine Day!	294
21.2	- Day 229: Christmas Eve, out into the bush	299
21.3	- Day 235: The Glasshouse Mountains	305
21.4	2014 Let's be 'avin ya!	307
21.5	- Day 242: Adelaide to Port Fairy	311
21.6	- Day 243: The Great Ocean Road	312
21.7	Sydney	317
22	**South America**	
	Day 254 - Arrival in Santiago, Chile	323
22.1	- Shipping	325
22.2	- Hitting the Pan American Highway	325
22.3	- Peru	327
22.4	- Columbia	329
22.5	- Columbia to Panama Shipping	330
22.6	- Panama, Day 276	331
23	**Central America**	333
23.1	Costa Rica	334
23.2	- Day 287: Mexico	337
24	**USA! USA! USA! - 26th February 2014**	345
24.1	Getting the Beast into the USA	345
24.2	- Day 296: The Alamo	349
24.3	- Day 297: The Texas Tornado	350
24.4	- Day 305: Getting my Kicks!	352

24.5	The Grand Canyon	352
24.6	- Day 311: Dallas to Houston	354
24.7	Barber Motorsports Museum, Georgia & 'The Dragon's Tail'	357
24.8	- Day 330: On to Daytona, Florida & Beyond	360
24.9	- Day 341: Heading North & New Adventures	361
25	**Canada**	
	Day 357	365
26	Ireland, Isle of Man TT, & Home	371
26.1	- Day 383: Dublin, Ireland Country #54	371
26.2	- Cavan, Ireland	374
26.3	- Day 387: Northern Ireland	375
26.4	The Giants' Causeway	375
26.5	- Day 389: The Isle of Man TT	376
26.6	- Day 396: Marco Simoncelli Tribute Ride	380
27	**England, Heading Home**	383

Appendix
   My Life in Pictures   387

CHAPTER 1
INCEPTION

Back in 2008 I didn't even ride a motorbike, I'd never done anything more adventurous than move from the north east of Scotland, to the bright lights of London to join the Old Bill. But motorbikes, riding a motorbike, now that took me longer to discover, but a mere second to fall in love with.

The catalyst for this was my dear old mum. She'd been diagnosed with cancer in 1999, went through all the treatment, had a double mastectomy, hysterectomy, and got the all clear. My parents had worked hard all their lives to give my older brother Doug and I the home and childhood many could only dream of. I can't and won't complain, we had it made as kids. Don't get me wrong we weren't spoilt brats, but we wanted for nothing and were loved the way all kids should feel loved by their folks.

So on the 2nd of August 2004 my folks emigrated to Spain to start their new lives in the sun, Christ they deserved a break for once. But mum's cancer came back on more than one occasion and she hit it with the vigour and strength I had come to admire her for. That woman was as strong as an Ox, a veritable bedrock of strength to rely on even with what she was going through and I'll always love her dearly. During her last year my mum became very at one with herself and life around her. I'd moved her back to live with me in Bromley, South East London whilst she went through yet another course of treatment (my dad worked in South Korea). We'd often chat about things, any things, and I remember watching Ewan McGregor & Charlie Boorman's 'Long Way Round' on one of the daily repeated channels on TV, moaning to her that I wished I could do something like that. I'll never forget her response as I've tried to live by it ever since. She said, "Never have regrets

Bruce SMART

about life, take care of those you love, and make everyday count. Live YOUR life." So within a week I'd booked my motorbike course (DAS).

By the time I passed she'd admitted herself to a local end of life hospice, St Christopher's in Penge, South East London. She knew the end was near and bless her cotton socks, she didn't want to pass away in my flat, a measure of the incredible and strong woman she was. I arrived on a brand new GSXR-600 in full leather clobber to see the grin and look of pride on her face as I walked into her ward. She held my hand and made me promise I'd live my dream to ride around the world. Her battle came to an end 5 days later on the 23rd of July 2008. I miss her dearly.

So that was that, the seed was now sewn, the promise made, I just had to figure out how and when I'd do it. Over the next year or so I kind of let it slip, like everyone else I just assumed I'd do the trip once I retired. I couldn't go just now, I had a mortgage, I had a job, I had a son….. I couldn't afford it!

I'd had a wee episode at work where a fine figure of the community had decided to pull a gun on me. I'd literally stared down the barrel of a loaded gun and heard it go click as the round misfired. That kind of scenario certainly makes you reflect on life, and it played on my mind constantly as I waded through day to day life over the months and years ahead.

One night I found myself out for a curry and a few beers with my good mates Woody, Turner and Boastie. As the beers slid down I began to tell the lads about my dream to ride the world and the promise I'd made my mum. I'd expected them to tell me to grow up, think it was just another crazy 'Bruce' idea and talk me out of it. Maybe it was the 'Tiger' beer, maybe it was just lads together, but to a man, each of the lads just told me to go for it. I was going around the world! Bollocks.

CHAPTER 2
PREPARATION

I began to seriously plan the trip in 2010, contacting St Christopher's to tell them what I was going to do and asking if they'd support me as my charity. Through my good mate Russ I also had a contact with the Born Free foundation, so they naturally also became a beneficiary of the trip.

Next came Riders for Health, the official charity of the motoGP. I was going to ride around the world on a sportsbike, more about this choice later, so it made sense to me to visit all the motoGP circuits as I travelled around the world. Naively I thought they may take an interest in the trip, even let me in to see the circuits or ride a lap or two. At the very least I thought they'd help promote the trip through their social media, but alas I got absolutely nothing from the circuits themselves, only what I managed to blag on the day.

Rider's (Riders for Health) initially jumped at the chance to be one of TeapotOne's beneficiaries and all was going well. Russ and I had gone to their Northampton HQ and met with their marketing and fundraising team. We'd been invited to the 'Day of Champion's' event at the Silverstone round of the motoGP. I was going to get interviewed on stage in front of a crowd of thousands. We had hit the big time and we weren't looking back. But then came the killer blow.

I'd contacted the motoGP several times via email to let them know what I was planning, but had never had a reply. I'd put a small banner ad on my website to advertise 'TeapotOne' and in it I'd used the motoGP logo to illustrate the connection to Rider's for Health and the fact I'd planned on riding around each of the motoGP tracks as I travelled the globe. In early January 2011 I received an email from a chap called Sergio Mathias who stated he was a solicitor for a company called 'Dorna', the holding company of the motoGP. In this email he stated it had come to their attention that I'd used the motoGP logo to 'Promote a product or service'. They instructed me to remove the logo or face legal action. I emailed him straight back apologising for any offence caused and assuring him that none was intended. I told him about TeapotOne, the connection with Riders' For Health and the fact I was planning on riding each of the tracks, all to raise money for charity. I also told him I was to be interviewed on stage at that year's Day of Champions event, and that I would gladly state that the motoGP was not affiliated to, or indeed backed, TeapotOne – if that was their wish. It seems they took offence to this.

I never got a reply from Mr Mathias, but I was contacted by Andrea Coleman, the co-founder of Riders' for Health. She thanked me for choosing them as one of my charities and thanked me for attending their HQ. However she also told me that Riders' could no longer act as one of my beneficiaries due to recent events. She stated they'd been contacted by the motoGP and that they were unhappy with my reply to their email. They were also unhappy that I was to be interviewed on stage at the Day of Champions and would have the opportunity to be negative about them in any way! So like that, Riders' For Health was wiped from the TeapotOne table, along with all the exposure and contacts it would bring.

2.1: The Bike

My good mate Russ worked tirelessly with me throughout the years of planning that led up to the trip. We'd obtained our first Corporate Sponsor in the form of MD-Racing. They are a motorcycle garage based in the South East of England, owned and run by a chap called Mike Dawson. Mike had been a chief technician with Ducati UK for many years. He heard about the trip through Russ and jumped at the chance to get on-board.

Following a short meeting over a coffee, Mike immediately stated he would supply and custom build the bike for the trip, but that it would have to be a Ducati! A DUCATI!! Despite my dream of doing the trip on a 'Gixxer', I couldn't turn down the offer of a custom built, fully serviced and supported package! So Mike went and sourced a 2005 Multistrada with only 2,600 miles on the clock. She was gorgeous and absolutely mint.

He set to work hard-wiring her throughout, changing the cans, fitting swanky 'Touratech' hard panniers, and generally turning her into a bomb-proof work horse. But when the news struck that Rider's For Health were pulling out, he decided that he too would have to call it quits. When they were on-board, he was willing to devote the time and expense to the project believing that the exposure through Rider's would reap his rewards. Without that, it was just going to be too much of a commitment, and so both MD-Racing and the bike were gone.

To be honest, and I don't want to sound like a spoilt brat here, I was actually relieved when MD pulled out. Since we had had the custom bike, I didn't have the same passion and enthusiasm for the trip. I'd lived and breathed 'TeapotOne', envisaged me riding and dragging a Suzuki GSX-R 1000 all around the world, through desert, rock, mud, jungle and track. The very fact it wasn't supposed to be able to do this type of journey was what appealed to me. I knew I'd get her through it and she'd return my loyalty. I KNEW my Gixxer would get me around the world. I knew it. And I just couldn't wait to get started, bring it on.

2.2: The Personal Life

And then there's me. Well, for years my mantra had been, "Stay single, Stay Strong!" To say I was bitter about the fairer sex would be like saying Hitler could be a tad intolerable. "Snakes with tits!"

When I came up with the idea of this project the only person I had to take into account was my son. I'd spoken with him about the trip and he was fully behind me. He knew it meant I wouldn't see him for about a year or so but he thought it was a brilliant thing to do. My son Ellis is truly incredible. He's my son but he's also my friend. We have a brilliant relationship despite only getting to see each other a handful of times a year. I speak to him a couple of times a month by phone and he'd spend time with me during his holidays. We've toured Scotland, France, Germany, Austria and Belgium on the bike and he loved it. Well he did until he got too big for the gixxer, so for now I think his touring days are over until he gets his own beast.

But now someone else had come into my world. Someone else had become my world. I've no idea how it happened but it did. Bang, wallop, almost in an instant she was there, part of my life and almost straight away I couldn't see a future without her?

Nikki is a fellow copper, a plonk, who works with me in the Diplomatic Protection Group – not famous for its plentiful supply of women, never mind beautiful ones, but I seemed to have acquired a rose. She's incredible and I love her completely. The thought of being away from her for so long made me feel sick, but the thought of not doing the trip was like a death sentence to me, simply not worth even contemplating. She'd toured the world, been there, done that, been about a bit(?) She knew right from the start that I would be going away on the trip and wouldn't dream of standing in its way, for that I love her dearly.

She would be coming out to visit me at various points throughout the trip and I couldn't wait to experience some of this adventure with her by my side. However it was weird to now have this added element. Prior to Nikki coming into my life, this trip was my life, my entire focus and being. I could see as far as the trip itself and then what would be, would be. If it took 5yrs then it took 5yrs. If I decided that I didn't want to stop then I wouldn't stop. The world was indeed my lobster and I wanted a good table!

But now I was well aware that I'd leave someone behind when I finally departed, someone whom I'd have a future with, and would need to get back home to start that future. Don't get me wrong, I was doing the trip, all 100,000 miles plus of it in all its' glory and all its' magnitude. I know I keep saying this, but I just couldn't wait to set off and finally become this adventure!

2.3 My Patron

I'd started a bit of a diary during the initial years of preparation, but as ever I'd update it very intermittently. I've based a lot of the early stages of this book on what I wrote and I feel this next bit should simply be lifted straight from that.

18th November 2011

So what's new with TeapotOne?

We now have an official patron in the form of PC David Rathband. David was the PC who was shot in the face by Raoul Moat in July 2010. Although going through some tough times in his own personal life at the moment….

(I never did finish writing the above paragraph, things always got in the way and I never got around to doing it. Unfortunately, before I did get round to it, the following tragic events occurred.)

1st March 2012 - Good Night PC Rathband, Sleep Well Brother

It is with the heaviest of hearts that I announce the passing of TeapotOne's patron, PC David Rathband. David was found by officers from Northumbria police at his home in Blyth yesterday, 29th February 2012 at approx 7pm and pronounced deceased at the scene.

After being shot in the face by Raoul Moat in July 2010, David had been left completely blind. He founded the charity, 'The Blue Lamp Foundation' to help emergency service workers who found themselves injured through criminal acts, such as he was. He fundraised tirelessly bringing it's work into the public eye and was a symbol of the courage and professionalism our police family should all strive to befit.

This is the very reason I asked David to be the TeapotOne patron and I was incredibly honoured when he said yes. Although I never got to meet him face to face, we spoke via phone, emails and texts and he seemed every bit the man I took him to be.

My heart goes out to Kath, Ash & Mia, his brother Darren, his family and colleagues.

The Final Inspection
The policeman stood and faced his God, Which must always come to pass.
He hoped his shoes were shining. Just as brightly as his brass.
"Step foreword now, policeman. How shall I deal with you?
Have you always turned the other cheek? To My church have you been true?"

The policeman squared his shoulders and said, "No, Lord, I guess I aint,

Because those of us who carry badges can't always be a saint.

I've had to work most Sundays, and at times my talk was rough,

and sometimes I've been violent, Because the streets are awfully tough.

But I never took a penny, That wasn't mine to keep. Though I worked a lot of overtime when the bills got just too steep.

And I never passed a cry for help, Though at times I shook with fear.

And sometimes, God forgive me, I've wept unmanly tears.

I know I don't deserve a place, Among the people here.

They never wanted me around except to calm their fear.

If you've a place for me here, Lord, It needn't be so grand. I never expected or had too much, but if you don't…I'll understand.

There was silence all around the throne Where the saints had often trod.

As the policeman waited quietly, For the judgment of his God.

"Step foreword now, policeman, You've borne your burdens well

Come walk a beat on Heaven's streets, You've done your time in hell."

PC David Rathband 1968-2012, Sleep Well Brother.

2.4 Sponsorship

When I started planning I imagined I'd get corporate sponsorship to cover a large part of the trip running costs. After all, why wouldn't they want to be involved. I was a member of the Prime Minister's illustrious Diplomatic Protection Group, riding a sports bike around the world for charity, to keep a promise he made to his dying mum, a distance never completed on a motorbike of that kind in that timescale before. One of my charities, 'The Children's Trust' were even familiar to the Prime Minister as his family had used their incredible services during their son's last year. Alas, I didn't even get a reply to the letter and emails I sent them. Naivety is a wonderful thing eh.

For nearly three years I tried every angle I could think of, cold calling, emails, letters, Facebook, Twitter, LinkedIn, website contact forms, even turning up in person at HQ's, events and some shows. Time after time I got the same response, "We've already allocated our charity funding for the years ahead", or "Ewan McGregor's already done that" were the favourites. There were, and still are literally hundreds of people a week contacting companies trying to get sponsorship for one idea after another, it's a tough old game.

I tried everything, explaining that I'd be doing it on a sports bike, it was for charity, telling them the back story, the magnitude of the route in the time allocated, but trying to get any finances from them was like getting blood out a stone.

There were a few exceptions. Vango are a Scottish outdoors company specialising in tents and camping equipment. They basically gave me their catalogue and said 'fill your boots'! Over the last year of planning, a few others came onboard. Garmin provided their Zumo 660 and all maps in their range, R&G provided some crash protection, Pipewerx an exhaust, Shoei provided their XR1000 midrange lid, SiDi gave their excellent Goretex sports boots, Spada provided a rain suit and gloves, and Kriega gave me free range to use their entire kit!

Although not finances, these donations were a huge help as it meant I didn't need to outlay my own money for the kit, but I was still a long way short of my calculated trip fund of about £35,000. I'd worked out my budget for the entire 18 month period, including food, fuel, some accommodation, shipping, visas etc. However I'd forgotten to recalculate this, as I'd expected the servicing, parts, tyres etc to be covered by corporate means, in reality the final figure ended up being significantly more!

I'd gone to the NEC bike show in 2011 and done the rounds with all the manufacturers and stalls. Through this I met a chap called Luigi on the Bridgestone stand. I remember giving him my sales pitch, something I'd done literally a thousand times before, watching his eyes begin to glaze and wander the surroundings, I thought there wasn't a chance in hell of getting anywhere with this. Like the gent he is, Luigi entertained me for the duration and we got on to talking about bikes and biking in general. I left there thinking that at the very least I'd actually talked to someone who was genuinely interested in what I had planned, but I didn't hold out much luck for Bridgestone's involvement.

Bruce SMART

How wrong can you be. A few months later I had Bridgestone as the official trip tyre supplier with unlimited tyres (where available) for the whole journey. Luigi's support throughout the trip was exceptional, the only one of the initial 'sponsors' to actually keep in touch, offer any help and show an interest in the project as a whole. In fact he's become a very good friend, top bloke.

Around the same time I also got a phone call from 'Fast Bikes Magazine' who ended up being my media partner. Through them I got to write a monthly article on the trip, giving a further PR vehicle for existing and potential sponsors, but also spreading the potential audience far wider across the globe. Without 'Fast Bikes' involvement I doubt I'd have got the following I did, I couldn't (and still can't) believe that's my ugly mug in the mag when I read those issues!

With only months to go before the off, I still had nowhere near the finances I'd need to do the trip. I'd already remortgaged to pay off debts and buy my bike (the Beast), so was struggling to fund it. I remembered watching that years Isle of Man TT and seeing one of the bikes with a load of names all over his fairings, of people who had contributed to funding his racing. It struck me that I could do the same here.

So, I created a 'crowd funding' site where people could donate £100 and get their name on the bike. For £200 they could get a company logo, or any picture within reason, on the bike and on the website, then set about PR'ing through my social media. It raised a couple of grand, so by the time I actually left I had just over £8K in the trip fund, hmm could be interesting!

Then there was Suzuki themselves. I chatted with one of their marketing team at the NEC wayback in 2010. Initially a stone blank no, when I mentioned that I wasn't after a bike as I'd be buying one anyway, but rather I was after some support in the way of servicing etc, their attitude changed. I was told that if I went away and got the bike, then they'd be prepared to offer a global servicing package, happy Days! It didn't happen, I bought a new Gixxer 1000 and Suzuki promptly told me they wouldn't be involved in any way? I tried many times over the next few years, emailing their PR chap Luke Plummer on several occasions, trying to let him know I wasn't just another flash in the pan, I WAS going to do this and I wanted Suzuki to be involved as I loved the bike and loved the brand.

It came to a head when I met Luke in person at one of the Horizon Unlimited HUBB meets in the UK in 2012. I rocked up to give a presentation on planning a trip like this, and whilst there I saw Suzuki had a big stand as they were launching their latest VStrom model. Walking up I introduced myself, explaining who I was and what I was going to be doing. At that point a chap turned around and looked me up and down, telling me he knew who I was and said I'd been bombarding him with emails? He then laughed in my face saying, "the bike won't do it, because YOU won't do it". I could've punched the prat in the face, and I hope he's reading this. This could've been one of the greatest pieces of marketing Suzuki could ask for, but they lost it because of one persons attitude.

2.5 All Wrapped Up & Ready To Go

To say I was excited would be like saying I'm a little on the lardy side! Under the help and expert guidance of Amanda Wooders at TravCour (www.travcour.com), visas were well under way and several already granted. With many more still in the queue ready to present themselves at embassies and consulates all over London & Europe, I was a long way from easy street, but the first steps had certainly been taken. There were a few tricky ones amongst them, most notably China and Saudi, and as it turned out, they weren't needed in the end anyway!

2.5.1 The Bike Wrap

I'm lucky to have an incredibly talented mate called Simon Clare who draws pictures for a living. His portfolio includes work for Disney, Warner Bros, Pixar, Looney Tunes, BBC, BMW & Coca Cola, and now 'TeapotOne' to name but a few! Si came up with the conceptual design for the bike wrap, and when I asked if he could incorporate everyone's names into the main fairing logo, I think he was just about ready to knock me out! I'm sure Si has found himself pushed to his very limits within his role as 'Chief Illustrator' here at 'TeapotOne'. He was responsible for my logo and merchandise designs, if you don't like them….. it's HIS fault! You can view his website portfolio at www.contact-me.net/

Bruce SMART

simonclare

So once Simon had come up with the conceptual design, it was over to Mark Lumsdon of Thunderline Designs (07860 709236 or mail@thunderline.co.uk) to actually wrap the bike itself. Mark has a long established reputation for quality work and an attention to detail that's second to none. Anyone in and around London during the Olympics is bound to have seen his work as he was part of the team who wrapped all the BMW's used for the games. He also frequently does work for Dobles of Coulsdon, the South's busiest Honda motorcycle dealership. But he'd never actually wrapped a whole bike before, until he met me!

I think you'll agree he did an incredible job. With only a matter of days to get everything printed out, put on the bike and ready to go for an impending photoshoot, Mark worked around the clock. Literally actually, starting at 2pm on the Tuesday and finishing at 6:30AM on the Wednesday morning!

2.5.2 The Lid

Well it wasn't just the beast that'd been getting a makeover. A lad called Lee Fareham of D-ZignUK.com does custom paint-jobs on helmets, so I dropped Lee a line. Less than 4 weeks later I had a spanking new scheme which looks stunning.

2.6 The Carnet

The biggest issue I faced in the build up to the trip was the Carnet de Passage. For those not in the know, the carnet is a bit of paperwork which is required in certain countries around the globe in order to take high value bits of equipment into and out of those countries. Effectively it's put in place to stop people buying a bit of kit, in my case a motorbike, which is worth X-amount in my home country, and then taking it to another country where it is worth 6X-amount, selling it and pocketing the tax due to my home country. Loads more info about them can be found on the RAC website at (www.rac.co.uk/travel/driving-abroad/carnet-de-passage/)

I could bore you for hours regarding the saga I had getting mine, but in a nutshell it went like this. 3yrs ago right at the onset of my preparation for the trip, I contacted the RAC (they are the carnet issuing authority in the UK) to get advice on cost and application schedules. I spoke with a great guy called Paul Gowen who was 'Mr Carnet' here in the UK. He was very helpful and knowledgable, listened to everything about TeapotOne, and advised me that I'd qualify for special discounts due to the nature of the trip. As my route would be taking in Egypt, which has the highest risk factor in carnet terms, I would be liable for 8 times the value of my goods during the first 12 month period of travel. As my bike was worth £10K, that was an £80K risk!! However with the discounts, I was told I'd need to pay a one-off fee of around £1,900 for the 1st 12 months, then a significantly lower fee for the 2nd 12months. Paul told me he'd be in touch in June of 2012 and that was that.

Well June came and went and there was no sign of the RAC, so I gave them a bell. This is where it got interesting as Paul no longer worked for them. The helpful staff told me they'd updated their systems and everything was done online now so just fill it all in and they'd get back to me in a matter of weeks.

July flew by and soon it was the start of August. I was getting nervous as I knew I'd have to start visa applications in a few weeks and I'd need the carnet for these, so I gave the RAC a bell again. Good job I did really as they were just working out my premium, and guess what? It was now at the £80K mark!! I explained once again what I was doing and that I'd been told I qualified for the discounts, only to be told that the RAC no longer offered these discounts and I would have to either stump up the £80K myself, get a business or bank to guarantee it, or I could go down the insurance premium route and I could pay £8K, with a view to getting £4K back when I returned!

To say I was a tad excitable by this point would be a slight understatement and I have to admit, my time in Glasgow wasn't wasted as some of the more colourful character traits came to the fore in a 5 minute tirade, aimed at nobody in particular! I couldn't believe they were doing this, not now, not when I was so close, not after I'd checked almost 3yrs previously to make sure I wouldn't be in this situation! No. NO. NO! I'll squeam and squeam and squeam, until I'm sick.

Anyhoo, the long and short of it was this. After many weeks of too-ing and fro-ing I was faced with a phone call from the RAC on the 30th August from a lovely woman called Jess. Now Jess had taken sole charge of my predicament and had been tirelessly fighting my corner and trying to get the price down. Unfortunately, this phone call wasn't good and she basically told me it wasn't looking favourable and I'd have to find the money somehow if I wanted the carnet. All along I'd planned on the 1st October as my leaving date as this is my late mum's birthday and she's the very reason I was doing it. But without the carnet I couldn't apply for some visas the next day, meaning the whole project would be delayed and the start date put back.

But it wasn't just a case of the project being delayed. If I couldn't find a minimum of £8K then I wasn't getting the carnet, meaning I couldn't go to most of Africa, the Far East, and even some of South America! The whole thing was looking like it was collapsing around me, I couldn't believe it! I was faced with the fact I may actually have to cancel the whole thing, 3 years of work all gone, so many people let down, so many doubters proven right.

I sat at my computer desk and stared at my email for a few hours, stumped at how the hell I was going to word all this to my sponsors and followers. By about 2:30pm that afternoon I was still in a state of shock when the phone rang. On answering I was met by the familiar voice of Jess from the RAC who sounded remarkably upbeat? "Have you cancelled it yet?" she asked. She then gave me the incredible news that she'd managed to get a huge discount applied to my case and the carnet would be mine for a tad under £2,500. What's more, it would be in my hands by 8am the following morning! I just about proposed to her over the phone.

So that was that. In the space of about 3hrs I'd gone from almost admitting defeat, facing the prospect of my adventure of a lifetime crumbling in front of me, to complete euphoria firmly back in the driving seat of the TeapotOne juggernaut. Life was good once again. I was back on for the 1st October!!

Blimey, I'll be going around the world then! It sounds weird I know, but I'd almost put this fact to the back of my mind through all these months and years of planning. It was always, "next year", or "in 6 months", but all of a sudden it was, "in 3 weeks"!

As soon as I had that carnet it was as if a massive green light had been turned on in front of me. It was full steam ahead preparing all the visa applications which had to be completed in advance of my departure. I opted to use a specialist to help with all the various visas for the trip, and after a bit of research online I found Travcour. They specialise in visa and passport services and have over 25yrs experience in the field. Lovely job.

I've got to say, when I first approached Amanda Wooders about my trip, I could tell she was slightly sceptical and almost dismissive of my attempts to include some of the more problematic countries. I'm sure she thought I didn't have a hope in hell in getting some of them, and although there were plenty more still to be applied for, we'd already secured most of West Africa! Just the ever tricky Angolan to go, rarely issued to overlanders for some reason, but I was feeling positive.

2.7 The Kit

With days to go, I had everything I needed, there was just the small matter of figuring out how to pack it all into the Kriega luggage and fit it all on the bike. Yep, I know I should've done all the trial runs already, but you know, things to do and all that! At the start of the year I learned that lesson when I arrived at Assen race circuit in the pitch black the night before I began my 'BSB Enduro Ride'. It was about -6oC and I'd never put the tent up before, how hard could it be?

Well I found out, resulting in me having to be rescued by a bemused marshall who let me stay in her caravan for the night. You got to love the dutch!

So this time I wasn't going to make the same mistake and set to work erecting the tent I was taking on the trip, the Vango Chinook 200, right there in my living room. Probably not the best move as, although only a 2 man tent and very compact and light when packed, it's a big old bugger when up!

I've no problem admitting it, when I first left I had a ridiculous amount of kit. You pack for every eventuality, not wanting to go without at any point throughout the trip. But the realities quickly set in once you're on the road and kit is simply lost, broken, given away, left behind, or simply found wanting. But when I first left, this is a list of everything I took:

3 boxer shorts

3 pairs of socks

1 pair of cargo trousers that could be unzipped to shorts

1 pair of shorts

1 pair of flip flops

1 pair of hiking shoes

5 t-shirts

1 fleece

2 shirts

Washkit

First aid kit

Rain suit

Winter gloves

Winter undershirt for riding

Winter long johns for riding

Thermal riding socks and inner gloves

Para chord

Firefighter

Matches

2x 3.5 litre 'Rotopax' fuel cans

Vango Venom sleeping bag

Vango inflatable mattress

Vango duel fuel stove, cutlery set, kettle and mug

Vango Chinook 200 tent

2 weeks of emergency ration packs

Chain oil

Engine oil and spare engine oil

Oil filter

Spare wheel bearings

Wheel brace and rear spindle socket

Tyre levers

Socket set, Allen keys, various screwdrivers

GoPro 2

GoPro mounting accessories

Small Gorilla pod

Cable ties

Gaffa tape

Electrician tape

Garmin SD cards with all their maps

1 paper map of the whole world

1 large hunting knife

Tripod

Carnet & trip paperwork (copies of logbook, passport etc)

Leathers

Boots

Gloves

Helmet

'Spot' tracker

MacBook Pro, cables, adapters, external hard drive

Nikon P510 camera

iPhone

Wide Brimmed hat

Mozzie headover

Bruce SMART

Babywipes.

Told you I over packed!

CHAPTER 3
THE TRIP

Launch Day & We're Off!

So it finally arrived. After almost 3 years of planning, a lot of begging, persuading, persistence and just plain brass neck, I was suddenly there at the Cenotaph in Whitehall, London, at 8am on Monday the 1st October 2012, bike packed and ready to be ridden 100,000 miles around the world. "What the hell am I doing?"

I can honestly say I hadn't been nervous at all, I just couldn't wait to get the trip under way. However all that changed at about 5pm on Sunday evening when I finally got my arse in gear and started to finalise my packing for the trip. I'd packed, re-packed, unpacked and packed again, probably about half a dozen times prior to this point. But the stack of kit just didn't seem to be getting any lighter. It was an obscene amount to be packing onto a bike of any kind, let along a litre class Superbike!

My son, brother and father had all arrived by Sunday and it was also the day that my life was to be given away in the form of furniture and belongings from my flat. All through the day complete strangers turned up and took away almost everything I owned. It kind of felt like my very existence was being eroded right before my eyes? All the bad things that are currently going on around the world all seemed to be being mentioned on the tv, in the papers, over the radio, in fact everywhere I seemed to go on Sunday it was just doom and gloom, or danger here and disaster there. My Nikki was there as my bedrock as usual, but as we went out for dinner one last time before the off, I just couldn't settle and only wanted to be back home so I could repack just one last time.

After very little sleep, and even less for Nikki - no, my snoring, it was soon early

Bruce SMART

morning and time to get this underway. I rode to the Cenotaph myself, leaving early as I was due to meet up with a good mate, Ray Walton of Twitter '@Jap_STi_3' fame, as he took on his own challenge of visiting all of the gold post boxes around the country!

Typically though, the Monday morning London traffic was horrendous coming into town from the South East, and as my beast was severely over loaded, I couldn't even filter efficiently. I arrived just short of 8am and too late to meet Ray, really sorry bud for letting you down. Ruth Allsopp and the team from 'The Children's Trust' were already arriving, as were the lads who were to form the traffic escort. My head was flying by this point, it was such an extreme mix of excitement, nerves and uncertainty.

As time clicked by, more and more faces started to appear out the cold morning drizzle. Walshy, my old mate from Uni was one of the first to arrive, and a face I've not seen in decades, yet it was just like old times. It was incredible to see so many people make the effort to come along and I can't put into words how much it meant. Thank you one and all, truly.

After what felt like minutes, it was soon time to get ready in front of the Cenotaph memorial for a few final photoshoot moments before the off. I'd just started to calm down and settle into it when Andy, of 'Andy Newbold Photography', asked for a picture of my Nikki and I together. This is when it really hit home for me, and standing there in the rain, holding this incredible woman, I realised I was going, I wasn't going to see her, my son, my dad, brother, family or friends, for a long, long time to come. I have to confess, I had a wee greet to myself, told Nikki I loved her, hugged my boy and family, and quick as you like we mounted up on the bikes, blasted the horns and we were off!

My apologies to everyone left standing in the street, I really didn't mean to just shoot off, it just all happened so quick! With our escort around us we made fluid progress into South London and out into Kent. With the rain increasing in vigour we were soon alone as a convoy of bikes cruising our way down to Dover, arriving with literally minutes to spare to check in and board the ferry! After another rapid set of 'thank you and goodbyes' to everyone who rode down, myself, Woody and Turner were soon riding our bikes onto the P&O ferry. The lads had booked themselves onto the ferry and were joining me for the first 2 days of the trip as I headed down to Le Mans, but more of this later.

As I got off the bike on the car deck of the ferry, my head was still buzzing with emotions and the adrenaline still soaring through my veins. Wheeling the bike forward to get her in to position to strap down, my outside foot slipped on the deck and down we went onto her side, BANG! I couldn't believe it, I'd not even left the bloody country and I'd ditched the beast already, NO!!!!!!!!! If ever 'R&G' wanted an advert of what their crash protection can do, this was it. Not a scratch, not even a dent! The bar end slider and crash bungs took all the contact, leaving the paintwork and wrap completely untouched. I reckon my severely overladen 'Kriega' luggage may have helped too though!

It took the 3 of us to get her upright again, but she was soon securely strapped down and we were seated upstairs with a warm brew in our hands! After what seemed like no time at all, we were in Calais, riding off the boat onto French soil. The rain was getting worse so we decided just to take the motorway and head straight to Rouen which would be our 1st stop for the night. After an hour or so the rain eased off and it became quite a pleasant afternoon as we rolled into town and found our hotel for the evening, slap bang in the old town part of the city. Dumping the kit, having a quick shower to warm up, we were soon out wandering the streets looking for some grub and a beer or two. A quality night was had, but I was ready for my kip when I finally got into my bed on Day 1!

ICELAND
NORWAY
NORWAY
SWEDEN
IRELAND
UNITED KINGDOM
DENMARK
POLAND
NETHERLANDS
GERMANY
BELGIUM
SWITZERLAND
CZECH REPUBLIC
SLOVAKIA
FRANCE
AUSTRIA
HUNGARY
SLOVENIA
ANDORRA
CROATIA
BOSNIA & HERZEGOVINA
ROM
FRANCE
MONACO
ITALY
SERBIA
MONTENEGRO
BU
PORTUGAL
SPAIN
ALBANIA
MACEDO
ITALY
GREECE
MOROCCO
MOROCCO
ALGERIA
TUNISIA
ALGERIA
LIBYA
WESTERN SAHARA
MOROCCO MAUR
MALI
MALI
LIBYA

CHAPTER 4
FRANCE & INTO EUROPE

I hadn't had any reply regarding the lap of Le Mans so decided rather than riding all the way there for just a picture, I'd go with the lads up to the Normandy beaches, and I'm really glad I did as the place is almost surreal in it's tranquility, when compared to its horrendous and notorious past.

If you've never been I urge you to go. It's just over the water from us in the UK and is a monumental part of our nation's history. Whether you agree with military conflict or not, those lads laid their lives down in a way we will hopefully never have to witness on that scale again. Just to stand on the beaches, look out at the sea and try to envisage what happened is almost too much to get your head around, yet the peacefulness and beauty of the various monuments and exhibits all along this coast, is a testament to tact and taste. A job very well done by all involved.

Having endured the motorway up, we decided to enjoy the limited twisties available in Northern France, I set the Garmin to plot a route avoiding all toll roads and motorways. Crikey, the route it took us was simply stunning in both quality of road, and the beauty of the various chateaus and villages it meandered it's way through. One we couldn't stop in but I'll certainly go back to was Bayeux, of the tapestry fame. The place is simply stunning, with a huge Cathedral located bang in it's centre, I'd definitely like to pop back there another time.

Later on we stopped for a wee coffee and quick natural (police slang for a toilet break) in a cracking wee village called Beaumont-en-Auge. As luck would have it we happened

Bruce SMART

to park outside a place called, 'Le P'tit Beaumont' and it turns out the owner is an avid biker. In fact he actually competes in the Dakar Rally and is taking part in it next year once again. I have to confess I didn't note his name, but the cafe website is www.leptitbeaumont.fr if you want a wee look at the place. If you're ever in that neck of the woods I thoroughly recommend their cappuccinos! What's more there was a group of Americans sitting across from us who also took an interest in the bike and when they heard about TeapotOne, they invited me to stay with them when I got to Seattle! Lovely job, this travelling lark is brilliant eh!!

So that was Day 2, what would the rest hold? The following morning Woody & Turner departed to head back to Calais and then home. As I awoke that morning it was like Day 1 all over again. I felt a bit sick, a bit jittery, like I actually wanted to go with the lads and head home to blighty. But that was ridiculous, pull yourself together ya great big fairy and get on with it!

I saw the lads off and they turned the corner out of sight, I was alone. I spent about an hour packing the bike, making sure everything was secure, everything was in it's place. I unpacked and packed again just to make sure. Eventually I was on the road and heading north east towards Belgium. Hitting the back roads to try and sample some twists and turns, progress was horrendously slow, I had to get a move on, I had to get there. Where I didn't really know for the end of day 3, but I had to get there!

As the rain came down once more I set the Garmin to plot a route via the motorways, not toll roads though – I'm Scottish. Pretty soon I was making good progress along through Northern France, towns and villages passing in a blur. Before I knew it I was in Belgium, and just as I was thinking of coming off the motorway and hitting the back roads, I was in the Netherlands. By now the rain was coming down like Niagra so I headed into Assen itself and found a place to stay for the night.

The next day I was up and out on the road arriving at Assen TT circuit nice and early to get the obligatory shot in front of the main sign. Unfortunately there still hadn't been any progress regarding actual laps of the motoGP circuits, so yet again it was just a pic and off.

Way back in April 2012 I did the BSB Enduro ride where I rode to each of the circuits used in the 2012 BSB Championship and completed a lap of each one (well the circuits that bothered to get back to me). I was lucky enough to get a lap of Assen during this so I couldn't feel too hard done by in this instance.

Soon it was back on the bike and "on the road again," now heading South into Germany, and the Nurburgring. I'd checked the cracking website nurburgring.org.uk the night before so knew I wouldn't have a chance to do a lap as it was closed to 'tourist laps' until the evening. I'd arrive too late, and would be leaving first thing the next morning, so that was that. But again I've been to the ring before, lived to tell the tale and wear the badge with honour, so I've got nothing to prove. That said, I'm defo going back as I've got lap times to beat and tyres to rip up!

I stayed the night at a cracking place right on the ring itself, called 'HOTEL An Der Nordschleife' owned and run by a great lad called Eddy Mathey. Very biker friendly with loads of rooms, capable of accommodating the single guest right through to parties of 20 or more, this place is perfect. With it's own in-house steak restaurant and bar, you've got everything you need right on your doorstep, including the ring itself. In the morning you open your window out onto your balcony and you can see, let alone hear, the cars and bikes roaring through the Adenau section of the circuit.

After a brief visit to the main car park where you normally go to buy your lap tokens, gather in the car park to talk near-death experiences, and generally drool at the motors and machinery on offer, I had to get back on the beast once more and head East to the Sachsenring, my next motoGP circuit, and off I went.

The roads in Europe never cease to amaze me. Even non-descript back roads are grin-inducing in their layout, and their surface quality is by far superior to ours in the

Bruce SMART

UK. With few exceptions, most of the tarmac is impeccably kept. I glided along through Germany, revelling in every twist, turn, hairpin and sweeper that came my way. More than once I caught myself looking at the Garmin display in awe as it looked like it had been drawn by a 3yr old with a crayon!

Soon enough I arrived at the Sachsenring, a weird setting for a world class motoGP circuit I must admit. It seems to be set in an industrial park bang in the middle of the town of Oberlungwitz, and to be honest, if you didn't know it was there you could easily go right by it. Set in a natural dip, or bowl, I suppose it's the perfect place really. Again there'd been no communication so I missed out on yet another lap, but I stayed a while to watch the cars that were hurtling around the track. It looked an amazing play-zone and I promised myself that I'd return soon to sample it on the beast for real. Alas, the obligatory pic would have to do for now.

With Germany now 'done' in my book, it was time to head East once more and head to the Czech Republic. Daylight was starting to dwindle as I got towards the border, so I found a campsite for the night off a back road in a farmers field. The Vango 'Chinook 200 tent pitched in no time and my gear and I stowed away for the night. Despite me being almost 18 stone and 6'3", together with the mountain of kit I've brought, there was a surprising amount of space within the tent and I slept like a log until morning.

Riding a motorbike is a therapeutic old game. You spend a lot of time alone with your thoughts, cocooned in your lid for long periods at a time with nobody to interrupt your thinking or logical progression. Me, I tend to think about boobs and food mostly, but hey-hum. After a while, even I can get a bit bored with just boobs, so it was on with the ipod, hit shuffle and let chance dance through the 6,500 songs on offer.

Bang, straight out the gate, 'ABC by the Jackson 5'! Lovely job, I was flying along beaming away in my lid, not a care in the world and starting to really get into this roadtrip lark. Soon I was at the border with the Czech Republic and just like that I was in. I've got to say, I'm loving this 'one europe' lark, easy as you like, no issues, no problems, no queues.

If you've ever fancied touring on your bike or car, just pack a bag and go. There's nothing to hold you back, just do it! (Well apart from the job, the kids….. "Live Your Life")

It's a big old place the Czech Republic, and even bigger when your sat nav decides it doesn't exist? Unfortunately, the garmin map for the whole of europe is too big to fit onto the device in one hit, meaning you can either have the UK, Ireland and most of mainland europe on it, or you have to sacrifice the uk to get Czech, Poland etc. As I didn't know this at the time, I got as far as entering the Czech Republic and then just seemed to be hovering in mid air, slightly off centre from a purple line going through the garmin display? Using my pigeon-esque sense of direction, and by looking at the sun deciding which way was West, I headed in the opposite direction along a main road for what seemed like hours. Eventually I picked up signs for Praha and we were back in business. Keeping off the toll roads I stuck to this main road right through the country. It was epic, similar to the South's A272 in parts with long sweeping bends, tight alpine sections, and thundering straights where you could get yourself in a whole lot of bother of the uniformed variety. As it was, I was carrying a small house on the back of the bike so my playtime was fairly constrained by normal standards, but I still had a go!

After a full days riding I began to descend into the main city of Prague and headed for the old town. I'd been here many times before on stag do's and birthday bashes, but this time was different being alone. I eventually found a home for the night and washed my kit in the sink, hung it out to dry, then headed into the old town to see the sights.

Now I'm a man of the world. I've seen a fair bit, experienced my fair share, and generally try to keep an open mind about most things. But, until proven otherwise to me, 'The Beach Boys' had obviously NEVER been to Eastern Europe when they penned their hit, "California Girls". Everywhere you look are stunning women, everywhere! My good mate Webby has a fairly enthusiastic penchant for Eastern European women, and I couldn't help but here his voice in my head as I wandered around this beautiful city.

Now it's not just the women that are easy on the eye, the cityscape itself is fairly impressive too. The place is full of impressive Cathedrals, Churches, museums and palaces, with cracking wee lanes intermingled around their footings.

After a while I stopped to grab some grub, then headed back to my room for the night. On the way I found this incredible old boy playing the violin in the street. The sound was just amazing as it swirled and swooned it's way down through the alleys and open courtyards of the place. He looked a lot like one of the armourers at my old work (sorry Matt!), and just stood their playing along to his own back track. I sat a while but it just didn't seem right to shove a camera in his face. I recorded a few minutes worth of sound and later posted it up on YouTube, such was the beauty of the music. Would you believe it, the guy later sent me a rant, saying I owed him money for copyright infringement as I hadn't sought his permission to record him in the street? So I took it down. Some people!

Guess what? It was STILL raining as I awoke on Day 7. That was 5 solid days of rain and it was only getting heavier, and colder! I woke up feeling a bit sorry for myself, missing my Nikki and feeling like I needed to sit in my pants on my sofa with a brew. But then I remembered, I'd sold everything I owned and was riding around the world on an incredible adventure. GROW UP LAD AND GET ON WITH IT!

Mounting the beast, I set the satnav for Oswiecim in Poland where I'd visit Auschwitz the following day, and headed off East into the rain. In no time I was out the city and gliding along the back roads of Eastern Europe. It's amazing how the territory and people change even across the comparatively close proximity of a border. But I suppose it's the same here in the UK with Wales, Scotland and England. You can be 5 minutes South of the Scottish border and folk sound completely different to those 10 minutes up the road!

The further East I ventured the more industrial the landscape became. Alpine forests and medieval looking Churches gave way to farm land and ancient looking factory buildings with large chimneys spewing steam and smoke into the air. The smell of burning wood and peat filled my lid and I was reminded of my childhood days at home in the

North East of Scotland, sitting with my family in the living room beside my old dog Glen and a roaring fire. Happy days.

One thing I noticed as I rode around Europe is the amount of alternative fuel being utilised. Everywhere you look there are windfarms and solar panel plantations strewn across the countryside. Every garage has a multitude of fuel types on offer, including LPG and electric! To be honest they put the UK to shame!

It had been a long day in the saddle by the time I reached Oswiecim late into the night of day 7. I'd planned on getting there much earlier and setting up camp outside the town. But the rain hadn't stopped, the temperature had dropped dramatically, and it had even started to sleet! So a quick flick on my phone revealed a cheap hotel right opposite the museum so that's where I headed and dried off for the night. I slept like a log.

Auschwitz is somewhere I'd wanted to visit for a long time. I'm not really sure why though? It's obviously an incredibly important monument in history to a time we should never forget, but the hard fact is that it's the site of millions of people's deaths. Surely this shouldn't be turned into a tourist attraction?

But I should never have even contemplated that as the museum at Auschwitz is the very epitome of taste, decorum and respect. If you get there before 1030hrs you can wander through the 1st camp – Auschwitz I, alone. After that time you must be accompanied by a guide, which is probably best as you get the full input told in a compassionate and informative manner. The guides take over 3hrs to guide you through both camps, Auschwitz I and then Auschwitz II – Birkenau, the eerily more famous of the camps, where the mass gas chambers and crematoriums were located.

As soon as you walk in you are greeted by the famous iron gate with the words, *"Arbeit Macht Frei"* held aloft them. Translated as, "Work Sets You Free", they were meant to put those entering at ease, thinking they were being brought in to start a new life under the Reich. The sad truth being that work did indeed set these poor souls free, but only after being worked to death, often in only a matter of months.

What struck me most about the 1st Auschwitz camp was that it wasn't the wooden shack appearance I had expected. The buildings were brick built, solid and strong structures, fairly impressive and military looking to be honest. But this is no surprise as they were originally intended as German army barracks. Originally set up around June 1940, Auschwitz was intended as a prison camp for around 150,000 polish political prisoners. Over half this number perished.

From June 1941 it began to receive over 25,000 deported prisoners from various nationalities. Again around half perished. Also at this time, around 15,000 Soviet POWs were sent to the camp where they received the harshest treatment of all. Almost ALL perished.

In March 1942 Auschwitz began to fulfill it's most notorious function as a death camp for the extermination of over 1.2 million Jews from all over the continent. Later in 1943 it began to receive over 23,000 Gypsies. Over 21,000 of them perished.

The main parade square typifies the Nazi's opinion of the Jews. Perverse, even by the Nazi standards, it's where they would hold roll call every morning and night, counting in each and every prisoner, even the dead ones carried back by their colleagues after dying whilst at work. If the numbers didn't match up, the prisoners would be made to stand there until they did, or the possible escapee/s found. Often this would last for hours, often into the night. In the depths of winter it could reach well below zero, so the SS built the guards a small cabin to shelter from the elements, right in front of the prisoners. Here they could watch souls perish right before their eyes in relative warmth and comfort?

Most of the gas chambers and crematoriums were blown up and destroyed by the nazis in an attempt to hide the truth about the Auschwitz camps. Only one now exists at Auschwitz I and is honestly a very sobering place to visit. You can't begin to imagine the fear and horror faced by those who entered that door. It almost wasn't right to go in, but I suppose it's there to learn from and so must be experienced.

Prisoners suspected of resistance involvement or planning escape were interrogated here, and as such it was a site of terror for those at the camp. After his tribunal in 1947, the camp SS 1st Commandant Rudolph Huss, was hanged here on the 16th April. A fitting end perhaps.

I left Auschwitz a little bemused at the severity of what went on there, the scale of what was involved, the planning and intricacy taken by those who perpetrated it's horrors. But at the same time I left glad that I had come, glad that I had paid my respects in a small way to all those lost within it's confines. There is a sign within the museum giving a quote by a chap called George Santayana, which says,

> "The One Who Does Not Remember History Is Bound To Live Through It Again".

Enough said.

So after a sombre morning, it was back on the bike reflecting on what I'd seen and heard as I twisted and turned my way back West into the Czech Republic and to the next motoGP circuit at Brno.

Yet again it's not what I expected as it's up the top of a hill set within woods on the outskirts of the city. If you weren't looking for it you'd certainly pass it by. As it was I WAS looking for it and very nearly did! Thankfully the Garmin had the circuit in it's 'Points of Interest' so I was soon plonked right underneath the main sign with the track careering overhead. "CLICK", and it was another one in the bag.

With the time kicking on I made the decision to get on the motorway and head for Vienna for the night. After the quality roads I had experienced, it was somewhat of a shock to be faced with the Czech motorways in the South East. Bearing in mind that the speed limit on these things is 130KPH (about 90 odd miles an hour) you'd expect them to be washboard flat. No, imagine riding over 1000's of road humps one after the other for mile upon mile upon mile, and all at over 80 miles an hour! I thought the front forks were going to blow out before I even got to Africa!

Eventually I crossed into Austria and all was right once again. The efficient Austrians supplied billiard smooth tarmac and a plethora of road signs, even I couldn't get lost here. Pretty soon I arrived into the centre of Vienna and stopped over at a hostel for the night after yet another downpour throughout the day. With only a few hours to sample her delights, I was soon out and strolling through the streets of Vienna, but I have to be honest, I'm not sure what the fuss is about? Granted I only had a couple of hours, it was night time and I was alone, ignorant of what was on offer. Everything seemed to be under construction, or in some state of repair? It's a bonny place don't get me wrong, and if you're into museums, you'll be in your element. Oh and if you like shopping - Nikki, you'd love it.

Another thing I've noticed on the continent is the driving. Each nation seems to have their own particular character traits. The French are typically very biker aware, practically mounting the verge to allow you to pass. The Germans are sticklers for the rules. If it says 80 then they do 80 and not a stitch more. But get them on the unrestricted sections and they plant the foot and keep going. It's a joy to ride behind them in the rain as they seem to read the road so much better than a lot of drivers in the UK, they hardly ever use their brakes and have a very fluent, controlled style of driving. This continues into Poland and also down into Austria where they seem to be even more conservative. If the speed limit says 50, then they'll do 40 just to be safe. Again they tend to be very biker aware, moving right out your way to let you pass. It was a joy to ride amongst my European brethren, well that was until one morning when I had my first near death experience on TeapotOne.

Riding along the back roads of Austria I'd just decided to stop and set the GoPro up to get some 'transitional' footage – see Austin Vince, I was listening at your film school! After setting the camera up I got on the bike to do a ride past and just as I got to a t-junction, a woman came out directly in my path forcing me onto the opposite carriageway, just as a truck was coming the other way! I've got it all on camera, I wasn't even going quick as I'd only just set off. She looked right at me too, and just pulled out. Muppet. Anyway, I lived, and got some good footage. I honestly don't think either she or the truck driver even noticed?

Anyway, I decided to slow it all down as I was about 5 days ahead of schedule by now. I'd been so pre-occupied with getting to the next place that I sacrificed actually meeting the people of the places I was going to. That had to change. Keeping to the back roads I made my way across to Salzburg where I planned to pop into the city centre, do a spot of sightseeing, check the t'interweb in a cafe somewhere, then pitch the tent enroute to the passes.

However the weather had other ideas. At this stage I'd never ridden in such rain as this. It was constant, freezing and HUGE! It was like riding through solid water in parts, coming in through my visor, my Gore-Tex boots began to fill, gloves sodden right through and every passing truck sent a tidal wave cascading over me. Progress was slow to say the least, so by 3pm I'd had enough. I stopped at a filling station, used my gizmo (phone) and booked into a hotel in Salzburg for 2 whole nights. What the hell, I was on me holidays! I'd stop over, dry everything out, do some proper sightseeing, update the blog, work on the next vid, and do some household chores on the web that needed doing, things like visas and finding a tenant for my flat!

That reminds me, if you're the person who rented my flat, only to pull out just before I left after saying you wanted it unfurnished – meaning I had to sell everything I owned, thanks very much. I now had an empty flat, no worldy possessions, and now nobody to pay my mortgage. Cheers. Thankfully I got a replacement tenant not too long after, but still lost a month or two's rental out of the trip funds. Right, back to the trip.

Salzburg, ah yes. I went for a wee wander around the place, it's not big at all, but even in the pouring rain and fog it is stunning. A real picture postcard, storybook of a place, famous for the birthplace of Mozart and the Sound of Music. I wandered around in the rain for about 4 hours all through the old part of town.

I couldn't come to Salzburg and not visit one of it's most famous sons' birthplace, so it was off to "Hagenauer House" at Getreidegasse 9, to see the house where Mozart was born on January 27, 1756. The building is named after the merchant and toy dealer, Johann Lorenz Hagenauer, who owned the building and was a friend of the Mozart family. Guess who swallowed the tour guide. Oh hang on, that could be read the wrong way?! Anyway…

But it's not just his music that Mozart is famous for in Salzburg. Oh no, his balls are also considered a delicious treat in these parts too. In fact throughout Austria you can sample these cracking wee tasty morsels, in the form of, "Mozartkugel" or "Mozart Balls". These pitsachio and nougat, chocolate covered balls are sold all over Austria now and are quite the treat. I demolished about a dozen before collapsing into a diabetic coma.

Ever heard of the 'Love Locked Bridge'? Apparently it's a tradition going back to Rome, but has now taken off all around the world, and Salzburg is no different. As I walked across the Markat bridge, I couldn't help but notice 100's, if not 1,000's of padlocks attached to it's fencing. At the time I'd no idea what this was about but took some pics anyway with a view to googling it when I got back to the hotel. Well here you go, this is what it's all about.

Apparently if you're in love in the city, you and your chosen one can come to the bridge and attach a padlock to the railings to signify you're ever lasting love and devotion for one another. Each of the locks are adorned with the names of the respective sweethearts, but every now and then you find one that has been scrubbed out! Ha Ha, love it! Who said romance is dead!

By the way, if you were the chap who was taking your bike test in Austria in-between Vienna and Salzburg, I hope you didn't fail because of me! This chap was the 1st biker I'd seen in a while so I stuck my arm out to say hello, as is custom on the continent instead of the UK 'nod'. Being a good egg the lad responded but only then did I notice he was wearing a learner bib and had an instructor/examiner behind! Hope they didn't fail you for that mate, you're still a biker in my book.

Austria is incredible, straight out of 'The Sound of Music' – funny that eh. One word of warning though, the Austrian old bill are VERY hot on speeding. They literally hide in the trees, bus shelters, or behind rocks to get you. If it says 70kph, do 65 or they WILL stop you.

I was gliding along approaching a wee town and looked down at the garmin to see what my speed was, as I hadn't changed the speedo from mph to kph. It showed 73 and it was now a 50 so I began to brake, looked up, and the 5-0 stepped out from behind a bus shelter with a speed gun! "Rollocks", thought I. Do I just cane it and hope that's that? Well, when you're a 18 stone bloke, dressed in white leathers, on a bike with this distinct a paint job, not to mention 600 weight of luggage on the back, I thought I may just stand out a tad. No way of talking yourself out of that one if they track you down. So I sucked it up, turned around and went back with my tail between my legs.

Luckily enough there was a Sgt there who noticed the old bill hat on the TeapotOne logo. He asked what it was about so I told him. "Ah, Kollege!" he said with a broad smile. Phew, lovely job, I told them all about the trip in a series of mixed up French, Auf Wiedersehen Pet German, and some language I may well have made up, but they seemed to get the jist. I dished out a few TeapotOne wristbands and tie pins and they let me on my way.

With that I made my way further South, the personification of safe, methodical and proficient riding. Well until I was at least out of ear shot, at which point I came across two more old bill waiting a few villages further down the road, the very point where I intended to open her up! Lucky one that, guess they were the back up for anyone who didn't stop for the earlier two.

I'd heard on Facebook about the Glossknocker Pass so decided it'd be rude not to pass by and cast an eye over this beauty. I rode feeling like a kid at Crimbo, eager to devour this famous alpine pass. As I pulled into 'Bruck' – one of the starting points of the pass, I crossed the bridge, saw the signs for it, rounded the first bend, and wallop! The road was closed off for maintenance works, NNNNNNNNNNNNNNOOOOOOOOOO!!!

To top it all off, it'd been raining all morning but just as I got close to doing the road the sun came out. It was set to be a perfect morning. Like a sulking fat kid that's not been allowed seconds, I stomped off on the bike, around a hairpin bend, and popped a wee impromptu wheelie, quite unintentionally, nearly scaring myself stupid. The added weight on the bike kind of put the centre of balance off so once she was up, she was up!

CHAPTER 5
ITALY & BEYOND

Now wide awake, I set off into the unknown once more. Within about 5 minutes I was riding some of the most spectacular roads I'd yet come across on this trip. Soon enough I was faced with what looked like a dead end into an industrial car park? I looked around and the road just seemed to end down a wee path that led to some houses, then a great big mountain? There seemed to be train tracks and what looked like a station, but the place was deserted. I turned around and retraced my steps a few times, but each time the garmin brought me right back here. In the end I'd hit the 'detour' button so many times, the garmin just gave up and said it couldn't calculate the route! Now I was buggered, so I stopped at a petrol station and asked how I got to Italy!

Turns out the satnav was right all along and it was indeed a station. On returning it all made sense now. There were a few cars patiently waiting at the end of the road, next to a wee kiosk. I joined the queue and waited.

Pretty soon I was on a train with the beast heading through a mountain to Italy, and all for 16 euros. After about 10mins we were at the end of the line and I rode off into peeing rain once more. No more than 5 minutes later I was presented with beautifully surfaced, twisting ribbons of Tarmac. Even in the rain the Bridgestone BATTLAX BT-023's stuck like glue as I aimed the beasts' nose South and twisted her open. Class, sheer class on two wheels, I was in heaven, and Italy, country number 9.

As I stormed down through the hills, the rain intensified and light began to fade. I found a wee spot to call it a night, high up in the Italian hills, popped to a local pizzeria

Bruce SMART

for a calzone and a beer, then went to bed dreaming of what had passed before me.

Day 12 broke with the sun high in the sky, temperatures already rising to sweaty level by 8am. Being a fat, Scottish bloke, I'm not meant to be out in this weather, least of all in a leather suit! I couldn't get on the bike quick enough, soon the air was rushing through and cooling the parts beer just can't get to.

Within about an hour I was passing through the Trentino province and although I was now down low, the scenery was just as beautiful. Arriving at Riva del Garda around lunchtime, I parked the beast up and grabbed an ice cream to eat by the lake. Life is tough at times so you need to just sit back a little don't you.

Refreshed I headed along the east bank of the lake, through towns like Malcesine, Lazise, before hitting Peschiera del Garda at the southern tip. The sun was low in the sky now, and seeing a cracking looking campsite by the lake, I decided to pull in and pitch the tent. At 14 euros it wasn't half bad, toilets and showers, Tv, restaurant, laundry and wifi all on site, happy days. Tent pitched, pizza, beer, and bed by 8pm. Rock'n'roll baby, yeah! I slept like a log.

The next day I headed East to San Marino to visit the Misano World Circuit, newly renamed the 'Marco Simoncelli Circuit' after the great motoGP promise who was taken so early from us the previous year. You can't help but notice you're in bikers territory as you enter San Marino. There are Rossi '46' flags flying high from garages, homes, shops, banks, EVERYWHERE! But I also noticed something else, something extraordinary really. Shrines at the side of the road, to Marco Simoncelli, and not just one or two. I even saw a full race rep bike laid at the side of the road, in Marco's '58' team design, with a flag draped across it with his famous, 'Ciao Marco' signature. Beautiful, and a fitting tribute to this great lad.

Arriving at the circuit I had a wee chat with the security guard who seemed genuinely interested in what I was doing and let me in for a quick pic and vid. You've got to love bikers eh. It was also my birthday, 36yrs old, how the hell had that happened? I still don't know what I want to do when I grow up, but it better involve bikes.

As a wee treat I headed into the centre of Italy, up into the hills where the roads twist and the hills soar. It reminded me a lot of the Trossachs in Scotland actually, only warmer. I found a cracking hotel for the night with an unbeatable deal going online, so I clicked it, booked it, packed it, job done.

I spent the next few days in Italy as I had a meeting with Bridgestone at their European test facility just outside Rome on Monday morning. Heading down from the hills I decided to aim for Rome and get a look at what all the fuss was about. On route I sampled some great roads and some greater place names! Ever heard of a wee place called 'Bastardo'?

Checking online it said there was plenty of parking outside the Colosseum so I thought it'd be great to get a pic of the beast outside the world famous landmark. That'd be the Crimbo cards taken care of eh. Well no, not at all. Who ever wrote that online had obviously never been to Rome on a Sunday. The entire city seems to be blocked off intermittently by the old bill in a way that makes no sense. They seem to do it once you're actually in, so when you try to get out, you can't. It was about 32 degrees and mid afternoon, I was in full leathers, astride a sports bike that was panting for clean, cool air to pass through her gills. The temp on the bike was reading 110, so I was not in the best of moods. If it hadn't been for the garmin, I reckon I probably would have just ridden straight through one of those blocks, but it showed me the way – eventually, and I was soon heading just outside the city for the night. Goodnight Rome, I will be back, just not on a bike.

The next day I made my way to the Bridgestone test facility but unfortunately I couldn't take any pics or vids. They had a photographer onhand and promised to send me some pics, but these never appeared. Safe to say, they were the perfect hosts, showing me all around this incredible place. Riccardo Ugolini and his team where a real joy to spend the morning with. They even arranged for me to go out in a car with their top test driver,

Bruce SMART

Cassera, who showed me the ropes on the various test tracks and skid pans on offer. This place should have been renamed, 'Stag World', it'd make a fortune! The hospitality shown by Riccardo and his countrymen is testament to a terrific country. Ok, they're driving may not be quite what we're used to, but they are the most hospitable, genuine and welcoming of people. As I would find out once again later on, read on.

All to soon it was time to hit the road again, heading north for Valencia, Rossi country. The obligatory rain had started to fall, with TV reporting a storm unheard of in centuries was about to hit North West Italy, exactly where I was heading. I decided to make up the distance and hit the motorways, arriving just outside Scarperia as the night closed in, in the full force of the storm.

As morning broke the skies had cleared and I rode through the sunshine, reaching Mugello before most folk where even up for brekkie. This is a stunning circuit, set deep in the Valencian hills, completely secluded from all around it. It oozes style and I'd wager your mortgage just to get a lap or two of it. But alas, once more it was only a pic and a vid, so after 10 minutes of drooling, I was back on the beast heading towards Monaco for lunch.

Preparing myself for a day on the motorways, I plugged into the ipod and was happily tapping my feet to some good old boogie woogie and Jive, when I started to feel some vibration between the legs. Behave. Thinking it was probably just the road surface I ignored it, now belting out classics from 'The Commitments' soundtrack. Life was good.

But then the vibration became more of a wobble, followed by an intermittent clunk, then crack, then screech. I'm no mechanic but even I didn't think this was normal! As I pulled into a services off the motorway, even with my ipod at full volume I could still hear this almighty screeching of metal on metal coming from the bowels of the beast. The looks on the bewildered members of public said it all.

Previously, at a toll booth I'd dropped some change down the side of the bike, and thought maybe somehow a coin had got caught somewhere in the engine room. Being well prepared I'd packed the socket to get the RG crash bungs off so I could remove the fairings. Oh hang on a minute, no I didn't. T%^t!

Asking around some parked up lorries, nobody had the right sized socket so I decided to limp off the motorway down into the local towns and villages to seek help. If you're ever after tyres, then the Italian/French med is where you want to go. Every 2nd place is a tyre fitters! I went from one to another without success when suddenly I spotted her. The familiar orange/red 'S' Suzuki logo high above a dealership down a side road, so I headed straight to it.

Unfortunately it was a car dealership, but he informed me there was a 'moto Suzuki garage' just down the road, passing me off with directions. Needless to say I got lost, ending up at yet another tyre fitters in Sanremo, about 20kms down the road. These lads were awesome, as one spoke good english and straight away they stated it was the bearing. As luck would have it there was a motorbike mechanic across the road, but 'Nemo' was currently away at lunch and wouldn't be back until after 5pm? It was 1:30pm, no wonder Italians live such long lives, they're never at work!

I sat there until after 5 with no sign of Nemo so returned to the lads at the tyre shop. After some head scratching, they got on their laptop, found a Suzuki garage, back where I'd been previously, phoned them up, explained what I was doing and what had happened, booked me in and got the address for the satnav. I love Italians!

With much hand shaking I was off screeching my way back to where I started. As I made my way down the last cobbled street in Imperia, I saw 'Moto Debona' laying at its' foot. Before I even pulled up outside, the mechanics were out, coming down the street and gesturing me to get off the bike and give it to them.

Within minutes they had the rear wheel off and instantly it was obvious what was wrong. The rear bearings had completely gone, I mean vapourised! They looked at me in a way I often used to look at my mum or dad when they tried to work a computer, and I felt less of a man.

They set to work stripping out the old bearings, all the while shaking their heads and giving me the kind of grins you give the village idiot! I know, I know, I know. But through some 'Ital-glish' they managed to figure out what I was doing, and all was forgiven. I was their hero! The chief mechanic there had racing trophies, medals, newspapers clippings, all covering when he used to race as a youngster. By the looks of it he'd been pretty handy, but this guy was treating me like some super star!

After a lot of to-ing and fro-ing, it became apparent that the bearings would have to be ordered in and wouldn't be ready until Friday, that was 3 days away! Still there was nothing to be done so the lady from the service desk said she'd show me a cheap motel and began to walk me down the street. We got about 300yrds when the young technician came belting after us to say they'd found a solution. It turns out they'd managed to get a set of bearings off of their own bikes and fit them into the beast, so now she was good to go! Gents you're both stars and I owe you massively. If ever I can return the favour, you only need to ask. Thank, thank you, thank you.

Once again mobile I rode through the night, straight across Southern France to some digs at a Formule 1 motel near Perpignan, arriving late and cream crackered.

CHAPTER 6
SPAIN & THE N260

Now feeling like Marco Polo, I, the intrepid explorer, awoke this day to bright sunshine. The birds were chirping louder than usual, the winds were warmer, the clouds had smiles, I liked today. With the beast saddled once more, I hit the motorways for the last stretch down to a town called 'Olot' in northern Spain. This was to be my Eastern start point for the fabled N260, a road held almost in folklore alongside 'the ring', 'Stelvio pass' and other automotive greats. Hundreds of miles in length, with countless corners of every degree, it's held by many to be the greatest motorcycling stretch of tarmac in existence. I was going to enjoy this.

Pulling over at the side of the road to fit the GoPros to the beast, 2 police solos came screaming round the bend from the hills in front of me, sunglasses on, teeth on show from the ear to ear grins they both displayed. They slowed and I expected a pull. Instead, they rev'ed their engines at me and gave 2 big thumbs up signs, before accelerating hard down the road. I like the Spanish police.

Now feeling untouchable, I took a deep breath and was off, instantly hitting hairpin after hairpin, weaving my way up and around the side of colossal mountains which went on as far as you could see. The onboard vid for this is available on the trip 'You Tube' channel (teapotonevids) so hopefully it gives you a sense of what it's like to ride this road. Now I use the word, "EPIC" quite a bit in this vid, and for good reason. It was. I've absolutely no doubt that the N260 in northern Spain is by far the greatest road I've ever ridden. I rank it even above the Nurburgring simply because it's a public road, with all the challenges that come with it. Make a mistake and it's a LONG drop. Awesome. EPIC.

Bruce SMART

To be honest, almost every day I spent in Spain provided incredible roads to devour with the beast. The country seems to be designed for bikes, of any style. Get your arse on your bike and get over there!

IRELAND
DOM
TED
NETHERLANDS
G
BELGIUM
FRANCE
ANDORRA
FRANCE
MONACO
PORTUGAL
SPAIN
MOROCCO
ALG
MORO
ALG

CHAPTER 7
PORTUGAL

I made my way down to Badjo and crossed over the border into Portugal, staying outside a town called Elvas for the evening. It was raining yet again but in the morning the skies had cleared and the sun was shining. Avoiding toll roads and motorways, I made my through Portugal with the Estoril circuit as my next destination. The roads were ok, but paled when compared to Spain. I was spoilt.

Arriving at Estoril it was once again only a quick pic, vid and a bite to eat at the roadside. Something I didn't know about was the memorial to Ayrton Senna at the circuit, following his tragic death back in 1994 in San Marino. A subtle tribute to a great man.

From here it was a quick blat down to Portimao circuit to meet my mate Micky Hutton. Micky had kindly arranged for me to stay with his family whilst he, his girlfriend and friends were over on holiday. In my haste to get there, I had another 'interaction' with Portugal's finest. This time I didn't get away with a few wristbands, instead it was 120 euros! But better than a ban which it would've been in the UK. A far better system in my opinion.

We had a great night down at a local bar in Silves with as much chicken, chips and beer we could throw down our necks. Lovely job, just what I was after. I can't thank Micky and his family enough for letting me stay. His aunt and uncle, Marion and Nigel Whistler, were the perfect hosts and their beautiful B&B was simply stunning. I was saddened to hear that Nigel passed away about a year later, he was a lovely man and my thoughts go out to Micky and his family.

CHAPTER 8
JEREZ & THE ROAD of BONES

It was back into Spain the next day with Jerez circuit as my first port of call. Usual story I'm afraid so just a pic and vid before moving on.

Soon back on the road, I was now heading for the town of Montoro in Cordova. A chap called Ken Birchall had contacted me through facebook and offered to put me up for the evening at his home with his family. As he'd mentioned there'd be beer involved, how could I say no!

As luck would have it, the route there was a cracking ride in the sun. I felt free as a bird, soaring along beautiful asphalt as the landscape enveloped me within. I was to meet Ken off a slip road in the middle of nowhere as he said he lived somewhere, "quite remote". He wasn't kidding. After a few beers in a local bar with Ken, Kris and their family, they led me to a side road that seemed to disappear into the olive trees. It didn't look too bad, and I'd no doubt face a lot worse on my future travels, so off I went following behind his truck.

I've got to say, I'm glad I'd had a beer as I don't think I'd have attempted it without a bottle of Dutch courage! (I don't advocate drinking and driving folks, it was a bottle of beer and we were on a dusty cart track in the middle of nowhere) Blimey, I doubt the Dakar crowd tackle anything like this! With Ken's advice of, "plenty of back break, LOADS of back brake", fresh in my mind, I leant on the rear brake pedal and just aimed the beasts' nose as we slid down the crevice, sorry drive!

But what was waiting at the end was more than worth it. Ken had been out there for about 7 years and turns his hand to just about anything. A cracking mechanic by trade (time served Suzuki too funnily enough), Ken has rebuilt his home to what it is today. It's simply beautiful, set amongst acres of olive trees and in the most stunning natural surroundings. Can't think why he left Blighty?

We spent the evening chatting away about bikes, Blighty, home life, everything really. Kris cooked a stunning roast pork dinner and the kids kept me well watered with endless cups of tea. It was a great evening and just what the doctor ordered after 3 weeks on the road. 1st class hosts and brilliant folks, thank you for your kind and generous hospitality, I hope I can repay your kindness one day.

Leaving that morning was like I'd had a week off the bike. I felt refreshed and ready for whatever lay ahead. Hitting the road, I pointed the beast south and twisted the throttle.

I'd been told through the facebook page about the Puerto Nueve Bridge in Ronda, southern Spain. Looking at the pics online it's pretty stunning stuff, so I decided to pass by on my way down to Gibraltar. Arriving in the town it was fairly easy to find the bridge, but actually parking the bike and getting off to see it was another thing entirely!

Seeing a couple of bikes on the pavement 2 mins from the bridge, I parked up and was just chatting to a chap who was asking about the trip when a local came over. He told me the local police were coming and would tow the bikes away if left there. True enough, they came around the corner and didn't look like they were up for any wristbands! I jumped back on and rode around, and around, and around, but still couldn't find anywhere to park up. There was a parking bay about 20mins walk away, but I just didn't fancy leaving all the kit, so left having just got a glimpse of this marvel.

It was a 'straight' run from Ronda down to Gibraltar but Spain had one last biking wonder up her sleeve for TeapotOne. Riding down through the mountains was a fitting way to leave the Spanish mainland behind. I fell in love over that week, the place is a pure bikers fantasy and I can't wait to get back there again, astride the beast once more, and devour everything it has to offer. Porno puns intended.

CHAPTER 9
GIBRALTAR the FRONTIER

For the next few days I was to stay in Gibraltar, spending time with my aunty Pat, her other half Laurie, and catch up with the years that had passed since we last met. She kindly arranged for me to stay at the Caleta Hotel right on the shore and next to the famous 'rock'.

I had time off the bike sightseeing with my Aunty Pat as a most informative guide. She took me to the local cop shop and introduced me to the constabulary. Pretty similar to my beat at Peckham I thought? It's amazing, you can go anywhere and old bill all look the same, all carry themselves the same way, and are all essentially the same. Just nice folk, there to help, naturally suspicious and protective of their own yes, but decent folk in the majority. Much like people as a whole, as I found out through my entire journey.

My first port of call was to the 'Pitstop' garage where the beast was to go in for a service. Aaron Vella was the owner and had kindly agreed to look after my baby, making sure she was fighting fit for the next stage down the west of Africa to Cape Town.

With her safely dropped off we wandered around the town for the rest of the day, aunty Pat introducing me to all the incredible historic sites on offer on this unique and proudly British frontier. Like the 5th Rosia Battery where Nelson's body was brought ashore after the battle of Trafalgar!

There is so much history to be found on this tiny outcrop of rock, it really is an incredible place to visit and I'd love to go back and spend more time there with the Mrs.

Bruce SMART

But it was also the first introduction to border crossings and the timescales that could be involved.

Getting into Gib is no issue if you're a Brit, especially on a bike. Getting to the front of the huge queues of traffic, one flash of your passport and you're waived through, crossing over the runway – yes a runway, before entering the rock.

However, leaving the next morning to go the short distance to 'motomania' in La Linea, Spain, was a different story. It took about an hour and a half to get to the front of the queue, followed by a short question and answers session from the 14yr old with a gun standing between the two points. Thankfully he let me in and I arrived at 'motomania' about 15 mins later to get fresh new boots on the beast, courtesy of Bridgestone.

The Bridgestone BATTLAX BT-023s are an incredible tyre. Their grip in any weather, on any road surface, is simply superb. The handling is lightning, almost feeling at first like the tyre is slipping on contact, it's that fast. The mileage available is nothing short of unbelievable, with around 14,000 miles out a front and routinely getting up to 9,000 miles out of a rear!

Back at the hotel I had loads of work to do. I hadn't updated the facebook page in a while, needed to update the website blog, the 1st episode of the vid series needed doing, and I hadn't yet plotted the route down through Africa! Unfortunately I had to say goodbye to my aunty Pat and Laurie, and never made it to see my cousin Clare – sorry Clare! I spent the whole of Tuesday afternoon and night working away in my room, but all the time, I could look out my window and see her.

Morocco, and Africa, was waiting…..

ITALY FRANCE
ANDORRA
SPAIN MONACO
PORTUGAL ITALY

MOROCCO ALGERIA TUNISIA
MOROCCO ALGERIA LIBYA
WESTERN SAHARA
MOROCCO MAURITANIA MALI NIGER
MAURITANIA MALI
MAURITANIA MALI NIGER
SENEGAL
GAMBIA MALI BURKINA FASO NIGERIA
GUINEA-BISSAU
GUINEA CÔTE D'IVOIRE BENIN NIGERIA CAMEROON
SIERRA LEONE TOGO
LIBERIA GHANA NIGERIA
EQUATORIAL GUINEA
GABON

CHAPTER 10
AFRICA

Europe started in the rain so it was only fitting that I should leave the continent in a similarly wet fashion. The clouds were looming low and angry black over the rock as I waited for my ferry at the port of Algeciras. The place was heaving and I later found out why. Apparently the next day would see a nationwide festival take place, and 1,000's of goats would be slaughtered for a feast!

At that moment I think I knew how the goats felt, I was absolutely kacking it! This was real unknown stuff for me, I'd no idea what I was doing, where I was going, or what awaited me. I sat there on my bike at the quayside and just took it all in, the sights, sounds, smells. The place was chaotic, cars were 'queuing' in a disorderly fashion everywhere, their occupants tooting horns, chatting amongst themselves, and with others 100's of feet away! I felt like I stood out a mile, which in a white leather suit, on a sports bike, I kind of did.

The ferry eventually rocked up over 2hrs late and a mad scramble to get onboard ensued. I just sat back and waited, following on behind. Once onboard the main deck was packed with people, everywhere I looked there were crowds, 1,000's of eyes staring at me. I had to get out the spot light so went out on deck, found a bench, sat down and watched Europe begin to fade into the horizon.

Soon enough a crowd formed around me and I thought I was going for a swim! But the Moroccan's are an incredibly welcoming people and they only wanted to know what I was doing, what bike I had, where I was going and for how long. As I explained my story, more gathered around until there was quite a crowd. The familiar questions were all being asked, why West Africa, why a sports bike, why on my own. I really warmed to these folk on the boat, they seemed genuinely interested and were very warm in their welcoming nature. 2 hours later we were pulling into Tangiers in Morocco. I had arrived.

As I waited for the hustle and bustle, or carnage as it would be better described, of people scrambling to get their cars, vans and trucks off the ferry to die down, I met a Belgian chap who was also patiently waiting to the side. We got chatting and it turned out he lived most of the year in Morocco, and had come back for this goat festival. It was during this chat with him that it became all too clear why all the crowds of people had gathered on the main deck as soon as they boarded the ferry.

Apparently you had to get a landing card stamped by police onboard the boat BEFORE you left. If you didn't get it, you didn't get into the country and were sent straight back! I flew back up the stairs, arriving at the office just as the last few people were leaving. I was the last to be seen, in a jiffy it was done, and I was back on the bike and riding onto African shores. It wasn't that different, just a port like any other port. Until I went around the corner and met my first proper border post. Guns, lots of guns and uniforms. Why was I nervous? I handled firearms every day at work and wore a uniform myself. But that was exactly it, 'I' was usually the one with the gun and uniform, I was in control. This time I was completely out my comfort zone, entirely at the mercy of strangers in a strange land. 50p, 1p, 50p, 1p…….. you get the picture?

It took about an hour to get through the border and customs, no problem at all looking back. The police were good as gold, very polite – as are just about everyone I met in Morocco actually, and those who spoke english were eager to know more about the trip and where I was going. They seemed genuinely interested, and the more they asked about the trip, the less they asked about paperwork, documents, etc. All ticks in the boxes and signatures where they needed to be. Lovely job, I was in.

There are no pics or vid from this first border, they didn't take too kindly to the presence of cameras so I thought it best to keep them stashed away! That 1st night I headed for the first major town down the coast, Rabat, and plotted up there for the night.

The next day I headed south for Casablanca, naively thinking it'd be like the movies. How wrong could I have been. I was more than a little shocked to see the place, not what I was expecting to be honest, but real, very real. I'm sure the downtown part of the city is just what you'd expect, but arriving by motorbike from within the country you need to go through these parts of town first, and it's here you see the real people, the real city. I suppose this is what makes over-landing as revealing and raw as it is.

But again, the people were incredible. I'd pull up at a set of traffic lights, and those who actually stopped would turn to me through their open windows and welcome me to their country. Grown men would beam a smile and rev an imaginary throttle, clapping their hands in excitement as the beast roared her approval! Brilliant.

Checking the garmin for suitable 'points of interest', I saw the 'Casablanca Lighthouse' so thought I'd pop along and take a butchers. The El Hank lighthouse, or 'Pointe D'el-Hank Light', is a famous Moroccan landmark dating back to the early 1900's. It's an impressive looking structure, strangely familiar in an unfamiliar land. I liked it.

I wasn't that taken with Casblanca to be honest so was soon back on the road heading south to Marrakesh. Now this was how I'd imagined Morocco to be. The hustle and bustle around the place was intense, traffic came at you from every direction. Red lights didn't seem to be a definite stop, lane markings in the road meant nothing, he who tooted their horn the loudest and took up as much physical space as possible was King. It was a thrilling ride, much like riding in central London to be honest. Dominate the road, let the 'Pipewerx' can roar nice and loud, and get your arse out of there pronto. I was nipping in and out of the traffic like a local in no time, it was brilliant. I was beaming in my lid, loving every second of this adventure now.

Soon enough I was at the walled city limits. Marrakesh itself is an ancient walled city, made up of loads of markets and trade areas, no use for the bike. I didn't fancy leaving her alone with all the kit stowed on her, nice as the people were, Morocco is famed for it's thieves! I parked up outside the walls, took some pics and footage, and just watched the chaos pass by.

10.1 - The Atlas Mountains

My target for the end of my 1st full day in Morocco was an ancient place called 'Ait Benhaddou' way out on the very skirts of the Sahara Desert, on the other side of the infamous Atlas Mountains. Well, what was I waiting for!

With my faith 100% instilled in the garmin Zumo 660, I followed it's route for mile after stunning mile, the landscape ever changing around me. The windy, noisy, litter strewn coast gradually became greener, the traffic thinned out, but the amount of people stayed the same. Everywhere I went there were people, standing in the middle of nowhere, walking through baron open lands, walking up insanely high mountains, just people everywhere? Where did they live, where were they going, HOW did they survive?

As you get outside of Marrakesh you can see the mountains looming high on the horizon, beckoning you closer. The roads become twistier as they begin to head skyward. It reminded me a lot of the great roads in Northern Spain, the views were equally spectacular.

I was in the zone now, flying up and over these majestic natural beasts, devouring their paths under Bridgestone rubber. As it moved into late afternoon, I began to descend over the other side, the Sahara beckoning me closer. As the light began to fade and the temperature drop, I turned off the main road and rode across gravelly sand into the horizon. In the middle of nowhere I pulled off the road, parked up, and pitched the tent. Now I was over-landing! Like THAT, somebody switched the lights out. Night night.

10.2 - Ait Benhaddou to Agadir

As the sun rose I awoke in the Sahara Desert. I'd planned on getting up early, setting the tripod up and doing a time-lapse of the rising sun. It would've been amazing. As it was by the time I woke up, the sun was well and truly awake and high in the sky! Sorry.

By the time I'd stowed the kit away I saw how close I'd been to my target the night before. There on the horizon was the most incredible vision, straight out of Indiana Jones, Ait Benhaddou, an ancient walled city dating back to the caravan route days. It's truly an awesome sight, one not to be missed if you're ever out this way.

Now picture the scene. A big coach pulls up and a large Moroccan guide steps off as if to claim this land his own. He's met by a fat white guy in white leathers, lying in the dirt taking pictures, not of the 1,000 year old historical site, but of the belly pan of his sportsbike. To add insult to injury, 40 Japanese tourists then poured off the bus and came straight over to me. Ignoring Ait Benhaddou, they waited patiently for me to finish, then one by one stood with me next to the beast and had their pictures taken. (Tommy Day I was thinking of you bud!) The guide gave up, got back on the bus, and visibly sulked. Can't blame him really.

As the tourist buses drove off, I finished packing up and started making my way South West, destination Agadir on the Western coast of Morocco. I was aiming at holding up here for the night with a view to heading down South and possibly entering Western Sahara by Sunday.

The route was superb, views every bit as awesome as the day before, and this time I made sure my wee travel companion 'Benji The Bear' got an airing. For those not in the know, Benji was given to me and named by the kids and young folk at 'The Children's Trust'. He was to be my only constant companion throughout the trip, and was hopefully a means for them to discover a little bit more about the world around them. Unfortunately, Benji was a casualty of Africa, never making it all the way around the world. Sleep well my friend.

What I do know is this, if the sight of a 6'3" fat white bloke, in white leathers on a sportsbike, doesn't draw enough attention, then the sight of said bloke getting a teddy bear out his luggage and taking pics of it certainly will draw a crowd!

Bruce SMART

Safely in Agadir, I was sitting in my hotel room feeling a wee bit blue and sorry for myself. It was Nikki's birthday and I was missing her, just a tad. Having spent almost 4 weeks by myself now and in a strange new world, I was missing the normal conversations you have with people. Just then the phone in my room rang and I answered to be met with, "Is this the guy who's riding a motorbike around the world?" Somewhat stunned, I went down to the reception to be met by Adam Barnett and his better half Jennifer. Fellow Scot's, from just up the road of my home town actually, they were on holiday in Agadir and were passing the hotel when they saw the beast. Being a bike nut, Adam had to have a closer look which drew the attention of hotel staff. They told them about me and that was that. Within 5 minutes we were sitting at the bar like old chums. Got to love bikers!

Cheers Adam and Jennifer, you really brightened my day, it was a pleasure to meet you both.

CHAPTER 11

FROM DREAM....
to NIGHTMARE

To this day, I find it hard to comprehend what happened during this stage of the trip. No individual incident seems enough to warrant such a dramatic decision to end the trip, and yet I know I made the right choice. In an instant the dream could be shattered, in one error of judgement, your time could well be up. Ladies and gentlemen, I give you Africa.

On leaving the hotel in Agadir I headed South through Morocco, aiming for my next country of Western Sahara. I've said it before, but I completely under estimated the size of Morocco. It is vast, and completely desolate in parts – or at least I thought that was desolate!

At the various checkpoints along the road, I'd been hearing for a few days that there was another Brit riding to Cape Town about a day ahead. I decided I'd try to catch him up and see if he fancied buddying up for the Mauritania/Mali section at least. By the end of day 29 I was still in Morocco, in the middle of nowhere as the sun began to set. I pulled off the road, crossed some sand to find a rocky dune outcrop, and parked up behind it to give myself some privacy from the road. Setting up the tent took no time, the 'Vango Chinook 200' is a doddle and doesn't even need to be pegged out as it's completely free standing. Handy in the sand of the Sahara – forward thinking me eh.

I've got to say, it was a stunning place to spend the night and with the full moon glowing brightly, I had a spectacular view from the tent all night. The next day I was up with the sun getting the bike packed and kit stowed away. On the road by 7:30am I hit the first fuel stop not long after, luckily it was open. Grabbing some fresh bread and replenishing water stocks, I was soon back in the saddle intent on reaching Western Sahara.

Having been fought over for many years between the Mauritanians, Moroccans, Algerians and Spanish, Western Sahara now appears to mostly be under Moroccan control, but is still listed as a separate country. So tick goes number 13.

It is simply stunning in it's remoteness, there truly is nothing there outside of the major towns. Many times I'd find myself just riding along a road to nowhere, massively long straight sections of tarmac, some of which would put the best British roads to shame, scything through huge seas of sand. With fuel stops few and far between, you really do have to keep an eye on your mileage to judge when you need to top up, and plan WAY ahead. The fuel stops can be as much as 100 miles apart, and more as you get further South through Africa, so this was all good practice.

I passed into the country without even knowing. No formal border, just yet another police checkpoint, of which there are plenty throughout Morocco. The local police are excellent, kind, polite and professional, bar one young lad who took exception to the fact I was travelling the world as he wanted to and couldn't afford it. He wanted a 'souvenir' for his trouble, so I gave him an, "I've met the Met" sticker and rode off! I didn't get a pic though sorry, don't think he appreciated it!

My route was taking me through all tarmac so far, mostly of great quality on the whole. The road I was on suddenly became quite remote and seemed to vanish ahead into a sea of sand. "It's finally here", I thought as I prepared myself for the epic crossing of the Sahara I'd seen others do on TV before. But alas no, it was just some dunes that had consumed the tarmac, so the going stayed fairly swift. At the last moment I saw a cavernous hole in the road, directly in my path. I couldn't avoid it so simply pinned the throttle to try and take as much weight off the front as I could. BANG, as the rear tyre smashed into this pitt! Bollocks. I stopped and took a look, the rim had taken a cracking bang and dented, but the 'Bridgestone BATTLAX BT-023's' seemed untouched, no bulging, no tears in the tyre wall. They truly are an incredible tyre.

I've spoken of the Bridgestone tyres before and I know you'd expect me to be full of praise for them as they were my tyre supplier after all, but they are simply a superb bit of kit. I've abused them beyond what any bike tyre would be expected to handle, let alone a sports touring tyre. They've been ragged around race tracks, pounded on the daily commute through London, scrubbed in through the green lanes of Surrey & Sussex, as well as ridden across the desert sands of the Sahara. They've handled snow & ice, rain that would float the arc, and scorching Sahara heat without skipping a beat. On top of all that they've provided mileage I never thought possible from any bike tyre, let alone tyres on a 1000cc superbike carrying 200 weight of luggage and my fat ass!

But I wasn't in Europe any more, there wasn't a Bridgestone tyre shop in the next town. In fact there weren't ANY tyres that would fit my bike for the next 8,000 miles until I reached South Africa! With a far more cautious pace now adopted I continued along the route, until in the distance I could see the back of another bike. Could this be the fabled other rider to Cape Town? I pinned her open again and soon rode up behind an ancient looking sidecar ensemble being muscled along by Robert. With a Brit plate proudly on display, I slowly overtook and gave a big wave, 'Hello'! We both pulled over and introduced ourselves.

Robert Cooper is a 63 year old retired mechanic, originally from Cape Town in South Africa. Having lived in Scotland for the best part of 25 years, he was now living his dream and riding a Ural combination from Dumfries to Cape Town. He'd no idea how long it would take, no real idea of a route, no visas, and absolutely no grasp of any other language apart from english and Afrikaans! And I thought I was under prepared?

We chatted briefly at the side of the road about our plans, but I got the impression Robert would much rather forge on alone so we agreed to keep an eye out for each other along the way. I've got to admit, the thought of tackling Mauritania and Mali alone didn't exactly fill me with joy, but it was great to know there was another face in the crowd that wasn't too far away. I rode for another couple of hours but as the sun began to settle out West, I found another cracking spot in the desert and lay camp for the night.

I'm not sure what did it, I'd hardly eaten anything over the last couple of days apart from a few bits of bread and water. But the dreaded 'Delhi-belly' struck with vengeance throughout the night and I hardly slept a wink. It was incredibly humid, with not a breath of wind to stifle the desert heat, meaning the air was thick with mosquitos. Not good when you're perched delicately in the dark with everything on offer!

I've had better nights sleep. So when the sun began to rise I wasn't all that keen to get up and on the road once more. But I was out of water and the temperature was rising high already, so I packed up the kit, got on the beast and rode through the sand, heading to the road off in the distance. But something didn't feel right on the bike, and when I reached tarmac it all became clear why. The back tyre was flat as a pancake. Bollocks.

A quick check of the tyre surface showed no visible tears or punctures so I could only assume it was as a result of the dented rim. Taking all the kit off again I got some of the compressed air cylinders out of the 'Air Pro' puncture kit I always carry under the pillion seat. Two cylinders of air had the tyre up to a good enough pressure for me to limp her to the first available petrol station that hopefully would have air available.

With a doubly sick feeling in my stomach now, I gingerly rode the beast South along the only road there was hoping the next fuel stop wouldn't be too far away. A check on the Garmin showed the nearest fuel stop was about 18Km, would the tyre hold? I was hoping that the tyre had gone flat during the night as the temperature had dropped, causing the tyre pressure, and consequently volume, to decrease. Relying on my schoolboy physics, I hoped that by riding on the tyre its internal temp would rise and therefore the pressure increase, effectively sealing the tyre wall against the rim – slim chance I know, but it was all I could do. Anorexic really!

It held and soon enough I was pulling up to a deserted looking shell of a building. As

I turned off the engine and sank further into the saddle, I rested my head on my tank-bag, frantically trying to think of a solution to this impending issue. At that point a guy stepped out of this 'abandoned' ruin and nonchalantly walked across the courtyard to a small outhouse, disappearing inside. There was the roar of a diesel generator and he merrily wandered over to me, pointing at the beasts' tank.

As he filled her up, I set about racking my brain for any schoolboy french I knew for, "air", "hose" or "flat tyre". Failing miserably I pointed at the soft back tyre and made a sort of 'hissing' noise whilst squirting an imaginary air hose. The bloke began to laugh aloud, then said to me in near perfect english, "You're tyre is pretty flat, do you want some air?"

Feeling a complete throbber I smiled and told him what had happened to the rim, explaining what the trip was all about. Like just about everybody I'd met throughout Morocco, the welcome in Western Sahara was equally as friendly. In no time I had the tyres up to pressure, a bottle of water, and some fresh bread for brekkie. Lovely job.

Setting off for the day I started to forget about the ropey guts and damaged wheel, and settle into the trip ahead. As you travel down along the West coast of Africa, each mile brings a new level of remoteness, mile upon mile of sandy seas stretching out as far as the eye can see in every direction. Intermittently you catch a glimpse of the ocean on your right as the road swings back to the coast, revelling in the sea breeze that brings respite from the overpowering heat of the desert.

I was making good time, the border with Mauritania my target for the end of day 31. Needing fuel once again I stopped at the last stop before the border, and guess who wandered over. Robert had somehow overtaken me either the previous night or earlier today, but I'd now caught back up. Realising we were pretty much travelling at the same pace, we decided it was probably best if we buddy up for the next stretch through Mauritania and Mali. Conversations with fellow travellers on the road, and research online through the Horizons Unlimited 'HUBB', suggested things were fairly 'active' at the moment in these places. Boko Haram and other fanatical Islamic nutters were currently rampaging around

Bruce SMART

Central Africa, having sacked most of Mali they were now heading in to Mauritania. Oh joy. If ever anyone stood out from their surroundings, it was me, on a sportsbike, in leathers, in the desert. I can't tell you how happy I was to have someone else around.

Heading off down the road, we trundled along at a steady 50mph, continually scanning the road ahead for potholes, dogs, camels, and the odd oncoming vehicle which strayed wildly into your path. Pretty soon we reached the end of the road, literally.

CHAPTER 12

MAURITANIA

The border of Western Sahara into Mauritania truly is a tale of contrasts. From Western Sahara you arrive on pristine tarmac into a small, clean compound area. An orderly queue of vehicles sits patiently in front of a gate, with a small office building to the side. There's a bureau de change, a few shops for supplies and a cafe/restaurant. Nothing about this place suggests anything of the horror to come.

Filling in some paperwork and showing the relevant forms issued when you first arrive in Morocco, the police officer stamps your passport, shakes your hand and wishes you, "Bon Chance" – 'Good Luck'. "Ominous", I thought, but knowing what I know now, I'm sure there was some pity in his eyes too.

As the gate is slid open and you ride from Western Sahara to Mauritania, the world changes. The road suddenly ends, replaced by rock and sand. The smiling officials are replaced by para-military like uniformed henchmen who glower at you with suspicion. The professional demeanour of the Moroccan officers now a distant memory, hyenas in uniform now patrolling their patch, looking for whatever scraps they can scavenge. Packs of blokes surround you, all shouting in your face to get your attention over the other. Some asking for money, some begging for money, some demanding money, a few simply attempting to take your money. There are no signs to tell you what to do, no officials pointing the way.

We formed a plan where one would stay with the bikes whilst the other went to sort their paperwork, the idea being we'd swap once one had theirs completed. But the men in uniform wouldn't have it, demanding we both went at the same time. With our kit lying unattended amongst the hordes outside, we were baffled with demand after demand for money for this, that, and everything. Pay to get the bike into Mauritania, pay to get ourselves into Mauritania, pay a tax on this, a tax on that. Eager to return as soon as possible to our kit, we parted with our euros (far preferable to even local currency due to exchange rates) at an astonishing rate!

Soon we were back with the beasts, lighter in pocket but surely that was that? More locals descended on us wanting money to show us the way out, but there was only one track ahead, so we declined and rode along the sandy trail. A sea of sand lay before us with one discernible track leading the way. As we rounded a bend and crested a summit, the track split into two with both trails heading off into a deserted, sandy distance. It was 50- 50, we picked the path to the right and followed our nose.

After about 10 minutes the track had become even more 'rural' but we were no closer to any buildings of any kind, or indeed ANY sign of civilisation. As we stopped to decide on a new plan we could hear shouting over the desert winds. Turning to face the alien noise we saw 3 guys frantically stepping their way erratically across the sand towards us. They were holding their hands up, palms straight to us and arms extended, then I heard what they were shouting. "Mines, Mines, MINES!!"

Unknown to us we'd wandered straight into a mine field and it was at that point that the surroundings became all to clear. All around us were the remnants of cars, rusted ruins in pieces where they rotted in their desert graves. Whether they halted there as a result of mine action I have no idea, but there was more than one natural carcass amongst them. I didn't check to see if they were animal or not.

Realising what we'd done my immediate reaction was to retrace our route back to the junction and take the other path. Looking back, we should have done exactly that, but hindsight is a wonderful thing. Immediately our 'saviours' volunteered their services to get us out our predicament, for a price of course. Not relishing the thought of riding through the sand and rock in the 40 degree heat in my leathers once again, and not particularly keen to get blown up either, we agreed a price and our guides began to show us the way across the field to the other path. Before reaching the safety of the road, he again demanded money, leaving us stranded once again when we refused. Forking out once more, we were soon back on a path of some kind before arriving at a dilapidated crop of out buildings in the desert. There were other vehicles parked up here with men in uniform emptying their contents whilst their occupants stood watching. Two soldiers/police with dogs came over, asking if we had any drugs or alcohol. Not convinced with our negative reply, they nodded in the direction of the first hut. Another guy in plain clothes asked for our passports and paperwork and 50 euros. When I asked why, he said it was for processing the paperwork so we could get out quickly. Tempting though it was, I'd been had over enough already today so ignored him and went into the hut. Inside the stinking building sat a couple of sweating guys in green police uniforms, slowly filling in bits of paper, ink stamping with vigour, and generally ignoring my presence.

Eventually one looked up, held his hand out and demanded our passports, driving licences, and bike paperwork. All the while the same civilian bloke, who had followed me in, was continually asking for 50 euros, now saying it was for insurance. The chap in uniform said nothing, didn't even look at this other guy, so I knew it was a scam. I politely refused the civilian guys offer of help, paid the 25 euros to the officer – funnily enough there was no receipt, and left the hut to join Robert outside. He then had to go through the same process before we were moved onto another hut, more paperwork, more 'fees' to the men in uniform and more attempts to scam us out of money by eager locals. After about 3hrs in the baking sun with no water I was fried and couldn't wait to get out. Eventually we were allowed to leave and we slowly rode across the rocky sand to a tarmac road that looked like it had been recently used for artillery practice. Shellshocked ourselves and with the sun quickly setting, we nervously scanned the Garmin for any campsites or places to stay nearby.

The town of Nouadhibou lies on a small peninsula off the coast of Mauritania. Although effectively in the wrong direction of where we wanted to go, the sun was setting fast and it turns out mine fields are a plenty off the road throughout the country, making wild camping a fairly 'exciting' prospect! We rode into the setting sun, passing checkpoint after checkpoint – some as little as 100 metres apart. All wanting the same thing. Money.

After about 45 minutes we arrived in Nouadhibou, and what a place. I can't help thinking that Judith Chalmers has probably never been here. If you look up, "arsehole of nowhere" in the dictionary, I'm pretty sure there'll be a picture of this place. It was horrific. Dirty, stinking, chaotic, imposing, and threatening. Large 4X4's would scream up behind us and slowly overtake, with men fully clothed in hijab's staring as they passed. Being more agile on 2 wheels, I was able to dodge the traffic as they pulled out in front, sometimes actually aiming specifically at us. Robert on the other hand was a far more substantial target and was hit several times, at slow speed. I honestly thought we were going to be taken away in the back of one of those trucks, never to be seen again. It was terrifying.

After what felt like hours, we eventually pulled up outside a large metal closed gate, oddly positioned in between some buildings. The rusted sign above said, 'Camping' and my heart sank. Had we come all this way through this hell for nothing? But then the gate opened, a nervous looking man peered out and quickly gestured for us to come inside. 'Camping Baie de Levrier' wasn't too bad actually, a welcome relief from the horrors and hostility of the town itself. Based around a sand courtyard, it has several rooms available as well as basic showers and toilet facilities, so was a welcome oasis for the night. It was here we first met Sam and Cat, a British couple travelling through north West Africa in their 4X4. They'd been to Mauritania before and were planning on passing through Senegal, the Gambia, and Mali before heading home. It was great to have a brief chat with fellow Brits and share some of our experiences so far. Before long, I'd crashed out on a mattress and was out for the count.

We awoke early the next day, keen to get out of the town before the majority of people were up. Luckily there was a fuel stop right outside the digs so we replenished our stocks and hit the road. Unfortunately there was no water or food, but we still had some left from the past few days, so we headed off into the desert. There was only one road so navigation wasn't exactly tough. There are no towns to speak of, just the odd collection of ramshackle huts or buildings at the side of the road. Police/military checkpoints abound throughout the country, each wanting the same info – passport, name, details, nationality, where are you going, where have you come from, how long will you be travelling etc. The majority of these were uneventful, not exactly welcoming but civil and straight forward. But you could never count on this, as occasionally one would want money for some 'insurance' you didn't have, or 'certificate' for this or that. Sometimes they'd just cut to the chase and demand money, loaded rifle loosely hanging in your direction.

Robert just about made me laugh out loud at one checkpoint. The young officer was trying his best to get some money out of us, saying we needed to pay for some non-existent bit of paperwork we didn't have. Bored with the continual fleecing, I was playing the dumb tourist when the young lad took some notes out of his pocket and showed them to Robert, hoping he'd take the hint and part with some cash. Robert's eyes lit up and he merrily helped himself to the officers cash and put it in his own pocket before starting the bike and beginning to ride off. The bloke just didn't know what to do and stood there open mouthed for about a nano-second before grabbing his gun. Luckily Robert didn't ride off and returned the cash straight away. We left quick sharpish and didn't look back.

We met up with Cat and Sam again a few times along the road, even managing to grab an ice cold coke at a road side cafe in the middle of nowhere! Maybe this place wasn't as bad as they said. I was really suffering in the heat by lunchtime and water stocks were low. The delhi-belly had returned with a vengeance, and with the added excitement of mines to dodge at the side of the road, constipation was certainly not an issue. After a few hours I'd stopped sweating, my vision now misty, narrow and blurred. I had a banging sore head and a constant screaming noise ringing in my ears. I wasn't in a good way and knew it. Our water supplies were dangerously low and there was nowhere to get any more. The next town was Nouakchott, a good couple of hours ride away.

I remember at one stage having to pull over yet again to deal with an urgent bladder moment. Trying to get back on the bike I could hardly stand, dizzy from dehydration and the heat. All I wanted to do was lie down and sleep, thoughts of my son and Nikki running through my mind. I knew I wasn't in a good way here, I knew I needed water badly and to get out the sun. But this just wasn't an option here, there was nowhere for either. I remember thinking at that point I might not see my Nikki again, never hold her, never have the life we'd planned. Was this really worth that? What a waste! Looking back now, I think that was probably the turning point for me where the trip stopped being an adventure and was now a very real expedition in survival.

Fast forward about an hour and I was leading Robert and I through the Sahara. The road was endlessly straight, stretching ahead into a shimmering sea. I was doing all I could to stay awake, riding with the visor up, jacket and gloves off to keep air moving over my skin, but careful to try to keep covered from the suns' powerful rays. Imagine standing directly in front of a hairdryer whilst you're in an oven and you'll have some idea of what it was like! You could hardly breathe, the air was so hot. All of a sudden we crested a hill and the road just vanished from underneath me. It was like reaching the top of a roller coaster! I was only going about 50mph but as the bike crashed back down onto the road the rear sub-frame snapped like a twig. A combination of the sustained weight of luggage I was carrying, my fat ass and the severity of the drop was just too much for the alloy frame and that was that.

I managed to stay on the bike, pulling over to the side of the road before falling off onto the ground. Looking back up at the beast I could see her back was broken, my heart sank. With still over 150Km's to go before the next town I thought I was done for. I look back now I'm in the safety of Blighty and it all seems a bit melodramatic, but at that point in time it seemed a distinct possibility!

Robert arrived after me having also bottomed out the Ural on the same sump in the road. Straight away he saw the issue with my bike and it dawned on him how badly affected I was by the heat. Realising we needed to get out of here quickly, he got me back on my feet, took some of the luggage off the beast and into his sidecar, and got me back on the bike. I had to sit far forward, jewels resting on the tank and half squatting on the foot pegs, so the next 2hrs were excruciatingly painful, but we eventually rolled into Nouakchott, finding the 'Auberge Sahara' Cat and Sam had told us about, with them already there to greet us. It felt like the weight of the world was lifted as I climbed off the bike that night, I wanted to kiss the ground and demolish a gallon of water. But most of all I just wanted to speak to my son and Nikki. Unfortunately the cell signal was pretty much non-existent and the advertised 'wi-fi' temperamental at best. I managed to get a few texts out to folk and a quick update via the FB page to alert people to the damage to the bike. As usual you were all brilliant, loads of offers of help and temp fixes came flooding in. It was great to have such support so far from home, I can't thank you all enough.

That night after I'd had a shower and some food and water, I found myself reflecting on what had happened over the last few days. I've had a few situations in my life where, had things gone differently, I wouldn't be here now. I've stared down the barrel of a gun at work when chasing a wanted suspect, thankfully it didn't go off, and this moment helped spark the whole project into life. A short time after this happened, I had the conversation with my mum where she said, "Never have regrets", and the rest is now history.

TeapotOne was the very focus of my life for the previous 3yrs. I'd lived and breathed it every day, spent many a sleepless night worrying about finances, visas, routes, sponsorship sources, and how to get it out in the public domain. I'd remortgaged my flat, sold almost everything I owned, sacrificed my relationship with Nikki at one stage, all to make this trip a reality. But that day in the desert, slumped in the sand and heat, I really questioned if the trip was worth all this, was it worth my life for this? At that point I actually regretted coming away.

It's incredible what some kip and grub can do to your spirits. I awoke the next day ready to take on the world so Cat kindly asked the chap who ran the auberge, if there were any local mechanics who could have a look at my bike. Within 10 minutes a guy arrived, took one look at the broken sub-frame and said he'd fix it for 200 euros. Concerned he'd just try and weld it, I made sure he knew I wanted a new part fabricated out of steel and he nodded agreement. 4hrs later he returned saying he couldn't make it out of steel, but he would solder and brace it. With no other option I had to go with it, so we were stuck in

Bruce SMART

Nouakchott for 3 days whilst the repair was made. Even here, we felt captives in the digs.

Stepping out onto the street you immediately felt vulnerable, people descending on you begging for money, pulling you this way and that. One evening we decided to venture out and eat at a local cafe. A chap came over and introduced himself, turns out he'd studied at Uni in Edinburgh and loved the Scots! At last, some generosity and kindness from strangers, just like I'd heard other travellers speak of. This had been conspicuous in its' absence throughout Mauritania to be honest. After a few hours we'd had some grub and a few drinks, nothing spectacular though as nobody had mentioned anything about the price despite us asking before ordering. We'd learnt very quickly to establish the price for anything in advance otherwise you were fleeced outrageously. Alas this was no different. This guy had spent the last couple of hours telling us how much he loved Scottish people, how kind and generous the Mauritanian people were, and how we were safe here with him. Asking for the bill, he quickly interrupted and spoke to the woman who ran the place in a local language. I could tell by the way they looked at each other and us, they were working out how much they could charge and get away with it. The bill arrived, 30 euros for two plates of fish, bread and 2 cokes. Not bad if I was in London! When I questioned the amount, we were met with a grin and he simply said, "You whites can afford this, it's nothing!"

By mid afternoon the next day, the local mechanic returned with the rear sub-frame patched up and braced back together. Although 'agricultural' looking, it'd do the job so I set about fitting it back on the bike. This being the first time I'd ever done this, it took a few attempts, a bit of pushing here, squeezing there, but eventually she was back. With all the wiring connected where I hoped it was meant to be, I turned the key in the ignition and the beast whirred back to life. That's a good start, at least the electrics seem to be working. Nervously I pulled in the clutch and pushed the starter as she roared into life, WALLOP! I'm not a religious man, but thanked whoever was looking over me, we were going to make it.

My plan now was to get to Dakar in Senegal. Once there I could arrange shipping of a replacement part, we could get Roberts' visas for the next few countries, and we could get supplies together for the trip ahead. Lovely job.

Day 35 started nice and early, we packed up the bikes, settled the bill for our stay and said goodbye to a few fellow travellers we'd met over the last 3 days. One of them was a chap called 'Micky', a Hungarian lad who was here planning and prepping the route for the 2013 Budapest – Bamako Rally (www.budapestbamako.org) Micky had apparently won the rally for the last X-amount of years on the trott, so the organisers asked him to sit out this year and help with the planning and prep. He was here with his Australian wife and it was great to sit and chat with them the previous evening, finding out about their adventures, as well as getting a few hints and tips for the 'roads' ahead.

The next obstacle was going to be the border crossing into Senegal at Rosso. This place is infamous as one of the worst and most corrupt borders in Africa, if not the world. There's another option at Diama but this involves about 50Km of really bad off-roading to reach from the main road in Mauritania. As I was on the gixxer, and it was already fairly delicate after breaking the rear sub-frame, we thought we'd just brave it out and go for Rosso. As it was, Micky was also going to cross at Rosso as soon as his car was fixed, (it was also being repaired by the same bloke who'd fixed my bike.) Micky knew a guy at the Rosso border so was hoping he'd be working and this may 'speed' up the process a bit, as well as make it slightly less expensive!

We hoped that Micky would catch us up through the day and we'd all go through Rosso together, so Robert and I headed off first thing. Yet again we struggled to get fuel and supplies as we left Nouakchott. Fuel wasn't too much of an issue, although you had to pay through the nose for it. I walked into a local shop to buy a loaf of bread and 4 big bottles of water. I didn't have local money left so attempted to pay with 20 euros. The guy wouldn't take the money and waved me out the shop. Having been in the desert without water a few days previously, I didn't want to repeat this again. Desperate, I offered the full 20 euros in return for just the water. At that, he picked up an AK47 from behind the counter and pointed it straight at me. I was getting kind of bored of all this now.

Backing out the shop slowly, I began to walk back to the bikes but was met by another chap who asked if I was ok. Expecting yet another fleecing, I remarked I was only after water in the limited French I knew. The chap replied in English, asking what the problem was so I explained I only had euros but they wouldn't accept it in the shop. As 'luck' would have it, this chap apparently owned all the shops in the 'street' so took me straight back and I paid 20 euros for 4 bottles of water and a stick of bread. I didn't argue, I didn't care, I just wanted out this bloody place.

We were soon on the road and heading South, destination Senegal, a place where everyone had said you'll see the real Africa. This was where the beauty, kindness and generosity was going to happen. I couldn't wait as I'd had just about enough of the place by now. As the morning progressed we slogged on through the building heat, the landscape slowly began to change as the odd speckle of greenery fought to break through the dry crusty earth. You could tell you were moving from 'Arab' africa to 'Black' Africa as the various roadside communities changed. In the north there were hardly any buildings or towns, and those were separated by huge expanses of absolutely nothing. But as you ventured further South we started to see more and more huts appearing at the road, until it appeared like the country was just made up of one continuous village. It was hard to find a vacant spot to pull over and have a pee!

You've probably noticed that there aren't many pics of this section, and there's good reason. The police in Mauritania seemed to have a real dislike to cameras of any kind. If they saw you with one they'd either take it for themselves, or make you delete what was on it. With random checkpoints springing up all over the place, I decided not to get the bike cams or regular camera out whilst on the road, in case we stumbled upon one all of a sudden. To be honest, I didn't want to get the cameras out at all as I feared they'd disappear in an instant should they take anyone's fancy!

We were nearing Rosso by lunchtime, the sun was high in the sky and the road had become horrendous in its' condition. Huge potholes littered the surface, often it was easier to simply come off the road and ride down the sides, but the ever present threat of mines limited how far you could venture. We rolled up to yet another checkpoint and were directed over to the side where a fat young lad in uniform sat in the shade. He mumbled something in French which I couldn't understand so I asked if he spoke English. Looking at me in disgust, he pulled 3 phones out his pocket and dialled a number on one. After a brief conversation in a language I couldn't make out, he handed the phone to me saying, "talk!" A very well spoken young lad introduced himself as David on the other end. He asked where I came from, what I was doing, where I was going, how many people I was with, all the normal sort of questions we'd been asked at all the checkpoints throughout Africa, so I didn't feel too alarmed. He thanked me and asked me to put the other guy back on the line, so I did exactly that. The officer then smiled and waved us on down the road. Not too bad then.

About 10 minutes later we arrived at the gates to hell. To give you some idea of what Rosso is like, think Mad Max and the Star Wars bar, mix it with the inmates of a maximum security prison, then chuck it in the oven for 6 hrs at 850 degrees. It was horrific.

A huge queue of traffic stretched back from a large, closed, solid, metal gate. Gangs of young lads were swooping over each vehicle like packs of wolves around a young animal, every way you looked people were coming at you wanting money, pulling at your clothing and kit on the bike. At this point a well dressed young lad came out the crowd and walked straight up to me. Holding out his hand he introduced himself as David, the guy I'd spoken to on the phone, and asked us to follow him to the front of the queue. Nervously we followed as he had a brief chat with the officers on the gate, it was duly opened and we were welcomed inside with smiles and open arms. All good so far, it was just a big open car park on the banks of a large river. The metal gate was shut behind us and we were now in the relative calm and serenity of the border post.

David then walked over with one of the uniformed officers and 3 other young lads. "Give me your passports, driving licences, log books, and money", he said. Somewhat taken aback I asked why. He just laughed and said to relax, he was here to help and would get us out on the next ferry. The policeman in uniform smiled away and again asked for the same documents. I asked how much it cost and was met with what you don't want to hear, "How much have you got!" Bollocks, I could see where this was going.

I'd read on various forums about Rosso, the general amount banded about seemed to be around $100-$200 each to get everything done. Others had got away with as little as $20, but this was after long delays and much aggravation. Earlier that day I'd split my money up in case something like this happened. I knew I had about $50 in my wallet and about another 40 euros, as well as some local currency. I also had about $200 hidden in small amounts around the bike and luggage. The rest of my money was safely hidden in a bug out bag I had stashed away on me, something my mate Ralph had taught me on the Hostile Environment Course I'd undertaken through VGSOE.

By this time Robert had got out all his paperwork and handed it over to one of the goons, so I followed suit. Great, now they had all our docs, why did I do that! It's crazy, I can sit back now and reflect on what happened and how I reacted. Hindsight truly is a wonderful thing eh. But at that time, in the heat of the moment, all we wanted was to get out of that place as quickly as possible. Just to get away from these people, this place, get some form of control back into our lives!

"Quickly, we can get you on the next ferry, come, quick, I need $100 for each of you and it will be done, come quick!" Like a mug I reached for my wallet, highlighting exactly where it was. In an instant the police officer reached out and took it from me, gun loose in his grasp. Smiling all the while, he and David emptied it of the notes, leaving the Sterling, Polish and Czech notes I'd acquired through the trip so far. I stood there stunned at what had just occurred. Had I actually just been robbed by a Copper? No way, not me, not like that, not that easily? With a smile they returned my wallet to me, and asked me to follow them to one of the offices so they could get the paperwork sorted. I could see other people up on the landings, travellers like us, so I felt a bit safer. I followed feeling how I assume the many goats I'd seen had felt before they became dinner.

After about 20 minutes wait, David came back and said we now had to get insurance before we would be let onto the ferry. I knew we'd need this but had assumed it would be included in the initial price, but no. We were taken back out of the relative 'safety' of the compound to a squalid office off the main road. 3 guys sat around a desk with laptops and sunglasses, David said something to them and they looked at Robert and I. "$100, one month" barked one guy. Basically they were charging us $100 for a months worth of insurance to ride the bikes through Africa. Trouble is this insurance isn't worth the paper it's written on, it literally is a formality to get through the borders. If you haven't got it, you don't get through until you do get it. It ranges in price from a few dollars to hundreds, depending on your patience levels and luck.

Now I didn't have much patience left by now, nearly as little as the money I had left in my pocket! Baring in mind we'd just been robbed at gun point, yet again, it perhaps wasn't clever to get too 'fruity' with these lads. But I was very hot, very tired, very angry and very pissed off with this place. My time in Glasgow was well spent and I let loose with a tirade that Rab C Nesbitt himself would be proud of. Thankfully I don't think they understood a word, but found it fairly amusing. This didn't help my mood, but at least they didn't shoot me, or worse.

They actually sat us down and gave us a couple of cans of coke, no doubt paid for through our own money mind you. After 2hrs negotiation I got the insurance down to $20 for both of us for 5 days. That would get us through this crappy place and we could sort out insurance for the next leg at a, hopefully, better border later on.

We were taken back through the big gate into the compound and back to the office blocks. Whilst waiting outside an office I got talking with a Belgian chap who was patiently waiting in the queue. I was fuming by now and he asked what was wrong. I explained what had happened and how much it had cost us. He stood there open mouthed and told me it shouldn't have been any more than about $30 all in. He lived in the Gambia and crossed here all the time so was used to its' ways. He had his wife and small child in a camper van waiting outside the main gate, back in that hell-hole. One of the goons saw he was talking to us so came over and said something in French. I've got to give this French lad his due, he was no mug and began arguing with David and his goons. Things were getting pretty illuminated, hands and voices were being raised all over the option! When the French chap was finished he got his paperwork and went to walk back down the stairs but was followed by one of the goons. Not liking the look of this I went to follow but immediately the French guy came back up with blood pouring from his lip, he'd been punched in the stairwell. He didn't hit back, didn't fight at all, just went straight to the police in the office and told them what had happened. They came out and looked like they were going to do something about this, well they did. They took the French guy away and we didn't see him again. Holy Jesus, what was this place like, what had we got ourselves into! I'm not afraid to say it, now I was getting scared.

The Hungarian chap 'Micky' – from the previous nights stay at the 'Auberge Sahara' in Nouakchott, then appeared and I could have hugged him! He looked a bit shell-shocked and said his mate wasn't working so he was having problems himself. We told him about everything that had happened to us and he shook his head. "This is Africa man, it's not good here" was all he could say. You know what you could do with Africa as far as I was now concerned, poke it!

Yet another ferry was now loading up and we still weren't on it. All of a sudden David appeared with our paperwork and gestured for us to follow him back to the bikes. I asked if it was all done now and he just smiled, stepping onto the ferry with all our documents and waving for us to follow. Getting on the bikes we rode them aboard as he walked off towards the front. I think I'd have throttled the little bugger if we were alone. As the ferry began to leave the dock he came back and handed me our logbooks, insurance papers and driving licences...... but no passports! I looked at him and asked where they were he just smiled and said we'd get them at the other side. I hated this, absolutely hated it. Being out of control to this extent is just not fun, not in a place like this where absolutely anything can happen to you and nobody gives a flying whatever. As the ferry pulled into the port on the Senegal side of the river, I'd decided in my head that Africa was finished for me. I'd had enough of people waving guns in my face, had enough of people fleecing me for every penny I had. This wasn't adventure, it was just madness and at the rate we were going, financial – if not also actual, suicide.

As we were taken to another hut more people descended on us, each asking for money for this and that, some just wanting money. David then said he needed another $100 each for our passports or we'd have to go back to the other side and go through it all again. I could only laugh now and explain once again that we had no more money left, he'd had everything we had. Sitting down in the sand we resigned ourselves to a very long wait and a possible call to the British embassy – which probably wouldn't help us as the FCO had warned against any travel to Mauritania in the first place!

Content that he'd got everything he could from us, our passports duly arrived and David was nowhere to be seen. Somewhat in a state of shock, we wandered over to the hut and joined the 'queue'. Eventually some men in uniform took all our paperwork, stamped them with vigour and returned it all, pointing to the customs building across the courtyard. We wandered in and sat down, waiting our turn. Eventually the desk officer asked for our carnets and duly stamped them, saying we had 4 days to get to Dakar where they'd need to be stamped once more. Another 10 euros each for this, then 20 euros to a fat bloke at the main gate, otherwise he wouldn't open it! As I wandered over to the beast I passed Micky who was now looking pretty worried himself. As he'd refused the 'help' of David and his goons, there now seemed to be an issue with his carnet for his car and they weren't letting him through. He'd have to go back across on the ferry, back through the Mauritanian border post and try at Diama. Jesus I hated this place, I couldn't wait to get out of this compound and onto the open road. I didn't care where it went, I just wanted on the bike and to get moving as far away from this hell hole as possible. The fat guy slowly slid open the metal gate and a sea of faces stared at us from the waiting crowd. I just put my head down, turned the throttle and rode ahead, not stopping until we reached the outskirts of the town with Robert close behind.

I was fried, completely and utterly fried. With only a little bit of warm water left we rode as far along the road as we could then set up camp for the night. I couldn't speak, could hardly stand and was awash with a mix of emotion. I set the tent up, made my apologies to Robert as I just needed to lie down and go to sleep. Lying in the tent I couldn't believe what had happened, I couldn't believe that I was now contemplating giving up, I couldn't believe that I'd let myself be put into a situation where I would be out of control like that, and liberated of my money. You start to think over everything that had happened, you see the guns again, you see the smirking faces of those who'd threatened you and taken your money. The last few days just caught up with me as I lay there in Senegal. In the space of about 5 days I'd nearly died of heatstroke twice, broken the back of the beast, had a rear wheel rim that couldn't hold air pressure, lost count of the amount of times someone had pointed a gun at me, and now been set up and robbed by the police. I called my good mate Russ, telling him I didn't know if I could do this any more and was contemplating giving up. Like the great mate he is, he listened to what had happened and just let me babble on and vent it out. Russ was the voice of reason, offering alternatives to simply giving up, like shipping elsewhere in Africa, or elsewhere in the world, and carrying on from there. But I couldn't think that night, I just needed to sleep. Finishing the call, I began to drift off to sleep but my Nikki called after hearing from Russ. It was the best feeling to hear her voice again and we spoke for a short while, I promised to get some sleep and call her tomorrow once I'd had a chance to think.

The next day we woke early after a rough nights sleep, both absolutely shattered but keen to get to the safety and normality of Dakar. I began to think of alternatives to just giving up. The replacement part was going to cost a fair bit and would take about 5 days to ship to Dakar. Even then it wouldn't be any stronger so I'd still have the same issue with carrying all the luggage on my return up the east from South Africa. To be honest I wanted out of Africa, I'd lost the heart for this place and without the heart and mind to do a trip like this, it just isn't going to happen.

So I was now looking at shipping to somewhere like Turkey or India and continuing on from there. However, if I went to Turkey I'd now face Russia, Kazakhstan and Mongolia in the depths of winter, where temperatures can reach over 40 below. This was just suicide and not a viable option. This left India or somewhere similar, but the cost of shipping here would mean I'd arrive but have nothing left to do the actual trip! I was kind of stuck.

Despite spending almost 3 years trying to source the funding for the trip, remortgaging and selling everything I own, and getting a last minute influx of corporate and private sponsors to advertise on the bike, I'd still never had anywhere near the £35K I'd needed for the trip. In truth, I didn't even have a third of that with things like visas, meds, and the carnet all eating into this before I'd even left British shores! I'd thought I'd at least get around Africa before the money ran out and counted on hopefully recruiting more corporate sponsors to help fund the rest of the trip. It was a gamble I know, but never in a million years did I think I'd ever contemplate giving up like this.

Throughout the long ride to Dakar I racked my brain for alternatives, there must be a way? But in all honesty, the last week had really taken it out of me and I just wasn't prepared to risk everything for this trip anymore. Adventure is one thing, but this was starting to be actual life and death.

Arriving at Dakar both Robert and I were kind of taken aback by the place. Contrary to the cosmopolitan and developed city we'd expected to find, Dakar is a dirty, polluted and overcrowded place. Traffic puts the M25 at rush hour to shame, thousands of vehicles tightly packed into the narrow streets, all belching out black smoke into the baking heat. People are everywhere, selling everything you could think of from the side of the road. As you ride along, people run alongside begging for money or simply shouting, "Give me money, Give me money!"

We found our digs just next to the main container port, thanks to a passing moped rider who noticed us looking lost at the side of the road. The hotel was a real oasis in a sea of shit, tucked away at the end of a side road right on the coast. Obviously he expected a 'tip' for his services, but we gladly obliged in return for the safety and serenity of the hotel compared to outside. I'd pre-booked the hotel over the t'interweb from the Sunday to Wednesday, hopefully giving me enough time to arrange either shipping of parts, or shipping of the bike should I decide to end it. But as we'd been held at the Rosso border the day before, we didn't arrive until Monday so the hotel wouldn't give us the internet rate. Brilliant, even the hotels scammed you in this place. 100 euros a night for somewhere you'd begrudge paying £20 for here in the UK. But it was safe, we could buy food and water from the beach restaurant, and it had internet – at times. Getting into the room we both just collapsed on our beds and slept for a couple of hours. As knackered as I was, I still couldn't really sleep, thoughts of the last few years running through my head, all the plans, all the risks I'd taken, sacrifices people had made. After some grub and a couple of beers, we sat talking about what had happened that week, what we'd expected from our trips, and the reasons why we were doing them.

Ultimately Robert and I were fairly similar and both had loved ones waiting for our trips to end. Robert was returning to his homeland in South Africa, a lost love and family waiting for his arrival. For him, he'd no option of shipping, he'd have to ride the bike down through Africa. Robert had spent time in the Middle East working for the US Army – I didn't ask, so was used to this type of environment. He also got a significantly different reaction on his bike to the one I got on mine. When Robert rode through a village people would run alongside, waving and smiling. When I rode through, I had people spitting at me and throwing shoes? I don't know why, but the hostility and resentment directed at me and the bike was a stark contrast to the kindness and generosity people had spoken about of these distant lands.

I awoke the next day knowing what I wanted to do, and that was to come home. I just didn't have the heart or mind to carry on through Africa, and this is what will get you through on a trip like this. It doesn't matter how reliable your kit is, how physically strong you may be, or how much money you have, you need to have the fire and drive to get through the bad times that will inevitably arise. The last week had beaten that from me and showed me where my true priorities lay. I wasn't the lone wolf I'd made myself become before the trip, I didn't have anything to prove anymore and had everything to get back to. I was going home to my family and loved ones, that was where my heart and soul was, not here. I told Robert of my decision and gave him the SPOT tracker so his friends and family could track his progress.

It felt like a huge weight had been lifted from my shoulders as I made the decision. I'm disappointed that I didn't finish the African leg of the trip, but I'd ridden a gixxer across the Sahara Desert, to my knowledge nobody else has done that.

The last few days in Africa where spent frantically organising the shipping of the Beast home to Blighty. I owe my cousin Dave a lot as he worked tirelessly with his contacts to help in any way he could. I went with Robert to various embassies around Dakar, arranging visas for his trip ahead. Just as we began to slowly relax from the hell we'd just experienced, our taxi driver decided to take us on a detour to his cousins carpet stall, despite us saying we wanted to go directly to the embassy and back to the hotel. As he turned into the market street, hundreds of people descended on the car, pulling at the doors in an attempt to get the rich white men out. I could see the terror in the driver's face, he knew he'd made a mistake, the crowd turned angry and began to rock the cab. Thankfully he saw sense and blasted the horn, revving the engine wildly as he made our escape through the streets.

Back at our digs, Robert and I both packed up all our kit, he was continuing on to South Africa and I was returning to Blighty a broken man. The next morning I stood and waived goodbye as he pulled out the yard and disappeared down the manic, traffic infested streets of Dakar. My heart sank as I was alone once again, my mind racing with the consequences of decisions made.

A few days later I rode the Beast to Dakar airport and dropped her off at the shipping yard. A few hours later I was on a plane back to Lisbon, and then Heathrow.

I had awoken from the dream.

CHAPTER 13
WE'RE OFF AGAIN

When it all fell apart in Africa, I've got to admit I was a mess mentally. That place is hard, really hard, it well and truly beat me. I'd spent so long planning the trip, working so hard trying to get the industry to take me seriously, and sacrificed a hell of a lot to get it off the ground. When I found myself back in Blighty I was awash with emotion.

Initially I was relieved to be home and out of that place, safe in the arms of my Nikki and family, back in familiar surroundings where I knew what was 'normal', what was expected, and safe! But soon enough I found myself yearning for the road again, quickly dulling to the monotony of normality and haven to a growing sense of failure and loss. I remember being in the Sahara and in a really bad way. I remember thinking to myself, "If I get through this, when I get home I'm going to make things right, I'm going to get on with my life". Here I was, back in my normal life and nothing had changed around me. It was situation as normal. But I wasn't normal, far from it.

As time went by I could feel myself growing distant to those around me, I couldn't accept that this was it now. Bridgestone and Fast Bikes had been fantastic when I told them I was coming home, they threw open the idea to break the trip down into smaller chunks with greater support. Initially this sounded great, something I could work around normal life and the job. However as weeks turned to months, it was dawning on me that this wasn't my dream, and for it to happen you have to be 100% committed.

Then out of the blue came a chap called Martin who I'd met at the NEC bike show whilst there with Bridgestone. Martin was the UK director of a company called 'Delta Energy Services', and he'd got in touch just at the point when I was coming home from Africa. He'd wanted to offer some financial sponsorship to the trip in return for some marketing material to highlight Delta's 25th anniversary. After a good chat at the NEC, we bid our farewells and that was that, or so I thought.

Fast forward nearly 6 months and I was sitting in their UK HQ in Coventry, chatting about bikes and drinking a cracking brew. In an instant a deal was done, leaving me a matter of weeks to get permission from work to leave for another 18 months, not to mention break the news to Nikki that I'd be going on another wee bike ride!

As usual Nikki was a rock, less than impressed, but she knew I had to do this, if not just for my own sanity and self-respect. I had about three and a half weeks to get everything ready before I was due to leave on the 9th May 2013. I'd be heading across Russia to Vladivostok so only had a short weather window in which to travel on the bike. Too late and I'd get caught in the wet and cold, making it impossible to pass on the beast. I also still had a valid Carnet de Passage so needed to get going in order to make use of it before it expired. In truth I just couldn't wait to get back on the road, I was going insane in this life of normality and needed to settle the demons that had grown in my conscience since my return.

There was the small matter of yet another broken rear-sub frame, this time it failed with only my fat backside on the back whilst coming off the M1 on way to a track day at Donnington! Somehow the threads in the main frame had been crossed, meaning some of the bolts holding the rear sub frame had worked loose over time. This had caused added stress on the remaining bolts and they failed. I had to get these heli-coiled and replace the rear sub-frame and bolts. Suzuki UK kindly offered me the frame at a discounted price, but I'd have to assemble it, put it back on the bike and rewire the wiring loom.

Thankfully I've got some cracking mates, so whilst Jimbo lent me his bike ramp, tools, tea and garage, Dave 'Pudsey' Varela lent me his technical wizardry and basically rewired the bike. What should have been a quick job taking a maximum of 1 and a half hours, turned into a 2-day affair including an evening in the pub!

You know when you put together some flat-packed furniture and end up with bits left? Well we had the opposite problem, we had a spare connector block that was just sitting there begging to be plugged into something. But what, there was nothing left? I lost track of the times Dave asked me if there was another lead anywhere, in fact we both looked all over the place. After almost 8 hours I'd had to accept defeat for the night and we were off to the pub to clear our heads, ready to attack it fresh in the morning. In a fit of anger I booted a carboard box that was sitting on Jimbo's drive, watching it sail into a flower bed. Feeling like a bit of a tit I wandered over to pick it up, and saw it lying there in the soil. A black cable with a relay and connector block. We plugged it in, turned the key, and vroom, we were in business. Bollocks!

With the beast now fully repaired, and with a set of spanking new boots courtesy of Bridgestone's new sports touring tyre, the BATTLAX T-30, I was all set to go. Work had kindly granted me a rapid career break meaning I wasn't due back in the cloth until the 2nd November 2014, so as I'd never really unpacked my kit, I loaded up the bike and awaited launch day.

Just like before I set off from the Cenotaph in Whitehall, where I intended to return on completion of the trip, sometime in early July 2014. I didn't want the big send off this time. It was amazing to have everyone along for the ride down to Dover, but I'd done that now and, to be honest, I just wanted to get underway again. Martin from Delta met me at an un-Godly hour, we got a few pics, then set off to ride North.

I was starting the trip with a tour around Scotland with some lads from the www.1000rr.co.uk forum. My mates Jimbo and Dave are members and had drummed up a load of support for me on the 1st trip. When it all went wrong some of the lads got in touch and kindly invited me on their inaugural Scotland tour. As I'd already got this planned I thought what better way to kick start the trip of a lifetime than with a bunch of

Bruce SMART

like minded idiots! Lovely job.

On the way up to the meet in Hawick, I stopped off at the Winding Roads depot to pick up a few last minute bits'n'bobs. This is a cracking site for the travelling biker, if they don't have it, they'll get it. Lovely folk to boot. Martin left me at this point so I headed up to Squires cafe in Leeds to meet a good mate Ray 'Wandering' Walton. I met Ray a few years back whilst competing in the RBLR1000. Since then we've become good mates and his enthusiasm for biking makes me look like a weekend warrior.

Ray and I were supposed to be doing the Nordkapp run together after I stood him up for a breakfast meet when I first got back from Africa. I promised him I'd get him a bacon butty and a brew, he just needed to name the place. Ray said Nordkapp and I immediately agreed, not having the faintest idea where it was! I got a wee shock when I googled it I must admit, but that's Ray for you. When he says to his Mrs, Jeanie, that he's just popping out for a ride, she doesn't ask what time he'll be back, but what day!

Unfortunately due to family circumstances Ray couldn't come with me on this part of the trip so we met up at Squires and I shared some grub and a brew with my good mate. I could sense his disappointment at not being able to come, but his family means the world to him and that's the measure of the man. Another time Raymondo, there's always another time bud.

From Squires I headed up to Darlington to meet David Iles, the brother of Bob Iles, the owner of Delta Energy Services. David is an amazing bloke, the warmth and generosity he offered a complete stranger was incredible to behold. He suffers from Lymphatic cancer and now offers guidance and counselling to fellow sufferers, such as Johnny who I met at David's house. He does an incredible job of fund-raising for the Lymphoma Association too, and as such Bob had asked if I would add them to my list of charities I was raising awareness for. I gladly agreed and after meeting with David, I'm proud to be associated with this incredible organisation and urge you to take a look at what they do. If you can spare any donations their way, that'd be even better, ta.

After a brew and another sandwich – got to maintain my reserves, I bid farewell to David and Johnny and headed north to God's country just as the rain began to fall. As luck would have it I'd left home to embark on my 70,000 mile journey around the world without my waterproofs. Not the best start I'll admit. Anyway, using that as an excuse I managed to keep just one step ahead of the heavy rainfall as I rocketed to the border, stopping briefly for the required pic at the border marker.

The Scotland leg was to take 3 full days and cover most of Scotland, ending on the Monday when we'd each go our separate ways. But first the lads had to experience Scotland on their bikes, simply one of the greatest places from the saddle. This is also where my good mate Dave got the nickname 'Pudsey'. Despite being an electrical genius, Dave is a bit ham-fisted when it comes to anything not connected with wires. Whilst attempting to change the visor on his Arai lid, he managed to break off one of the side pods, making the lid almost unusable! But never fear, there is NOTHING in this world that gaffa tape can not fix. With the added security of some black insulation tape, we soon had him back on the road, looking scarily alike the 'Children In Need' mascot, Pudsey Bear! And so, Dave "Pudsey" Varella was born, and you know it will never now die!

After meeting with the remaining Scottish contingent at Peebles, we all made our way to the Cove at 'the ferry' for a photo op underneath the great Forth Rail Bridge. This is an incredible piece of engineering by any standards, and an instantly recognisable image.

Our destination for the end of day 2 was to be Grantown-On-Spey, so we headed off for the next stop at Knockhill Circuit where we'd got a couple of parade laps arranged. With the rain coming down it was a good job we were chaperoned around the circuit, front and rear, to ensure everyone behaved. It's a brilliant wee circuit and I vowed to get back there one day to sample it's curves, inclines and declines at full throttle. That said, we still managed to get some knee down action, I only wish it was caught on camera. What a great PR shot for the new BATTLAX T30, loaded up with luggage and still getting a knee down in the rain!

Bruce SMART

Next we headed off at a rate of knots through central Scotland, passing up through Glenshee and stopping in this spectacular natural wonder. Writing this, I've ridden through some of the most breathtaking scenery I've ever seen, but there are parts of Scotland which rival anything I've witnessed, and Glenshee is one such place. Folks it's on your doorstep there in Blighty, just make time when you can, and get up there to sample it. Simply stunning, and the roads are out of this world too, just watch out for the sheep!

That night we each sat at the hotel bar recounting tales of individual riding prowess, and more than one, "Oh Shit!" moment we all have every time we saddle the beasts. As usual, Dave, Jimbo and I were propping it up until the last, and on the way back to our room, Dave found the courage to finally fulfil his quest for the glorious 'knee-down' moment! (No not that kind!!) We found an abandoned mobility scooter on the way back to the room, so took advantage of the situation to get a few pics! (see the pics at the end of the book).

The Scotland tour was one of the best times I've had away on the bike. It involved one of the most 'impressive' runs I've ever participated in whilst heading up to John'O'Groats from Inverness. The lads wouldn't believe me that it'd only take about an hour and a half to cover the 125 miles or so. 95 minutes later we were sitting having a brew looking out over the Pentland Firth, silent in a state of shock! What a simply awesome run that is, and to the lads that came that day, one word sum's it up. "BOWWWWWWwwwwwwwwwww-wwww!" (Lee that one's for you bud ;-))

I could make a book and vid out of this tour, but it's not my baby to share. The lads over at www.1000rr.co.uk have that honour and if you want to share it, you'll need to join them. If you're a biker you can't go wrong. It doesn't matter what you ride, just as long as you ride. Obviously if you happen to ride a Fireblade they'll probably talk back to you!

After saying farewell to the lads, I headed South alone to meet with Delta at their UK HQ in Coventry, then Bridgestone at their Warwick UK HQ. It was great to meet up with both groups of folks who have helped me so much in getting the project from a dream to reality, and share some of the excitement and build up with them.

Over the next few days I headed down South West to Lands End, before returning back to London where I was due to pick up my Russian visa before crossing the channel.

Well it wouldn't be a TeapotOne 'outing' without some kind of issue with the beast, and this would be no different. I'd stopped at a petrol station in Penzance and when I tried to start her up again, nothing? I tried all the normal culprits – side stand, kill switch, clutch, but still nothing at all. I tried bumping her, to the amused looks of the crowds, and she roared back into life, lovely job.

An hour or so later I pulled into another services in Ilminster and was faced with exactly the same predicament. Waddling around the forecourt, I was struggling to get enough momentum to bump her into life once more, when the lady from the counter came out and told me about a motorcycle garage just around the corner. Now this was fantastic news, but I was in the middle of nowhere, there wasn't even a 'corner' for it to be around? This guardian angel gave me directions down a farm track and low and behold, there I found Andy and his little den of biker haven.

You know you're in good hands when the mechanic is surrounded by all manner of models, each in various stages of repair, hands dirty with grease and oil, yet he's emanating a calm and confident aura about him. I was practically having a heart attack at the thought of my ignition switch not working, yet he calmly walked over to the bike, jiggled this and mumbled at that. Straight away he said, "that'll be shite in your clutch sensor, often is with these Jap'uns!" With that, he pulled in the clutch, pushed the ignition button and the beast roared to life once again? "I've got the touch", is all he said as he gave the clutch a squirt of GT85 and wiped her down. We talked about the trip for the next wee while then bid our farewells. Andy, you're a legend mate, thanks very much for returning my faith in the beast.

Bruce SMART

So it was back to London on the eve of day 7 where I was to meet up with Nikki for a quick brew before she went to work. I'd left the week previously for a year away and forgot my waterproofs, so ever my saviour, she brought them with her too! After a quick goodbye I was back on the road, but minus the Russian visa! There had been changes to the visa application process right at the time I had applied, so for now at least, I still had no Russian visa. It'd be in the hands of the biking Gods for now, so with that I ventured back across the Channel and onto mainland Europe once again.

CHAPTER 14
UK TO THE ARCTIC CIRCLE

Leaving Blighty I arrived once more on the shores of France and turned left. I've done this route many times now and just wanted to get some miles under my wheels so pushed forward through Belgium, into the Netherlands, arriving in Amsterdam late into the evening.

My mate Russ had managed to organise a contact in the city through his brother Daniel. Jo Swabe is a fellow Born Free lover and is at the very forefront of animal welfare across the globe. She had very kindly offered to put me up for the evening, bang in the centre of Amsterdam.

For anyone who's never been to this place, two pieces of advice. One – If navigating via satnav, give yourself plenty of time for 're-routes'! It's a nightmare of a place to drive around, and I've ridden in Rome! Two – Go. Definitely go. It's not at all what I had pictured in my head, although there's plenty of that if you want it, but there is so much more to the city. I only had a few hours quite late on in the evening, but there was more than enough to keep me occupied and make me want to come back for more another time.

If you're into art then this is the place for you as there are countless museums, exhibits, and random works scattered throughout the city. From the world famous 'Rijks Museum' which houses artwork from the likes of Rembrandt, to an incredible art-deco original cinema – The Tuschinski Theater, Amsterdam is bursting with culture of every kind.

After a good few hours wandering around the city it was time to head back to the flat and get some well earned kip. I was absolutely shattered, not sure why really, but for about the first 2 weeks of this trip, I was cream crackered every day? (I later found out that I'd actually developed a heart condition whilst on the trip!)

Days 9, 10 & 11 saw me get my head down and eat up the miles. I'd never intended to stop in any of these countries to be honest as I knew I had massive mileage to cover later in the trip. As it was, the Netherlands and Denmark didn't throw up any great surprises as far as biking goes. There were a few bikers out, but the roads were fairly non-descript, causing little stirring in the bike leathers.

Northern Germany on the other hand, now this is a country that can be relied upon to cater for any kind of biker. You just need to come off the motorways and within minutes you'll find yourself a diamond stretch of tarmac. I'd never sampled the very far north of Germany before and this route gave me a great incentive to go back with the lads on tour.

I met loads of bikers at the various petrol stations and rest stops along the way. It was great to stop and chat for a while, hearing about their exciting plans, sharing at bit of knowledge of various routes and places to stay, as well as spreading the TeapotOne gospel!

Soon enough I was in Sweden and only I would time it just right to arrive the night of the eurovision! You couldn't get away from it, every bill board, every tv channel, every radio station, people actually thought I'd ridden there for it? Believe me I hadn't, but did anyone see that nutter from Romania? That had to be a bet surely!

To my knowledge, there's not too much of note that originates from Sweden, apart form ABBA & IKEA of course. I may be wrong, but nothing is sparking the cranial matter as we speak. As Bjorn & Co weren't thumbing for lifts along the way, it was down to IKEA, every bloke's favourite place to wander alone, yet worst place in the world to be if you're with the other half! I spotted my first one quite early on into Sweden so had to stop at the roadside a take a quick snap.

Now I know there is so much more to Sweden than I've seen here, and I wish I'd given myself more time to see this magnificent country. But I had to be in Stavanger by the following Tuesday, nobody else's fault except mine. I'd been asked for a date when I'd be there, and that seemed like an achievable timescale, and it is if you're just putting your head down and getting on with it.

What I've quickly realised is this. The knack to 'adventure' travelling, when you really meet the people of the country and sample what it has to offer, is to come off the main roads and meander your way through. Stop wherever you want, sit for a while and absorb what's going on around you. People will naturally come over to you, brought in by the bike, wanting to know more. Everyone has a degree of wander lust, everyone has a dream to hit the open road, everyone wants to see what else is out there, and you're their realisation of that dream!

Alas Sweden will have to wait for another time as I motored my way up the western coast of this beautiful country. Soon enough I was at the Svinesundsbron bridge which spans the Svinesund gorge, a natural border between Sweden and Norway. It's a fairly impressive sight as bridges go, with the views all around equally so.

NORWAY
NORWAY
SWEDEN
NORWAY
DENMARK
POLAND
NETHERLAND
GERMANY
SW
CZECH
UNITED

CHAPTER 15
NORWAY

By mid afternoon on day 11 I was now in Norway, heading for it's capital city of Oslo. Almost straight away the roads and countryside seemed to change. What had been fairly non-descript main roads up the coast of Sweden, with rolling hills and fields abound, became snake-like ribbons of glorious tarmac, twisting their way through ever increasing mounds of forest strewn rock. I'd been warned of the roads in Norway, in that they were notorious for being bumpy and uneven. But at this early stage I found none of that, only fantastic, well kept, sticky bitumen which egged you on with each twist and turn, taunting you to twist the throttle ever more.

I arrived in Oslo and headed straight for the city centre where I'd found a fairly cheap (by Norway's standards) hotel room for the night. With the bike safe and sound in underground parking, I grabbed a quick shower, had a butchers on the t'interweb for the places to see, armed myself with my camera and hit those mean streets. It was a glorious evening, only the 2nd time it hadn't rained since I'd left London almost 2 weeks previously.

I spent a good couple of hours just wandering around the city centre, being the proverbial tourist, taking pictures of everything and anything that caught my eye. It's weird, my job in the real world see's me more often than not standing at the Downing Street gates, looking out on the world as tourist after tourist wanders by, camera around neck, oblivious to anyone else around them, focused completely on whatever's directly in front of them. And now this was me, I loved it.

Like Buckingham Palace, Oslo's Royal Palace sits atop the main street in the city centre, Karl Johans Gate. It's surrounded by a beautiful park, which is well used by locals and tourists alike, and looks over the city. Unlike our palace, there are no gates around it, you're free to wander right up to it's walls if you like, but you'll soon be met by the soldier on sentry duty, rifle in hand. The choice is yours.

As I walked down Karl Johans Gate towards the busy main centre, some music caught my ears and guided me over to the National Theatre, around another main square area. I sat and listened to the buskers, recording their cheery music for use on my vid series and dvd, so keep an ear out when it's finally done.

It was at this point I noticed the bikes. There outside the Hard Rock Cafe was a line of beautiful sportsbikes – ducati's, yamaha's, suzuki's, bmw's, each immaculately on display in the evening sun. I must have looked a right knobhead in my flipflops, surrounded by beautiful architecture and history, snapping away at a bunch of parked up machinery! But this is my art, my true love, and I ate it up.

Further down the street, like the bad kids who sit at the back of the bus, I found the cruiser and chopper brigade, chrome polished to within an inch of their lives. Aside these beautiful machines was a fine example of an American hotrod, again impressively finished and on display for all to see. I love this sort of thing and could spend the entire evening just wandering up and down the lines of machinery, smudging up the paintwork.

Content with my nights engine porn, I wandered down the length of Karl Johans Gate, taking this turn and that, and generally just meandering around the city centre. After picking up a bite to eat and a drink I set my sights on the hotel, head down to iphone in hand, religiously following google maps as I went. At this point I got a phone call from a woman called June Helene Larsen who told me to go back to Karl Johans Gate and meet her boyfriend?

As it turned out, my good mate Gordon had toured Norway about 10 years ago and met many a friendly biker, many of whom he had stayed in touch with. On seeing that

I was now exploring this incredible country, Gord' had put the word out amongst his Nordic brethren that there was a mad Scottish bloke in town. June had seen through the Facebook feed that I was in Oslo, so had contacted her boyfriend who was a biker in town and was at a biker meet in, yes you guessed it, Karl Johans Gate. 20 minutes later I was standing next to those same beautiful machines, chatting with Petter Meuem and his mate Roger. Ain't the t'interweb great eh!

It was brilliant to just chat bikes with fellow petrol heads, discuss best routes, machinery, sights to see and places to go. Petter and Roger, thank you both for an enjoyable evening, it was an absolute pleasure to meet you. Thanks also for the info about the Arctic Circle Raceway, I can now confirm that it is an incredible circuit, certainly one to put on your list! Cheers lads.

As I walked home, just yards from the hotel, I came across a sign outside a TV station that read, "Live Your Life!" Was someone sending me a message I wonder?

Day 12 and I was up a bit earlier than I'd planned, courtesy of someone choosing to make toast in their room a 5am! A few more hours kip, once the fire brigade had left, saw me back on the bike and heading out of town, destination Stavanger. I'd chosen to avoid the main roads, electing instead for the twisty back roads over the mountains. After sitting on the E18 south to Drammen, I took the E134 and followed it Westwards. Within minutes I was open mouthed, continually wanting to stop to take pics and vids for all to see.

Heading higher into the hills, I could feel the temperature dropping as the scenery just got hotter and hotter. As I turned off the E134 onto the E45, I passed through Raudholmane national park. What an incredible place to be, it was like something out of a BBC nature series, I could even hear Sir Attenborough's voice in my head as I looked around in awe!

My own personal nature documentary continued for hours as I travelled along the E45, then onto the E42, where it gave new meaning to my adopted phrase, #EPIC!

Bruce SMART

As evening began to settle I joined the main road to Stavanger, the E39 and headed north to this oil capital of Norway. I arrived in the centre of town at about 7:30pm and after a quick scout around, discovered that this was WAY above my price bracket. I needed to stay in Stavanger for at least 2 nights, and as it turned out 3, so I was on an economy drive as best I could. Having stayed in a fairly cheap place in Oslo, I found another thorn hotel just outside the city in a district called Sandnes, which coincidentally was where my main sponsor, Delta, had their HQ.

The whole point of going to Stavanger was to visit the HQ of Delta Energy Services, my new principal sponsor, without whom this trip simply couldn't have happened. Unfortunately the main man, Bob Iles, was away on business so I was left in the capable hands of Ole Bang to show me around. We had a great morning chatting about the trip, the work Delta carries out, Norway, and how Ole was once the Norwegian Go-Kartin Champion – twice!

Ole then showed me where I could get my bike serviced in Stavanger, leading me to a cracking place called 'Bikerstreet'. After ensuring I was all booked in, Ole left me for the day and set about chasing up the local press for our photo-op. With the beast now booked in bright and early the following morning, and with the rain beginning to come down, I headed back to my digs to catch up on admin, and sleep!

But as happened in Morocco, my phone went early in the evening and I spoke with a chap called Quentin Ross, an expat now living near Stavanger, who'd been following on facebook and saw I was in town. Quentin had arrived with his two young daughters in tow, so I popped down to meet him and chat about the trip. It was great to yet again be welcomed so warmly by complete strangers in a foreign land, and what's more, HE BROUGHT BEER! He gets my vote.

The next day I dropped the beast off at the doc's then caught the bus into town, getting the usual funny looks as I wandered around in a white leather suit, adorned with logos a plenty! Stavanger really is a great wee town. I'd grown up in the north east of Scotland due to my father being in the oil business and Aberdeen being the oil capital of the UK. I'd always heard of Stavanger, especially once my dad went to work in Norway for some years, and I'd always assumed it was some mega-city, a centre of industrial might, bursting to capacity with people, cars, industry and capitalism. How wrong could I be! It's a cracking wee place, a mixture of old and new yet done in a way that maintains its charm and character. It has a real homely feel to it and you're completely at ease just wandering the streets, sitting at the many streetside cafes, and just generally taking it all in.

As well as oil, Stavanger is home to a bustling cruise ship port. It makes an impressive sight to see these leviathans of the seas moored up directly opposite a main road, literally metres from someone's home or business! It just highlights how deep these fjords are!

If you come to Stavanger, there's no getting away from the importance the discovery of oil has had on the port. Here you'll find the Norwegian Petroleum Museum and as the name suggests it's all about oil and it's discovery. To be honest I'm not overly interested in oil, I suppose I take it for granted that it's there. Quite shameful really when you consider my own family has reaped it's rewards through my dad's employment in the business, as have so many other friends and family. So I thought I'd at least pop my head in the door and fly the flag – so to speak.

I've got to say I'm glad I did, it really is an interesting place and you can easily while away an hour or two just wandering around. If nothing else, there's plenty of buttons to push, big model oil rigs and ships to play with, films to watch, and even stuff for the grown ups like actual drill bits, sub-sea exploration vessels, pipeline displays and other 'oil stuff'?

Having done my sightseeing I headed back to Bikerstreet, picked up the beast and went to the hotel, only to hear from Ole that he'd managed to secure an interview for the biggest newspaper in Stavanger, the 'Aften Bladet'. I popped back into town, met up with Ole and April from the paper, and headed back to the oil museum for a quick interview.

Bruce SMART

We had an enjoyable hour or so there, chatting about the project, it's origins, the charities, and my plans ahead.

After 3 days stationary, it was great to get back in the saddle and back on the road. I spent the next 2 days riding north towards the famous Trollstigen, or 'Trolls Road', a spectacular stretch of twisty road through an incredible national park, but more on this later.

The journey there was equally impressive as the town of Stavanger rapidly gave way to the rugged natural beauty of the Norwegian coast line. It's littered with over 45,000 islands making up a truly incredible natural environment in which to just wander and explore. These islands are connected by a series of tunnels, bridges and ferries. Life on the road here is a series of connections, surrounded by natural wonders I've yet to surpass, it is truly humbling to be amongst this place. GET HERE!

I finally arrived at the northern end of the Trollstigen, setting up camp at a great campsite called 'Trollstigen Camping & Gjestegard'. It's a beautiful place to set a base if you're ever in this gorgeous part of the world. The actual troll's road is only about 10 minutes drive/ride away and the facilities available are fantastic.

After a great nights kip in my Vango kit, I headed off to tackle the legendary Trolls Road. This is a set of 11 hairpin bends that wind their way up the cliff face, to a height of over 700 metres and with an incline of around 9%. The road is the national 63 route, and during high season see's over 2,500 vehicles passing through it's twists and turns on a daily basis. Thankfully, I arrived only a week after the road was opened so traffic was light.

Like the Stelvio Pass, the Troll's Road is a delight to see, and many dream of riding it themselves. But the reality is a bit different as the hope of gliding effortlessly up and down this stairway to heaven, leaning tightly into each bend, scraping your pegs or knee, rapidly give way to scatterings of gravel and rubble across the pathway, and oncoming motorhomes hogging the whole road. Don't get me wrong, I loved it and would certainly ride up and down the route again, but the practicalities are such that it's more of a nerve wrangling endurance exercise until you reach the safety of the summit and can then claim, "I've ridden that. Smashed it!"

But what a summit it is, the views across the Trollstigen mountain ranges are simply amazing. I was caught completely unawares by their presence when I reached the top, smacked in the face by the most welcome and beautiful natural wonders. What a place.

Continuing north on my way to Trondheim, I pointed her nose towards one of the most iconic stretches of road known the world over, The Atlantic Road. At just over 5 miles in length, consisting of 8 bridges and several causeways, it connects the municipality of Averoy to the mainland at Eide, along the county road 64. During the winter months, wild storms ravage this stretch of coast, leading to incredibly dramatic shots as traffic makes it's way over the roller coaster-like main bridge, Storseisundet bridge.

I have to confess, I was slightly deflated when I actually saw this in person. The pictures you see in the magazines are far more dramatic than its sight in real life, not taking anything away from the actual engineering feat. I suppose the fact it was a flat calm day didn't add to the drama or majesty, but I just couldn't find the right camera angle to truly illustrate the scale and angle of incline/decline of the bridge up close. The real magic happens as you ride over Storseisundet, rapidly climbing to it's peak, blind to what lies on the other side. Suddenly you breach it's summit and descend into a sweeping turn back to land, fantastic. I could ride over that bridge time and again, and I did if I am to be honest, all in the name of cinematography you understand. After spending time playing with the bridge, I once again headed north, my final destination for the evening being Trondheim.

A chap called Emil Larsen had been following the project since reading about it in Fast Bikes Magazine many moons ago. Emil and his girlfriend very kindly offered to put me up for the night, and if that wasn't good enough, there was pizza and beer on the menu too. I broke many speed limits getting there, but along the way there were yet more stunning views to behold. This place is just awesome!

Bruce SMART

Arriving in Trondheim I was met by Emil on his mates R6, the sound of the can music to my ears. I followed him through the streets of Trondheim to his cracking flat, unpacked the bike – eventually, and got her safely stowed away in his underground garage. Yet again the hospitality shown to me by complete strangers really is astounding, Emil you are a true gentleman bud and I thank you from the bottom of my heart for the welcome you and your lovely girlfriend gave me. A great evening of banter, and the promised pizza and beer was had as we chatted about the project, what had happened so far, and mused about what lay ahead.

The next morning Emil joined me for a stretch of the journey north as we rode along the E6. It was great to have someone to ride with again, enjoying the twists and turns of the road as it cut it's path through forests, fjords and mountains. After a few stops we eventually parted near a wee place called Grong and Emil headed back home. Mate if you're reading this, thanks again and I meant what I said, you are more than welcome for a return trip in Blighty, any time.

After parting ways, I continued to head north along the main E6 route. Despite being a main road, the scenery continued to grow in intensity and the twists and turns just went on and on and ariston. I stopped for a while at a petrol station, refuelled both the beast and I, and took in what was around me.

By the end of day 18 I was in the small town of Mo I Rana, just short of the Arctic Circle. I'd found a great wee campsite on the outskirts of the town and set up camp for the evening. Little did I know that it was to become home for a wee bit longer than I'd planned!

At 5,500 miles the rear tyre was looking at bit sorry for itself and as the next leg of the trip would see me heading into the wilds of Lofoten and onwards to Nordkapp, I thought it best to get her changed now rather than tempt fate in the middle of nowhere.

As luck would have it, Monday was a bank holiday in the UK so try as I might I couldn't raise anyone in the Bridgestone UK office. I happened to mention on the facebook page what was going on with the tyre, and to my amazement, within about 30 minutes, a chap called Sture Endresen rocked up at the campsite and showed me where there was a tyre shop in town! I love this place, and thank you once again Sture, top lad!

Unfortunately the shop didn't have any Bridgestones and only dealt with Pirelli, but thankfully my mate 'Luigi' monitors the twitter and facebook feeds with vigor and was soon on the blower to offer his assistance. Leaving it in his capable hands I set off to meet another facebook contact, Stian, at the Arctic Circle Raceway. You've got to love social media, within the space of about 3 people I now had contact with one of the caretakers at the circuit and had complete free access for the afternoon!

The clue is in the name really, but the Arctic Circle Raceway is the most northernly circuit in the world and was opened in 1995. Specifically built for road racing, it also offers enduro racing due to the presence of the midnight sun.

It really is a stunning circuit, set in the amazing natural beauty of Norway. If you've done 'the ring' then this has to be added to your list of things to do on the bike. Absolutely brilliant and thoroughly recommended. As I've mentioned before, winter in Norway had only just ended about 3 weeks prior to my arrival. Nobody had been on the circuit yet so it still had loads of moose poo and gravel strewn across the top 'north pole' section – that's my excuse for going so sedately at least!

The new Bridgestone BATTLAX T30 rear tyre was promptly dispatched to Skjærvik's Scooter & MC shop just north of Mo I Rana, so I headed up to get the new rubber. Bjorn at Skjærvik's was a cracking bloke who made time to help, swiftly changing the tyre and stopping for a while to have a chat about the trip. Everywhere I went in Norway people were only too eager to help, to hear about my plans, and to offer whatever help they could. It's a truly fantastic country.

Bruce SMART

With new boots now on, I pointed the beast's nose North and followed the E6, destination Skutvik to catch the ferry over to Svolvaer in Lofoten. It was a beautiful day, as it had been almost every single day since leaving Stavanger, and with 24hr daytime there was no issue with failing light. I was really enjoying the ride now, well and truly into the journey and loving every second of it. Norway is just a fantastic country, continually throwing up surprises around every bend. Just when you think the scenery can't get any better, 'BHAM' have that!

Nothing, NOTHING, had prepared me for what I found at Skutvik. I'd arrived 20 mins after the last ferry for the day had left so found myself riding around this tiny little village looking for somewhere to stay. The two guesthouses were still shut, not yet ready for the tourist season, but I remembered I'd seen a sign for camping on the way into the port. Retracing my steps I saw the sign - "Ness camping". Must be an omen I thought, so took the turning off the road and followed my nose. About 10Km's later I found another sign for 'Ness camping' sending me down a tree lined track. At the end I found a simply beautiful site, right on the banks of an incredible bay. "This'll do nicely" said I, and all for only £15! (Bargain by Norway standards).

I quickly pitched the tent as the mozzies were in attack formation, my great big, bald heed the main target! Out of biking gear I grew a pair and ventured out into the cooling evening, Wow!

The owner of the site said the views further around the 'Ness' - Norwegian for peninsula, were even more beautiful, but I'm afraid I took her word for it as I was cream crackered. After sitting on the shore for a while, I retired to my castle and slept like a baby.

After a good lie in the following morning, I spent some more time on the shore before packing up and heading back to the port. I'm glad I got there early as it was already busy with lorries and tourists a plenty. I had over an hour wait in the scorching heat, it was already 28 degrees by midday, so I took comfort in the shade of one of the lorries and devoured an ice cream. Well, I'm on my 'hod'ilays' after all!

Soon enough we were all aboard the hour and a half ferry over to Svolvaer on the Lofoten islands. I must confess, I'd never even heard of them before this trip, but what a truly magical natural spectacle they are. The Lofoten islands jut right out of the North Western coastline of Norway, forming a huge and imposing rock wall along the skyline. Human habitation in these islands can be traced as far back as 250BC, with viking heritage deeply ingrained in the local populate. The views of the islands were every bit as dramatic as I'd been led to expect.

Soon enough I arrived at Svolvaer and was met by Karina Paulsen and Tom Larsen, more friends of June Larsen. Karina & Tom had kindly got in touch through facebook and invited me to stay with them whilst in Lofoten and show me the sights. They met me at the quayside with a few other bikers in tow, Harald, Gretta and her husband, and we went for something to eat at a stunning seaside place.

After lunch we took a long ride back through the islands, eventually crossing onto Hinnoya, the largest of the Lofoten islands, and home to Karina and Tom's beautiful abode in Lamhagan, on the banks of Kvaefjord.

The views from their home were stunning, sitting on their terrace as the sun slowly sank, with a can of beer in one hand, and the smell of BBQ whafting through the air. That would surely be hard to beat, only bettered by having the other half there with me to share it. I tried whale meat for the first time, and although I hate to admit it, it was sensational! A mixture of steak and liver in taste, cooked to perfection by trained chef Tom, it was a dinner fit for a King. It was great to sit around the table with their family, two sons Ruben and Tom, and chat about life.

After grub Tom & Karina took me along to see the midnight sun as it settled on the water before rising up to another day. Problem was, we were a tad too late so it'd already set and was rising once more by the time we got there! It was still an incredible sight, 2am and you still needed shades!

I'd been dealing with 24hr daylight since arriving at Trondheim a week or so earlier, but this far north it really was as bright during the night as it gets during a summer's early evening. Funnily enough it didn't stop me sleeping!

It was a late'ish rise the next day as I awoke to a great unexpected surprise. Tom had been up early to wash Karina's beloved bike, and couldn't help himself. The beast hadn't seen soap since the day before I left Blighty, way back on the 9th May. She'd been through over 3 weeks of varying weather, ridden over 5,000 miles of varying roads, and was in a pretty sorrowful state. I wasn't sure if Tom was joking when he pointed at her afterwards and said, "I didn't know she was red and white!"

After some quick maintenance - lubing the chain, checking tightness, making sure various bolts were still in place, I packed her up once more and we all set off for Halstad, where we were to meet another biker, Andrei.

From there the guys were going to escort me all the way to Bjerkvik, where I'd leave them and head north towards Alta, some 500-600Kms away. Along the way we picked up a couple of other bikers who rode along with us and drifted off at various stages. The biker spirit is well and truly alive in Norway, the kindness and generosity you experience from bikers all over the world, seems to be magnified here to a different level. What a place.

We even saw a moose off the roadside in low lying woodland. I went to slow down and get a pic but as soon as the engine note changed, he was off into the woods and out of sight! None the less, I've now seen a wild moose. Tick.

Now back on my own I had to give it some 'lemons' to make up on progress after the late start. Although there was no impending darkness, I still like to get somewhere by about 8 at the latest, so had some mileage to cover.

It was great to be back on the open road once more, free as a bird to glide along wherever I chose. This is what I live for, this is what I dream of. Perfect.

Or so I thought. Now, I'd seen some amazing sights in Norway over the last 2 weeks, but what came next took it to a whole new level. The Lyngen Alps, a mountain range running along the East of the city of Tromso, forms a natural rock curtain between Tromso and the mainland to the East. It is truly superb to behold, forcing me to practically stop right where I was and just gaze. It reminded me of the scenery from, 'The Lord of the Rings', magical, majestic and mystical.

I must've stayed there for some time, maybe half hour or so, but it was such a beautiful scene to witness. As the clouds moved, so the sun's rays would dance across the face of the mountains, revealing a spectral of light better than any light show I'd ever seen. I've been to a couple of places on my bike now that could only be bettered by having someone there to share it with. This was just a place. Very special and it'll stay with me always.

I rode for another hour or so before finding somewhere to stay in a place called Reisafjord. I set off early the next morning, determined to reach my goal of Nordkapp, some 250 odd miles further North East. It doesn't sound a lot I know, but 250 miles on these roads is hard going. Often you're down to 40mph or less, dealing with potholes, sand and gravel sections, or just wandering wildlife and campervans EVERY WHERE! Then there's the ever changing scenery, it just never gets boring.

After almost six hours of hard riding, the rain had begun to come down in sheets as I made my way up the last section of coastal road to Nordkapp. It's only about 80 miles but feels like it goes on forever as the road clings to the rugged coastline. There are about 3 tunnel sections, the longest of which is about 7Km in length, and I can't tell you how cold it gets inside. The longest actually goes under the sea to join the Nordkapp island to the mainland, and by the end of it you're desperate to feel the warm air once again.

I'd typed Nordkapp into the satnav and was clinging to it's estimated arrival time as I battled the elements and my own weariness. But as I arrived at the town of Nordkapp, I realised that the actual Northernmost mark I was looking for was another 18 miles along an even more isolated road. Bugger.

Soon enough I was riding along the long approach road to my destination, surrounded by wild reindeer and tourist's campervans! As I pulled up to the tollbooths I thought they may be like those at Lands End and just wave through a biker? Nope, £25 irrespective of how you got there, how long you were staying, and why you were there. Fair enough I suppose, but they were mighty impressed with the beast and my plans!

I've got to confess I didn't really have any idea as to what to expect there. I knew there was a monument, but that was about it. I just wanted a pic to show I'd been there and to pass on to my good mate Ray Walton who'd been unable to join me for this section of the trip. So that's what I did, after almost 3 weeks on the road, 5,500 miles, 9 countries and 2 back tyres, I took a few pics, had a look around........... and left.

The thought of riding that stretch of road again, through those tunnels, in the wind and rain, was almost too much. I knew there was a small town called Honningsvag just South of the town of Nordkapp and for a brief minute I toyed with the thought of seeking shelter there. But then I grew a pair, sucked it up and pointed her South.

Thankfully the rain and wind eased the further South I went, and after a few hours I was approaching the town of Alta once again. I'd noticed a sign for camping when I passed earlier in the day so was only to happy to seek refuge here for the night. Unfortunately once again it seems like I'd beaten the tourist season and the place seemed empty. Or was it?

I could just make out the form of two chaps through a reception window so popped around the back of the wooden building and chapped on the window. A gent opened the door and I asked, "Hello, do you speak English?" He looked at me confused like, then replied in his best Doncaster accent, "I should bloody hope so lad!"

Frank Edwards and Pete Jones were two chaps heading back down the way I'd come up the West of Norway. Pete had already cycled from Gibraltar to Calais previously, yes I said CYCLED, and he now wanted to join the continent up by cycling from Nordkapp to Calais. Here's people telling me I'M mad? Frank was Pete's support vehicle and the two of them made me feel very welcome indeed, cheers chaps. They'd arrived sometime earlier and met the owners of the site who'd basically left the place open for them, and said to pitch their tents wherever they like. All we had to do was just leave some money in an envelope in the outside postbox when we left in the morning. It was a cracking wee site with free hot showers, full kitchen cooking facilities, even a sauna!

After pitching my tent, grabbing a good shower, and some well earned scran, I retired to the banks of the lake to record a farewell piece to camera on Norway. I genuinely will miss this place, it's beauty and it's people. I can't recommend it highly enough for anyone, just remember to remortgage before you come though!

After leaving Alta I made my way South to the border with Finland, stopping briefly at my first police checkpoint this trip. A quick check of my driving licence and an on the spot breath test, (I told them I couldn't afford to drink in Norway, not at £9.60 a can!) I was soon on my way. I crossed the border after a couple of hours and continued South for the next 900 miles or so, practically all in a straight line!

The North of Finland is fairly alpine and the odd stretch of road can be quite fun on a sportsbike. But soon enough you're just on a straight path through an ocean of trees, as far as the eye can see, trees. Oh, and mozzies! I finally got to meet a moose here too, but nearly a little too close for comfort. I came round a bend and there about 500 metres ahead were two big moose just standing in the road. I stopped the bike quickly and reached for my phone to grab a pic. As I looked at the screen to frame the shot, I caught sight of the big bugger now stampeding straight at me down the road! Hitting the ignition switch the Beast roared into life as I twisted the throttle to rev her hard. Thankfully this did the trick as both moose darted off the road, away into the dense forest.

Bruce SMART

After 2 days solid riding I arrived in Helsinki which was to be my base for the next 4 days as I got the next vid episode (or episodes as it turned out) completed and uploaded. I'd found a cracking wee hostel in the centre of town called, Hostel Dormus Academica that was fairly reasonably priced, whilst allowing me scope to do some wandering around.

I'd also arranged to meet Andy McGrath, a mate of big Gordon's, who'd kindly allowed me to get my Russian and Mongolian visas sent to his place. They'd finally been issued so it was a lifesaver having Andy's address to use. It was an absolute pleasure to meet Andy and his mate Scott, cheers for a top night of beer and banter, and for giving me the whistle stop guided tour of the sights in Helsinki ;-) Top lads.

Leaving Finland, you travel by ferry across to Estonia where I stopped by the old Pirita road racing circuit to pay my respects to Joey Dunlop at his memorial. Leaving Tallinn I headed South once more, riding through Estonia, Latvia and Lithuania. There really is nothing to report here. the roads are depressingly straight, literally 100's of miles of never ending tarmac with only trees for company, intermittently broken by the odd little town. Despite this I've seen loads of bikers, each continuing the universal biker salute of a wave or nods as we pass by. Love it.

CHAPTER 16
TRANSFAGARASAN HIGHWAY & ON TO RUSSIA

After the none-descript nature of the road south from Estonia through Latvia and Lithuania, Poland comes as some relief as the occasional bend is introduced back into your day. The further south you travel along its eastern border, the more alpine-like the roads become as you begin to twist and turn through forests and hills. I made good time on the mileage, covering Poland in about a day and half, ever watchful of the road surface, wildlife and local plod!

Now this started very promisingly as the road and surroundings became almost Austrian like in appearance. But the road conditions quickly deteriorated the further south I went. Following the satnav route it was a mixture of main and back roads, but I quickly realised that the minor roads were no place for a sportsbike! Even on the main roads the presence of potholes was frequent, so I behaved and just plodded through.

Approaching the border with Hungary I noticed the satnav said I had to take a ferry? Strange as I hadn't seen any mention of this anywhere else. Blindly I followed its directions through ever narrowing roads, until I was on no more than a single lane track winding its way deep into a wood. The presence of fresh cut tree logs and heavy machinery debris on the road didn't instill me with confidence, but I decided to just go with it and see where it took me.

A dead end, that's where. The road just slid under the water of the river down a muddy slip road, as I looked across its 200m span to the road on the other side. Around me where the remnants of a one time working border post, a few huts, a red and white painted barrier, all very atmospheric but bugger all use to me now. With no other option but to turn around, I retraced my steps back to the next main junction and plotted my next move.

Soon enough I was back on the road, and a good one at that. As I watched the 'border' with Hungary loom towards me on the garmin screen, I rounded a beautiful left hairpin bend, a simple pole marked its spot. Bang, I was in Hungary.

My route literally took me through the top North Eastern corner of Hungary meaning I was in country for no more than maybe 45 minutes. As I sat at the border post with Romania, memories of Rosso came flooding back, but I needn't have worried. It took about 10 minutes in total, the officers were nothing but polite, and like that I was now in Romania. Lovely job.

I was getting used to crap road surfaces now, the continual juddering and shaking through the handlebars was only occasionally interrupted by an eerie silence as I hit fresh, smooth bitumen. Bliss. The west of Romania, at least the route I took, is fairly bleak. Straight, Soviet-like roads march you east through one small village or town after another. The places reminded me a lot of Morocco actually, lots of rubbish lying in the street, horse and carts making an increasing appearance as people's predominant mode of transport. But the further east you travel, you begin to see a change in the landscape as green begins to make an appearance, as do hills and mountains on the horizon. I entered the area of Transylvania and began to wind up and down hills on some beautiful sections of road, all heavily policed by truck after truck. Whilst on the subject of trucks, a word of warning for you. Slovakian and Romanian lorry drivers are a class of their own. They are complete and utter psychopaths, who think nothing of running you off the road if you're in their way. Their overtakes are ridiculous, I still can't work out how I've not witnessed complete carnage, yet. Anyway, rant over.

I included Romania in my route for one reason, the Transfagarasan Highway. After seeing Top Gear vote it, 'the best road in the world', I knew it was a road I had to ride.

Built in the early 1970's it was a strategic military road. The Soviet's had invaded Czechoslovakia back in 1968 and the then Romanian leader, Ceauşescu, decided he needed a way of getting his military might across the Carpathian mountains should the Russians try a similar move against them. It took 4 years to build the 90km stretch of road, mostly with military personnel, costing over 40 soldiers lives during its construction.

In typical 'Smart' luck, I arrived at the northern end of the 'DN7C' road in Cartisoara in glorious sunshine, which quickly became dense fog and rain as I began to climb into the mountains. Soon I was in complete blanket fog, the glorious views I had dreamed of seeing, completely obscured by a wall of grey. But something else struck me straight away, the road surface itself was terrible! It was covered in potholes, landslides, gravel and sand, not at all how it had appeared on 'Top Gear'? It turns out yet again I'd timed it well. They'd only just opened the road that month after the winter, so they hadn't yet begun repairing and clearing it ready for the onslaught of tourists. Ach well, I was there so lets just get on with it.

After an hour I'd ridden roughly half of the road, stopping frequently in awe of what presented itself to me. You just can't appreciate the scale of this road, the engineering undertaken in its construction, until you're on it. It truly is 'epic', if only the road was in better condition. Only then would it be a superb riding road, but there'd no doubt be many fatalities as it's not somewhere to take lightly.

I'd booked myself into a hotel I'd found online some days previously as it was time to wash the pants and socks, as well as get some admin done online. The Hotel Piscul Negru is located right on the Transfagarasan and is about half way along its length. It's a great place to stay, the rooms are massive, the food superb, and the welcome was like I was with family. It's not a bad price either, £20 at the time for a night, brilliant!

The beast was in a real sorry state now, I don't think I've ever seen her so filthy as the 6 weeks on the road had taken it's toll. Arriving at the hotel I was met by 'John', a Romanian chap who'd lived and worked in London for a year before returning to Romania to start the hotel. After introducing myself he recognised the Scottish accent and straight away any barriers came down. He made me feel like a lost brother and was eager to talk about the bike, my trip, where I'd been and where I was going. I tentatively asked if there was anywhere I could wash the beast and he immediately got to work rolling a hose out from the kitchen area to his back porch.

He even provided buckets of warm, soapy water, sponges and cloths! I felt terrible as his spanking new sponges were instantly turned to grotty, oily rags as I scrubbed the bike clean. But I needn't have worried as John was right in there with me, helping to wash the bike, following after me to hose her down. All he wanted in return was a wee pic on the bike in his chef whites. Brilliant stuff.

After dinner that evening, John sat with me chatting about life in Romania and what to see, and expressed his concerns at how westerners viewed his people. I must admit, my only experience of Romanian's had been through work, so it wasn't particularly positive to say the least. As was becoming the norm on this trip, every day's a school day, my eyes were being widened and my perceptions altered. The hospitality, kindness and generosity proffered by John to me was truly humbling, I felt like family to the man and his staff at the hotel.

Soon enough the drink came out and a small little shot glass was presented to me at the table, John smirking all the while. The thought of waking up in a bath of ice crossed my mind, but quickly vanished as common sense prevailed. 'Tuicha' is a Romanian delicacy made from fermented plums? I've got to say it was beautiful to drink, like a fruit based whisky! As the conversation progressed, the bottle slowly emptied. Lovely job.

The sun was shining bright in the blue sky the next morning, so I was up and out the hotel early doors, eager to get the rest of the Transfagarasan done before turning around and doing it again in its' entirety. John had also told me about 'Cetatea Poinari' – an ancient fortress set high in the rocks at the southern end of the road. This was the one-time home of 'Vlad The Impaler' and rumored to be one of the settings Bram Stoker had in mind when he created Dracula. There were over 1,300 steps up to the castle from the roadside so it was going to take a few hours to do, but I was assured the experience was worth it.

Setting off down the road I've got to admit I was slightly downhearted by the quality of road surface once again. If anything it was even worse in the lower lying areas, with large amounts of sand and gravel lying on the apex's of bends throughout. There's also a distinct lack of fuel on the road so make sure you fill up either in Cartisoara in the north, or south of Curtea De Arges in the south. After filling up I found the entrance to the castle, and it was closed! It seems I was just too early in the season as lots of the tourist attractions weren't yet open to the public. You'll just have to google it to see the pics, or better still get down there yourself and experience the place.

Just north of the castle the main Transfagarasan begins to wind its' way up into the mountains. You quickly arrive at the Vidraru Dam, an impressive concrete structure signifying the southern start point of the road.

As you make your way alongside the lake, you begin to twist and turn skyward, slowly at first, before beginning the ascent to the hills. Soon enough you're up in the God's, snaking through mile after mile of sweepers, hairpins, and glorious 'serpent-like' waves of road. If only the surface was in better condition this would truly be the greatest motorcycling road in the world, but in my humble opinion, I still think the N260 in northern Spain beats it. Road condition aside, the views are truly superb.

After about 2 hours it was all over, I'd ridden the whole length of the road, now in both directions. Personally I think south to north is the best route, starting at the dam and working your way high into the mountains. Each time you round a hairpin bend you get to look back at where you've been, the view is just breathtaking. If you go, try to wait until mid July as the works should be complete clearing all the winter debris etc, hopefully the surface will be better too. It honestly is a marvel of a road, one which I'm glad I've now ridden and experienced. But as a motorcycle road, if you want smiles and grins, then

Bruce SMART

nothing has beaten the N260 in northern Spain.

I did find a stretch of road to the east of Romania though that was a complete surprise. As you head east out of the wee town of Bretcu, you suddenly find yourself winding your way up along gloriously smooth, fresh tarmac (the E574/route 11). There is bend after bend of knee down heaven, with excellent sweeping curves, forest lined passes and beautiful wee villages along its length. If you're out this way, it's a must for sure.

My initial plan had been to ride from Romania, into Moldova, then into the Ukraine before entering Russia. I'd had a few folk get in touch with warnings about both Ukraine and Moldova, and eventually I'd decided to bypass Moldova by taking a more northern route up through Romania and into Ukraine. Well that was the plan anyway.

Trusting the satnav I popped in 'Kiev' and followed the directions. I'd learned to double-check the routes by looking at the overview map once the route had been calculated. But what I didn't do was zoom in. So, as I arrived at the Romanian side of the border I went through the normal procedures.

Every border is essentially the same. You have to exit a country and then enter the next one. Each has the same constituent parts, a police stage and a customs stage.

First it's the police checkpoint: - Hand over your passport, V5 (logbook) and insurance if asked. Answer any questions put to you, very little normally, and sit back and wait. Sometimes it takes minutes, sometimes it takes hours, but eventually they come back and waive you on to the next stage, customs.

Second stage, customs checkpoint: You do exactly the same here, hand over the documents, fill in any paperwork they require, answer any questions, and wait. You then officially leave that country and are sent on to the next stage, entering the new one. This consists of exactly the same process, police and then customs. Simple as that, when it goes well. An absolute infuriating brain fart when it doesn't!

But here it was no problems at all, I was through the Romanian side in about 25 minutes and crossed a bridge to the next stage. The Ukraine, or so I thought. You can imagine the sudden gut wrenching feeling that descended upon me as I rode off the bridge, only to see a great sign saying 'Welcome to Moldova'. Bugger. I'd heard all sorts of horror stories about this border, not in the violent or dangerous sense, just it was bribe central and subject to huge delays at times. The heart was racing already, and the temperature inside my race suit rose rapidly.

Straight away the first thing they asked for was insurance and I said I'd buy it there at the border. His face lit up and I could see the cogs turning. He led me to a small back room but then encountered a problem, the insurance chap was nowhere to be seen, apparently he'd gone home early? Contrary to what I'd heard, this border officer was only too helpful. He hurried around for about 20 minutes trying to find some way of getting the insurance before returning and telling me I'd have to go back to Romania to get some. To be fair, I was only too happy and did exactly that, only this time I did a 3 hour detour heading north through Romania to get to my original intended border with Ukraine. So although I didn't get stamped in, my wheels have been in Moldova, that'll do me – tick. Looking back I'm gutted I didn't go on into Moldova, I've met a few Moldovans throughout my trip and as usual they were fantastically friendly people. At the time there were horror stories about the section of the country to the east, and the crossing in to Russia. Mafia gangs ruled this section and had declared themselves almost a separate state to the rest of Moldova. I just went for the easy route, and undoubtedly missed out on some beautiful country and people. Ach well, next time.

Arriving at the correct border this time I went through the usual steps. I'd heard the Ukraine side could be a nightmare in terms of delays and bureaucracy, and dreaded the prospect of having to buy my insurance here. After handing over all my documents I sat and waited for about 45mins as uniformed officials dealt with the dozens of cars and lorries all waiting patiently. To my surprise smiles were abound here, both from the officials and public, it seemed a right cheery place actually. The police officer came back with my paperwork and waved me through, pointing down a road where a uniformed Ukrainian guard could be seen checking paperwork. This is it I thought, now I've got to deal with the Ukrainian side, this is where the fun will start!

As I pulled up at the guard, he held out his hand for the small white piece of paper you get at the first stage of the process. It gets stamped by various people and lets the guard at the exit point know you've been through the processes successfully and can leave/enter. This meant I'd actually already gone through the Ukrainian border checkpoints without realising? Where was all the corruption, where were the delays, the bribes, the grief? Hmm, there was a theme developing here.

To my surprise the guards eyes lit up when he saw the bike and he began to smile. "Yamaha, Yamaha?" he asked excitedly. "No, Suzuki GSXR" came my reply, expecting to be relieved of it very shortly. He was like a kid at Christmas, calling over other guards who all flocked around me like I was Valentino Rossi at his home grand prix. They loved it and were asking all sorts of questions like how fast it goes, who did I race for, why didn't I have a BMW!!! Then to top it all off, the main guard then twisted an imaginary throttle and said, "Wheelie, you can wheelie, go, go, GO!!!!" I didn't need any more instruction than that and officially entered the Ukraine on the back wheel of a screaming GSX-R. Lovely job.

That was probably the last time I reached any sort of speed in Ukraine as the roads in the west of the country are absolutely pants. Pothole ridden, full of corrugations and a patchwork of repair work, means you're in for a very bumpy ride. That's if there is any tarmac on them at all. Despite being on the main motorway from the west of the country towards Kiev, there are sections that now resemble a farm track. The surface is so badly destroyed that it's 1st gear and 5mph as you crawl over and around the huge gaping holes in its surface, sliding over grit, sand and gravel. I rode for around a few hours before taking refuge in a roadside motel for the night. Once again I was the centre of attraction for the staff who all came out to look at the bike and this fat bloke in a white leather suit. Fair one, I must look a right eejit!

The security guard came and found me as I was lubing up the chain, pointing at a closed gate around the back of the motel. He gestured for me to follow with the bike and opened the way to the staff car park, pointing at a covered area next to a barn. He even brushed the floor clean of sawdust and dirt before he'd let me put the beast there for the night. I motioned for him to sit on the bike if he wanted, but he smiled shyly and declined. Turns out he actually went and got a sleeping bag from his office and slept at the back door all night, guarding the bike! I was already experiencing just how friendly and helpful the folk in the east are. They'll literally give you the shirt off their back.

The next day I was up and out on the road, aiming to cover the 200 odd miles to Kiev in maybe 4 or 5 hours due to the bad road conditions. But as you get about 80 miles outside Kiev, the road suddenly becomes silky smooth, perfect bitumen and a joy to ride on. I nearly pulled over and kissed the ground! I'd booked into a hotel in Kiev as I wanted a day to sight-see around the city, as well as do some laundry as I was now kicking up a tad!

Armed with a city guide on my phone, I headed out to explore in glorious sunshine. Kiev, or Kyviv as it's locally known, really is a great city, a mixture of the new Europe and old Soviet in clever balance. It's a city you can just wander around, turn any corner and there's something to see due to its varied history.

For nearly 300 years it was the centre of the Kyvivan Rus, a mighty Eastern Slavic state whose territory ran as far as the Black Sea to the Baltic Sea. It protected Europe from the invasions of the savage nomads and was often invaded itself, but this Slavic stronghold fought off the invaders. Eventually the Kyvivan Rus state fell apart and during the 12th and 13th centuries parts of its territory fell under the control of Moscow and Poland.

The city has suffered nearly a 1,000 years of invasion, from the Mongol Tatars through to the Nazi's during WWII, where 40% of the city was destroyed by the Germans. The retreating Russians then destroyed much of the original Khreschatyk Street, now a famous shopping street.

Bruce SMART

You can see a part of the original Kyviv main gate at 'The Golden Gate'. This is a joint architectural/archaeological exercise where the original remaining section of wall and gate, are carefully entombed in an exact replica. Well worth popping to see if you're in town.

The whole city is just full of historical landmarks, both ancient and modern. From the Golden Gate, St Sophia's Cathedral and St Volodymyr's Cathedral, to the last remaining statue of Lenin, Independence Square and The Friendship of Nation's Arch. Hundred's, if not thousand's of years of varied history can be seen all over the city.

One thing I didn't get a chance to see until I passed it riding out of town, was the 'Motherland' statue. This 68m tall steel statue is of a fierce female warrior who holds a 12 ton sword and shield. It completely dominates the city skyline when you arrive from the East, well worth a visit if you can.

As well as all the history, Kiev has a quirky and modern feel to it. Every type of bar and restaurant can be found here, so you can always find something to suit your taste. If all that fails, then just come for the women. Kiev has a reputation for having the most beautiful women in the world, and having now seen a fair old chunk of this rock I can safely say they weren't lying! (I was only looking dear!)

Unfortunately I only had a day here so it'll have to join the growing list of places I'll have to come back to. Leaving the hotel the next day I ended up chatting with another Brit called Julian Stevens, who just so happens to work for KTM. We had a great chat about bikes, travelling, the roads in Ukraine and Russia, as well as the now infamous KTM/BMW decision of the Long Way Down. Julian if you're reading this mate, it was a pleasure to chat with you. Experiencing new places and meeting the locals is always brilliant, but it's great to be able to just chat bollocks with a fellow Brit every now and then. Cheers bud.

CHAPTER 17
RUSSIA

The roads heading east from Kiev were better than those in the west, but not by much. The poor old beast was being shaken to her core over every inch of travel. Soon I was at the Russian border but I needed to get my 'green card' insurance for the bike. As promised there was a wealth of huts/kiosks available right at the border, each eager for your business. I'd done a wee bit of research on 'Horizons Unlimited' beforehand regarding prices and was expecting to pay around $50 for 3 months worth of insurance. They quoted me $100 and when I questioned it, they showed me their printed tariffs. I tried various other booths, but they all seemed to go from the same sheet, none willing to openly undercut the others? So I paid the $100, got the insurance and rode into the border checkpoint.

I started the whole process just after 1pm and rode out the Russian side a little before 3pm. Not bad at all going by some people's experiences there. I found both the Ukrainian and Russian officers to be nothing but professional and polite. One Russian guard even babysat me through the whole form filling scenario, who knows what I ticked, but I got in without any problems! One bit of advice to anyone doing a border like this for the first time is this. Try to follow someone else in to the border, and go where they go, do what they do. If you're unsure, just wait a minute and watch what everyone else is doing. Or just simply ask, you'll always find someone who can either speak or understand enough English to get you through. 100's of people pass through these borders every single day, so remember, it's not impossible, just relax and it'll all be fine. If only I'd known this in Africa eh!

I ended up camping behind a forest the first night in Russia, thinking I was well off the beaten track. Two things: I wasn't, and the mozzies here are like jumbo jets with teeth! A few times during the night, cars would drive right by my tent into the woods. There wasn't any road so who knows where they were going or what they were doing. Mind you, they were probably thinking the same about the idiot on the sportsbike!

I was eaten alive in the 20 mins or so it took to set up the tent that night. I haven't got a single picture as all I wanted to do was get into the safety of the tent away from them. But I did take some video so you'll have to get the DVD to see for yourself. – See what I did there?

Leaving the next day I had a mild, 'Oh shit!' moment. After packing everything up I could whilst inside the tent, I was in full riding leathers, complete with wide brimmed hat and mozzie net, as I packed everything onto the bike and took down the tent. After about 30 mins I was ready to go, but where were the keys and satnav? I ended up having to unpack a few bags before finding them safely stashed away inside a t-shirt? Moral of the story, have a set place for your kit and ALWAYS put it in that place when you're not using it. Lesson learned.

The ride to Moscow from the border was fairly uneventful to be honest. Either I was just getting used to the roads, or they were fairly rideable in most places. They're almost always bumpy on a sportsbike's hard suspension, but there didn't seem to be the huge craters evident throughout the roads, like in Ukraine. There is a huge amount of roadworks going on so some stretches of road are nothing more than uncompacted hardcore, large, sharp blocks of stone that you have to just teeter over and hope they don't pierce the tyres! There was 1,000's of miles of this to come as I headed to the far east of Russia, so I may as well get used to it.

17.1 Moscow

I was only supposed to be there for 3-days, but 9-days later I left Moscow having made new friends and experiences in a city which took me by surprise. I never expected Moscow to be a rose, but the warmth, generosity and kindness shown to me has touched me deeply. I've vowed to return once again once my trip is complete, yet another place to bring the long suffering Mrs to in the future.

The plan was to arrive in Moscow on the Tuesday, drop the beast off at the mechanics for a full service and new boots, meet up with a mate of a mate, spend a day sightseeing, then head off either the Thursday afternoon or early Friday morning. Well that was the plan.

I arrived in good time on Tuesday 18th June'13. It was sweltering hot, almost 30 degrees and being a tad rotund, as well as being dressed head to foot in a leather race suit, I was leaking to say the least.

I'd booked myself into a hotel that was fairly central to town and the 'MudFactory', where I'd be getting the beast serviced. I'm getting used to the looks I draw on the bike everywhere I go. It gets attention at bike cafes in Blighty, so imagine the reaction as I ride along dirt tracks in the middle of nowhere. But in Moscow there's a surprisingly large motorcycle culture here, and it's not just the Harley's and enduro style bikes. Sportsbikes are king in the city of Moscow, with gixxers in particular the hot favourite. That said, only the keen eye picks the beast's true pedigree out at first glance, so there's still a degree of, "what the……!?"

As I pulled up to the security gates of the hotel, the guard eyed me with suspicion as most Russian's tend to on first glance. Happy that I was no threat, he gestured for me to come in and followed on foot behind. I dismounted my steed, removed the lid and took a deep breath of air, he just stood to my side, watching, beaming quietly. I smiled and began to unpack the kit, but could tell he wanted to say something. I'm embarrassed to say that my Russian is practically none existent. It's only once I arrived in a country that I realised how naive and pretentious it was of me to expect folk to speak English. From then on I did my best to at least be pre-armed with the basics, such as 'thank you, hello, goodbye' etc.

Before I could attempt my best 'Rusk-lish' the guard pointed at me and said, "Polskie,

Slovak?" then pointed at my number plate. You see I've got the Scottish flag with the letters, 'SCO', but most folk don't seem to recognise the flag, automatically just reading 'Slovak' or the like. As I spoke he smiled and said, "Ah Engliskie", to which I replied, "No! Not Englishkie, Scottish!" and held out my hand. His face lit up with a smile, laughing out loud he took my handshake and offered to take some bags. Sometimes it pays to be different.

I quickly got settled into the room, refreshed from a shower after a long, hot day on the road. I made contact with my mate Dels' pal in Moscow, called 'Ali'. Del had kindly put me in touch with Ali over facebook and Ali had offered to meet me one evening and show me some of the city. Arranging to meet at a nearby metro station, a plan was formulated for the evening that involved whiskey and cigars? It turns out old Ali Albetkov is quite a connected man in Moscow, so fairly shortly I found myself being whisked by his driver to a swanky part of town and deposited at a funky wine bar, full of smart looking Russian lads, each savoring a plethora of quality cigars! I fitted right in in my flip-flops, Craghoppers and travel shirt.

But I needn't have worried, as the welcome was as warm as the sun, especially when Ali introduced me as the 'Mad Scotsman riding Russia on a Gixxer!' It turns out it was not only a meeting of the Moscow cigar aficionado club, but it was also their guest speaker night with a chap from the 'Dalmore' Whisky brand on hand with samples of their finest! I couldn't have timed it better. It was a cracking night of quality cigars, whiskey and company, I even found out about the beautiful 'Dalmore' Whiskey's heritage. Yet again, every day's a schoolday when on tour!

After a wee search on google I found a free walking tour of Moscow so booked myself on and headed to the meeting point, early on day 42. If you're ever in Moscow, I can't recommend the tour highly enough. The guides are informal, friendly, knowledgeable about their subject, and speak impeccable English. It lasts about 2-3hrs so would be amazing value for money at £30, never mind FREE!

The wealth of history and architecture on offer in the city is incredible, a plethora of various styles and periods, all intermingled in a relatively small space. As we wandered along I listened to stories behind each famous landmark, whilst marveling at sights I'd only ever seen on the news! It was weird to think I'd grown up with Moscow being the focal point of, 'the enemy' in the cold war. A place to fear and be suspicious of, and whilst I appreciate times have changed significantly, I can't help but think my mum and Aunty Jan must have had a great giggle here when they came on a girls holiday back in the 80's! In fact I got a good indication of what communist cuisine must have been like during their absence, as my dad was left to do the cooking! Boiled eggs that would make a squash ball seem appealing, and burnt toast. Good times.

During the reign of Ivan IV (Ivan the Terrible) – trade routes with the West expanded exponentially, to such an extent that he decreed it was necessary to have an English court in the city to deal with the increasing amounts of English traders subject to disciplinary action. Well, that and he was trying to get into Elizabeth the 1st's knickers at the time!

So he built a special 'English Courthouse' and gifted it to Elizabeth the 1st, where it remained a symbol of little Britain and eventually became the first British Embassy in the world. See, I told you I'd teach you something didn't I! (Christ I hope I was listening properly and got it right! Blame the tour guide if I'm wrong.)

Soon we wandered onto the edges of the famous 'Red Square', setting eyes on the instantly recogniseable domes of St Basil's Cathedral. The history of the place is both lengthy and complex so I'll not pretend to know it and bore you here. It's well worth a google and you'll also see what it looks like inside. Stunning place.

Moving onto the Kremlin itself, it was pretty special to actually be standing there in front of the place, looking at the very seat of Russian political might. A place so many people once feared and revered, and to be honest many still do to this day. Having obtained a very small insight into this political world through my current role of employment, I found it particularly interesting just to observe the comings and goings of the place, noting with interest at how similar many of the processes were. I found myself chuckling as

Bruce SMART

I wondered if the Russian police officers on guard had the same varied topics of conversation we share at Downing St? God I hope not, there's not enough room for that level of depravity! I wonder how you say, "Wallop, 50 yards, left, towards" in Russian?

Ok so I'll admit it, I'd never heard of 'Gum' before I went on this tour. A few folk had recommended I visit it through the facebook page, but I'd no idea what it was. I must confess I wasn't all that fussed when I heard it was a shopping centre on the tour either. But what a place! The place is huge and the last place you'd expect to see in a communist stronghold. Even during the dark days of communism in Russia, when shops ran empty forcing people to starve to death, or travel many miles to queue for days just for some bread, the 'Gum' shopping centre was fully stocked with the finest goods available.

It really is an impressive place, and even if you don't have the slightest interest in shopping, as I don't, you can still easily loose an hour or so just wandering around, taking in the plentiful supply of local attractions – see what I did there? 'Vury nycee!" WALLOP, wallop, wallop!

Around the back of Red Square there's a big old building that sits empty. There's a funny story to this place, it's a hotel that has still not been finished, despite being built during the rule of Stalin. The architects came up with 2 final designs and showed them both to Stalin side by side. He was supposed to sign off on which design he wanted, but signed directly in the middle of both. The architects were too scared to ask him for clarification so it was built as a combination of the two, one half as one design, the other taking the form of the other!

There's a similar story to the main Koltsevaya, or 'circle/ring' route in the Moscow metro too. Apparently planners came to Stalin with their plans for the underground system and placed them before him, awaiting his approval. Allegedly he placed his coffee cup on the table, on top of the plans, and left the room without saying a word. The engineers removed the cup and saw a brown ring on the plans, realising that this was exactly what they needed! Taking it as a sign of Stalin's genius, they built the Koltsevaya and it has since been 'brown' in colour as a mark of respect to Stalin.

That evening Ali had planned another night out, this time at a Georgian place, where he'd planned to school me in the fine traditions of Russian wining and dining. As you've probably heard, Ruskies like their vodka, and like the Chinese with tea, there's some etiquette to go with it.

Well, when I say etiquette what I really mean is that they eat a variety of salted food with a shot of vodka. And when I say a shot, I mean a bucket of the stuff. But it's not like the vodka we get in Blighty, a Russian wouldn't even wash their floor with Smirnoff. True Russian vodka is actually quite nice, and even in the measures I was being served, is fairly pleasant to knock back. But the salted red-cabbage, Jesus don't touch that stuff, it'll blow the eyes out your skull, much to the amusement of Ali and the waiting staff!

On completion of the meal, I found myself being dressed in traditional Georgian dresswear, or at least that's what the staff and Ali told me? Personally I thought I looked more like a cross between Rod Stewart and Kenny Everett!

By now it had transpired that the beast needed a lot more work than first thought, she'd been through the wars in Slovakia and Western Ukraine, so was in quite a bad way. But it wasn't an issue as the tyres that had been sent from the UK had still not arrived either. The post in Russia is notoriously slow and unreliable, with items taking in excess of 3-4 months to arrive, if they do at all! My mates Bob and Chris at 'FWR tyres' in Kennington, London, had sent some Bridgestone BT-023's over and I could track my tyres through the parcelforce website. But as it'd taken 2 days to get to Heathrow, I wasn't holding my breath!

By now my new mate Ali had very kindly moved me into his flat in the north of the city, so I was camped on the floor in his living room. The Russian people are staggeringly welcoming and hospitable. They truly treat you like family and go out of their way to make you feel at home. Ali announced that he'd acquired some tickets to see 'Depeche Mode' in concert that night and asked if I'd like to go. In all honesty I wasn't overly fussed about going to a concert, and had never really listened to much Depeche Mode, but thought I'd accept out of politeness and just go with it.

Am I glad I did, what a cracking night, and I never knew I knew so many 'Depeche Mode' songs! Cracking stuff. The Russian crowds are mental too, they really get into it and the stadium was ram packed right from the off. My old mate from my 'TSG' days, Fletch, would be green with envy as he's a devout fan! I could just hear what he'd be screaming if he knew I was there. I'll not repeat it here.

For the next few days I just had to sit and wait for the tyres to arrive and the repairs be completed. I filled my time by working on the next YouTube vid episode and blog update, as well as putting together the full onboard vid for the Transfagarasan Highway.

Ali came up trumps yet again when he announced that he'd arranged for me to meet the editor of the biggest motorbike magazine in Russia, 'MotoReview'. The editor, Vladimir Zdorov, had ridden the route from Moscow to Vladivostok many times on a variety of bikes, but never a sportsbike so was intrigued to meet me. How could I say no!

Vladimir was a font of knowledge, drawing up a list of contacts for each stage along the way and giving me some pointers on fuel strategies and the like. As we sat at the table discussing the forthcoming trip, it seemed like it was all laid out there for me. I almost felt a bit cheated of the adventure, how wrong could I have been! As it turned out, I tried contacting half of the contacts but none replied, so nothing is ever set in stone on a trip like this. You just roll with each day as it comes.

So this is the part I couldn't wait for, the return of the beast into my sweaty wee mitts. I'd dropped her off in a sorry state to Vladimir at the 'MudFactory' workshop some 9 days previously. During that time he and his mechanic Alex, had done an incredible amount of work, often working straight through the day and night. They'd stripped the bike down to her frame, disassembled the engine and component parts, cleaned and lubed everything, even going as far as stripping the wiring loom and connector blocks, replacing everything they could along the way. When I picked her up she was almost showroom once again, I couldn't wait to get back in the saddle.

Eventually I got the call that she was ready to pick up, and without hesitation I was there. Vladimir and Alex had done the most amazing job I had ever seen. The Beast was like new, purring effortlessly on idle, each gear change like a hot knife through butter. Everything felt right, everything felt solid, and I had the confidence that every single aspect of the bike had been personally checked by Vladimir to make sure it was at its best for the trip ahead. Alex's wife Nastya had acted as an interpreter the whole way through, and she'd told me that Vladimir loved the idea of me taking a gixxer across Russia. He took it as self-pride that the first gixxer to cross his country would have come out of his workshop, so he had put everything he could into making sure it was as good as it could be. That is exactly what I wanted to hear, but unlike in some places in the UK, I knew that he meant that and had done the work himself. Many times back home I'd put her in for a service, paid a hefty bill, only to wonder if they'd actually done the work they said they'd done? 'FWR' tyres is another cracking wee garage who'll give you that personal touch. Chris and Bob are both bike nutters who live and breath the machines. Well worth a visit if you're in South London.

But I digress, I was in Russia and in the best hands possible. If you're ever in Moscow and need some work done on your bike, then I can't recommend MudFactory.ru highly enough. That was without doubt the most thorough and complete service I've ever experienced on my bikes, the service is truly second to none. To the extent that were they in the UK, I reckon I'd travel to wherever they were in the country just to use their services. Awesome work.

So with a 'new' bike and new boots, I was now ready to continue my challenge across this huge country. It's almost 7,000 miles to Vladivostok and includes 7 different time zones! The scale is absolutely mammoth, but I couldn't wait.

Bruce SMART

Saying farewell to Ali that morning, it struck me how much this man had done for me over the last 9 days. He'd welcomed me, a complete stranger, into his life and his home, on the basis of an email. He'd babysat me through my first few days in Moscow and ensured I was best prepared for what may lie ahead. I could never thank him enough, only offer a simple return of favour should he come to my home in the UK. Ali mate, if you're reading this, I meant every word. You're welcome to my home whenever you're in Blighty, thank you, thank you, thank you!

On a trip like this, you don't have time to fanny about. You meet people and very quickly must decide whether to spend time with them or move on. Those you do spend time with become good friends very quickly, simply because time is not on your side. Personally I feel I can open up to complete strangers far quicker than I do at home. Maybe it's some sort of safety mechanism, maybe I'm just a tit? Whatever the reason I loved being on the road, and relished each opportunity to meet new people and explore new things. Life was good.

The feeling of being back on the road again after a lay-off is hard to describe. Akin to a junkie getting their next 'fix', the 9 days I'd been off the beast felt like 9 months. So sitting astride her once more and riding through the heavy Moscow rush hour traffic was as if I was floating on air! I devoured each and every mile as I headed East in glorious sunshine, my destination for the end of the day was the city of Kazan.

As usual fate doesn't always let you get off with it that easy, and halfway between Nizhny Novgorod and Kazan I was suddenly enveloped in one of the most sudden and impressive storms I'd yet witnessed. An incredible dark line loomed in on the horizon, I began to wonder if maybe I should pull over and don the waterproofs, when 'bang', down it came. As if someone had picked me up and thrown me into a lake, I was drenched in seconds, unable to see out my visor and the road conditions making riding practically impossible. I looked for an escape and saw a sign for motel to my left, job done.

The quality of roadside motels in Russia can be a bit hit-and-miss at times, much like the cafes, or KAFEs (with Russian F – looks like a zero with a line through it). As I approached this one I thought my luck was out as it appeared derelict, apart from some building workers who'd been caught mid-mix of cement outside. But alas no, it was open for business as usual as one of the workers took me inside to the reception room on the 1st floor. After much pointing, loud 'Russ-glish' and many exasperated looks from the lady, I eventually found myself in a room with a bed, a desk, and a tv that didn't work. But it was dry, there were few mozzies, and I could get my stinking leathers off for the evening. That'll do nicely, ta!

Waking early the next morning to bright sunshine, I was soon back on the road, arriving about 4hrs later to the beautiful city of Kazan. Set at the confluence of the Volga and Kazanka rivers, the city is awash with history and culture, and is regarded as the 3rd capital of Russia. It's also been named as the 'sports' capital of Russia and is holding the 2013 Summer Universiade – the 2nd biggest sporting event in the world, next to the Olympics!

Everywhere you go in the city you see evidence of its preparations, new roads, new buildings, sports stadiums, flags, McDonalds and Coca-Cola (2 principal sponsors!), it's almost like being back in London during my last summer of 2012. The place is buzzing and as ever the Russian people are only too welcoming once you make contact with them.

In fact, the 2018 Fifa World Cup is being held in Russia, with Kazan being one of the host cities. So get yourself over here if you're coming for the football, it's an amazing country!

The most dominating feature of the city as you first arrive is the glorious 'White Kremlin'. An impressive white walled fortress enclosure, set on a hill at the entrance to the main city, it's now a world heritage site and well worth a visit. Kazan even has its' own 'leaning tower' in the form of the Syuyumbike Tower. The story goes that Ivan the Terrible besieged the city because the Princess of Kazan refused to marry him. To save her city she agreed, but only if he could build the highest and most beautiful tower in 1 week. He did

Bruce SMART

it, so she threw herself off the top. Woman eh, ye cannae please them!

There is a lot more to the city, but as usual I hadn't planned on staying long, merely an overnight stop on the way to a further destination. As it was I awoke the next morning with my first dose of 'Delhi-Belly' this trip, so spent another day in the city, albeit restrained to my room!

I left Kazan early on the morning of day 53, my destination was to at least reach the city of Ufa, if not beyond to Chelyabinsk. It was all going swimmingly, I should've known what was to come over the next few days, but first some personal grooming?

A chap called Edgar Barons had been following the facebook page since I just missed him when travelling through Eastern Europe. Edgar had got in touch to ask if he could treat me to a shave and a hair cut at one of their many salons. Believe it or not, this is the first time I've ever been offered a shave, and it's been a LONG time since I ever needed a haircut, but in the heat I was experiencing (sometimes up to 34 degrees) I was suffering. I'd planned to leave it until I got to Japan or South Korea before I shaved, but now seemed as good a time as ever seeing as Edgar was very kindly offering. So, armed with an address of a salon in Ufa, I headed off to be made beautiful!

Best laid plans and all that, I got to the shopping mall but couldn't find a salon. To be honest I've no idea what to look for, so found some young folk hoping they'd speak 'Rusglish' and did my best effort. Somewhat bemused by a fat, sweaty, bearded guy in leathers, warbling on in foreign, pointing at his bald head and making scissor signs at his beard, I think the message eventually began to sink in. One of the lads produced an ipad and got google translate up. Typing in my request, he looked at me the way a disappointing dad looks at his son when he tells him he wants to be a ballet dancer, then walked me through the mall to a beauty salon, full of women who wouldn't look out of place in the Sopranos! Entering the shop, the assistants just gawped at me. They obviously knew nothing about it, this couldn't be the place. I tentatively tried to ask, but they spoke no English. I'd live with the sweaty beard, so turned around and left.

I got some food, then headed back out of town on the beast. Later on I received a text from Edgar apologising for sending the wrong address! Mate if you're reading this, not a problem it's the thought that counts and I really appreciate your very kind offer. I'd have only stunk out the salon anyway!

That evening I'd made it past Ufa but was hit with a wave of fatigue so decided to make camp for the night in some woodland roughly halfway between Ufa and Chelyabinsk. Way off the road down an old track I found a perfect spot, one well used by campers it appeared as there was evidence of previous camp fires and tent spots. Soon enough I had my home set and as I lay in the tent I soon drifted into a deep sleep.

I awoke with a start as a large gentleman stuck his head into the tent, barking something in Russian. I nearly laid my own special kind of egg! You hear all sorts of stories of the dangers of wild camping in Russia. It's not just the bears you must be wary of, there are a few stories of foreign travellers who have been murdered in their sleep at the roadside, so you must be careful where you position your camp for the night.

I had a large hunting knife with me on the trip, for general 'outward-boundy' type stuff like chopping firewood, making bits and bobs, well just because it's what you do, isn't it? Actually it makes light work of cutting my bread so that'll do me.

Anyway, the thought ran through my mind that maybe this was the time to brandish said knife and fight my corner. But no, there was something about this guys demeanor that suggested he was more friend than foe. Unfortunately he spoke no English and I no Russian, so after some pointing and smiles it became clear that he only wanted to camp next to me with his family, for their safety! So that night I had guests, life was good.

I've grown to like camping now, not particularly enamored at the thought in the early stages of the trip, I now almost look forward to a night in the wilds. I find I get a good kip in the tent, forced to sleep early and awaken when the sun rises, you get a good early start feeling refreshed and ready for the day. Sometimes.

After an early start, I rode up behind another biker who was giving it some stick along some good sections of tarmac. Feeling good, I joined in and we 'dog-fought' our way through the bitumen skies, battling for the lead. It was a right giggle after so long alone, especially on fairly questionable surfaces at times. Eventually I needed fuel so I waved goodbye and pulled off the road.

Much later on I'd pulled over at the road side, scouring my maps for the appropriate turn-off to a town called Ishim, which would negate the need to enter Kazakhstan on the way to Omsk. Who should pull alongside but my friend from earlier. In good english he asked where I was heading, and it turned out he too was riding to Vladivostok! He was part of a large group of Russian bikers who were participating in a 10,000Km rally from St Petersburg to Vladivostok – 'Crazy Russian 10,000Km'. Establishing we were both heading to Ishim, he invited me stay with his group at their motel that evening, and we were off.

Carrying on from the morning's antics, we sped off along the road at a grin inducing pace. The road surface had deteriorated now, often breaking into sporadic bouts of broken bitumen, festooned with large crevices and potholes. But it was livable, even on a superbike like mine. My new comrade was leading and hit an almighty pothole, inducing the largest tank-slapper I've ever witnessed. The guy was like a rodeo cowboy riding his bucking bronco and holding on for dear life! Somehow, he managed to stay on but was visibly shaken so dropped back and I took the lead. Slowing the pace we carried on for an hour or two before pulling over at a Kafe for some refreshment and fuel.

So, last leg to Ishim, this was a near legendary section of 'road' in Russia. My first proper Russian test and a chance to see what all the fuss was about. Fuelled up we headed off with my new mate once again taking the lead at pace. Flying along I was happily weaving my way through a few bumps and holes in the normal section of road, when 'BANG', out of nowhere I rode over a large bump in the road. Nothing spectacular compared to what I'd encountered before, but I think a combination of speed and weight on the frame meant it just couldn't cope. Crack, the rear subframe broke for the 3rd time. Bollocks.

Pulling over to the side of the road I felt sick. The last time this had happened on the trip it lead to the end for me as I failed in Africa. Surely this wouldn't finish me again, not now, not here? A wave of dread descended as I looked around and could see only the ever-expanding horizon around me. What the hell do I do here then!

Bikers being bikers, my new mates were soon back around me, gasps and friendly chuckles abound as they looked at my broken bike. But quickly they matter-of-factly stated, "It is ok my friend, we have a van and mechanic. I call, he fix". Job done.

Over the next 5hrs we stood at the roadside waiting for their support van to arrive. More and more bikes arrived, some not even part of the rally group, just bikers being bikers and stopping to offer any help they could to a stranded colleague. You get this in the UK, in fact I've experienced this everywhere I've been to, but when you are really in need of help, completely out of your comfort zone, it's the best feeling in the world.

Soon we had over 13 bikes at the side of the road, with nationals from Russia, Moldova, Ukraine, Poland, Slovakia…… and Scotland! The Russians had music on their bike stereos, the 2 Poles had beer, and we all had food of varying guises. Sharing it amongst each other, it had almost a festival feel and we joked that next year, we would have a Kafe and music stand here for an annual bike festival in honour of the event!

Eventually the van arrived and the guys set to work securing the beast on the back, whilst I gathered my ridiculous amount of kit together and chucked it in the van. I thought I'd learned from the first trip attempt in Africa, I'd really tried to scale down my kit for this trip, only taking what I deemed as bare essentials. But here I was in the exact same predicament, and looking at my kit as it lay at the roadside, I suddenly remembered what Nick Sanders had said in an article in Fast Bikes. He stated he could take everything he needed to go around the world in his tank bag. If it didn't fit, he didn't really need it. This was going to have to be the approach I took from now on, time to get serious.

For now I was just a passenger in this groups voyage as we headed off into the night bound for their motel in Ishim. Soon enough we reached the infamous section of 'bad' road I'd heard so much about. I could see why, it's not so much a road as more a 20Km dusty track which, many moons ago, was once a road. To be honest it didn't seem as bad as some of the roads I'd ridden in Western Ukraine, but I was safely aboard a van being driven through it. A very different scenario to riding it yourself.

Soon enough we arrived at the motel and I was welcomed by the lads who'd already arrived like a long lost brother. Complete strangers to me, they extended their hands of friendship, taking me to their bikes, offering food and vodka a plenty. I found myself sitting in their mobile clubhouse (just one of the motel rooms they'd decided to use) faced with a table full of salted food and glasses abound, filled to the brim with vodka! Visions of the night in Moscow where Ali had briefed me on Russian vodka customs, came flooding back as I remembered the horrors of the red cabbage. Ach well, when in Rome eh.

A glass was offered and it was rude to say no, so armed with a bucket of vodka I soon had a suspicious yellow tomatoe-like food thrust into my other hand. Drink vodka, deep breath in, eat food, that was the routine I had to follow, and my new friends sat staring at me with wide mischievous eyes. It reminded me of my rugby days when you were nominated for a 'dirty pint' after mucking up in a game. You knew it wouldn't be good if you had to drink it, but if the shoe was on the other foot, you couldn't wait to watch the onslaught!

Knocking back the vodka and taking a deep breath in of air, your head straight away becomes light and your whole body tingles as if bathed in ice. Biting into the fruit I was relieved to find it wasn't half bad actually, a fair kick to it for sure, but thankfully it didn't make me cry or throw up like the red cabbage! It seemed like I passed that test as the lads clapped and patted me on the back, shaking my hand once more. As the second and third glasses were poured, my new van colleagues announced that we would have to go. We were going to drive all night to Novosibirsk where they had arranged for a mechanic to repair my bike! That was over 1,000Km away, these guys were incredible.

I said goodbye to all my new friends and was soon once more being driven through the night. Chatting with my 2 new colleagues I soon realised how fortunate I actually was. The main chap was called Gennady Filosof Shatov and it transpired that he is somewhat of a legend in Russian biking circles. In 2009 he rode solo around the world, visiting every continent and 37 countries, in almost 2yrs. He was the first and only Russian to do this, and has the scars to prove what an adventure he had. Following an altercation with 3 machete wielding locals in Africa, he now has a scar down the left side of his face which, when combined with his deep thick Russian accent, pirate-like long hair and biking denim waistcoat and bandana, gives him the aura of a man you just don't mess with. But a nicer more genuine guy you couldn't wish to meet.

The other young chap was called 'Maxin', a Moldovan – as was Gennady, who shared the driving duties around the clock. One drove whilst the other slept, that way they could keep moving 24hrs a day, always one stage ahead of the riders so as to sort out accommodation and any repairs required by the team. It was a very fluent operation, a joy to witness in the relative comfort of a bystander. As I sat in the front of the van I got to spend time with each man, chatting about our lives, our countries, politics and women. What more is there to life really? I got a great insight into the Russian pyhsche through talking with them, Gennady only too happy to state, "Russian man, if he like you, you like brother, he give you his blood. If he hate you, he take your blood, you die. It is very easy". He looked at me and smiled, holding out his hand he said, "Brother!" My mate, Gennady Shatov, thank feck for that!

We arrived on the outskirts of Novosibirsk by around 1630hrs the next afternoon, meeting several waiting folk who greeted Gennady with almost superstar status, yet a warmth only akin to a close friend. The man was certainly a celeb here and although I couldn't understand what was being said, you could tell by the way people were captivated by his every word, that he was a top story teller. After a few hours of eating and drinking, I was told that I would be staying with Mark and Irina Cherepanov at their home in the city.

Bruce SMART

Costa the mechanic would wait with my bike for some transport, then take it back to his workshop to do the repair. He'd then contact Mark and arrange for the bike to be brought back to me. Absolutely amazing, in a daze I thanked everyone for all their help, helped get the beast off the back of the van, then said goodbye and thank you to Max and Gennady. In a matter of minutes they were gone and I was being sped into town in the back of a tiny Suzuki Jeep!

Mark, his wife Irina, and their son Gleb, were the most amazing hosts. To them it was second nature, they've housed hundreds of intrepid overlanders passing through the city, so I was nothing special. But for me, this was yet another example of the outstanding Russian hospitality displayed across this vast country. It is truly humbling to experience and I hope I manage to maintain their way of thinking when I finally get back home, ready to pay back my dues to other folk I meet on my home turf.

As I only planned on being in the city for 2 days tops, my first evening there was a whistle stop tour of the tourist sights. A very young city, being founded in 1893, it's regarded as the capital of Siberia and marks the centre of the old Russian empire. It's a city bustling with science and exploration, the huge academic district a booming suburb in itself.

It's also a major transport hub in Russia, marking the crossing of its' two main railways, the Tran-Siberian and Turkestan-Siberia. This has helped it grow to become the 3rd largest city in Russia, behind Moscow and St Petersburg.

Tourism-wise there's not a hell of a lot to see really, lots of museums and theatres, and a growing shopping presence, but I was quite happy to just chill. I had plenty to be getting on with as the next vid episode was due as was the next Fast Bikes Mag article. So I just got on with it and got them all done.

I spent a total of 4 days in Novosibirsk, by which time 'the master' (the mechanic who was fixing the bike – I never got told his actual name) had worked his magic and the beast was back. Mark and I took a 'shortcut' in his beloved Jimny jeep to go pick her up, the off-road capabilities of his wee jeep were impressive, as was his navigation skills through forests, back yards and public parks! We had a scream flying along through the dirt at break neck speed, Mark constantly attempting to beat the traffic grinding it's way along the main highway in rush hour. He took us down public footpaths, into woodland areas, across wasteland alongside the railway line. Children applauded as we fired by, whilst the general Russian public didn't batter an eyelid. It's Russia!

Eventually we popped out right near the workshop and I was soon reunited with the beast. 'The Master' had done a grand job, his argon welding impressive to behold. He'd even added some bracing to each side, distributing the load down to the footpegs.

As is the Russian custom, the master kindly offered us some tea or coffee and we ventured up some rickety iron stairs to a place above his workshop. What I found completely blew me away, the guy had over 20 sportsbikes up there, filling one room completely and even had a GSX-R750 sitting pride of place under his TV in the lounge. The guy was my hero!

After several cups of coffee and even more laughs, Mark and I headed back to his home through the busy Novosibirsk traffic. Although I'd only been off the bike for 4 days, it felt like 4 months and I'd been clucking like a junkie to get back in the saddle. The feeling back astride the beast, despite being constrained by the traffic and 'interesting' Russian roads, was sheer ecstasy.

Back at the apartment, Mark's sister and eldest son had joined us for dinner. As it was to be my last night, the vodka came out, with accompanying salted food, and I was introduced to some Yakutsk specialities (Mark's hometown). I can't believe I didn't get any pics, but I've got loads of vid footage so it'll all be in the DVD.

As is custom, the guitar came out once the vodka began to flow, and Mark and his son Daniel entertained us well into the night. It was a cracking evening spent with my new

Russian friends, a real insight into general life here in this wonderful country. I keep going on about it, but the kindness and generosity I experienced in Russia is something that will stay with me to the grave. I love this place.

The previous nights celebrations had taken their toll and I awoke late on the morning of Day 59. I'd wanted to get an early start to cover the 1,000Km or so to the next major town, Krasnoyarsk, but best laid plans eh!

Having broken the subframe 3 times now, I'd decided it was time to get medieval on the kit front and really strip it down. I spent almost 3 hours packing, repacking, unpacking, going through my kit taking out more and more stuff, until eventually I just packed what was left, got on the bike, and left. Saying goodbye to Mark and Gleb felt strangely emotional, like I was saying goodbye to family I wouldn't see again. I'd only been part of their lives for 4 short days, but this family had opened their lives up to me, shared their home, their food, basically babysat me during my hours of need. I couldn't repay them, only offer similar hospitality should they ever come to Blighty. I hope one day they will.

Back on the road again I pointed the beasts' nose East and set sail. About 3 hours into the ride I'd pulled over to refuel. As I left another biker rocked up beside me, motioning to pull over. Turns out he was heading to a small bike festival out in the woods somewhere between here and Krasnoyarsk. He asked if I'd come with him and his girlfriend, so I thought, "Why not!"

About 2 hours later I found myself riding into some woodlands, way off the beaten track. I'd no idea where I was, no idea who these people were, and had no idea what they were doing here. I only knew that there were about 100 drunken Russian bikers rampaging towards me as I got off the beast in the forest. Straight away vodka was thrust into my hand, warm handshakes all round and smiles aplenty. No need to worry here then!

It turns out that the chap who stopped me on the road was called Alex, and guess what, he was a Russian cop. He'd called ahead as we rode to let the guys at the festival know there was a mad Scotsman coming who was riding a gixxer around the world. They went crazy and treated me like a long, lost brother. Fed and watered, I was taken around the camp and introduced to the various members of the bikers club from Novosibirsk. It turns out that loads of the guys were actually Spetsnatz, the Russian Special Forces! Looks like I was safe as houses here then. Luckily enough I'd brought a few badges and stickers from my work so distributed these amongst the lads. It's customary in Russia to exchange gifts when you first meet, nothing special, just a simple token gesture.

Now Russians seem to love a Goldwing, they're everywhere, on every type of road, in every town across the country. To the uninitiated, the Honda Goldwing is one of the biggest, lowest and most cumbersome bikes you can get. Think of a sofa on 2 wheels, it has cruise control and even a CD player/stereo. They have a cult following around the world but are not your general choice for bad roads, much like the sportsbike.

But here in Russia they seem to love them, and cruise happily over the bumps and potholes present on most major roads. I've even seen a few carving their way through the mud and sand of the off-road sections! Mind you, they gave me much the same amazed look as I passed them on the beast. They do like to bling them up a tad too, neon lights, extra horns, even spinners and lowered suspension.

One of the guys took me to his pride and joy, turning the ignition I was blinded by a Christmas Tree on 2 wheels. It was incredible, like something out a Spielberg movie. He proudly told me it was the only one in Russia and that it'd cost him over $30K to get it all done up!

The next morning I had some serious miles to make up so got on the road early after saying goodbye to my new friends. The road surface through most of Russia is much the same, a patchwork of tarmac and concrete, with plenty of snakes of tarmacadam repair works holding it, mostly, all together. The problem is you never quite know what you're going to get. Huge craters lie semi-submerged along your path, catching you unawares if you're not fully switched on at all times. Sometimes you just can't avoid them, your wheel crashing straight into deep holes, sending a violent spasm directly up through the bikes frame. The beast took an absolute pounding, each jolt and jar as if someone was kicking my own child.

I'd aimed to get to Krasnoyarsk by the end of the day but fell short by about 150Km, so found a cracking spot way off the road out in some fields. As usual I had the Transiberian Railway for company throughout the night, as you do pretty much from Novosibirsk all the way to Vladivostok. Thankfully, the mozzies weren't too bad here either, I reckon it was one of the best nights sleep I had in the whole of Russia.

I awoke early the next day and got back on the road. I'd cleared Krasnoyarsk by 8am and was soon at Kansk, where the road became 'agricultural' for a short 5-10Km section. It went from good tarmac to just plain rock, sand and earth, but this was still the main motorway across the country? It was to become a common theme across Russia, some stretches of road they just don't bother about.

I had almost 800 miles to cover today, so these off-road sections were seriously hurting my progress, not to mention the beast, and my back. Early afternoon I noticed a momentous occasion was approaching, the beast was soon to turn 50. 50,000 miles that is. Not bad for a 2yr old bike eh.

The rest of the day was spent battling through large sections of unmade road, to simple stretches of tracks through the earth, rock and sand. The longest was around 40km in length, I thought it'd never end! In the heat of the afternoon, the dust would just hang in the air, clogging your eyes, nose and doing untold damage to the bike's air filter.

I arrived in Irkutsk late in the evening of day 61 and was absolutely hanging. It'd easily been the hardest day yet on the bike, I was hot, sweaty, filthy and cream crackered. All I wanted was a bed to kip for the night and a shower, GOD I WANTED A SHOWER. But I'd not booked anywhere up yet so just headed for the centre of town and hoped I'd come across a motel or cheap hotel.

The first place that I saw, The Marriott. Well there was no way I could afford to stay there, but I struck upon a cunning plan. Wi-fi, they'd certainly have wi-fi, so I pulled up outside the main entrance, drawing a nervous look from the porter at the door. I swear if he'd had a gun he'd have drawn it. Without making eye contact I got my phone out and searched the available networks. Bang, got it, and in 5mins I'd found a cheap'ish hotel, clicked it, booked it… you know the rest. Less than 25mins later I was in a shower in a nice clean room, cold beer in hand. Perfick.

Whilst there I got a message from a Kiwi chap called Andrew Edwards on the Horizons Unlimited HUBB. He mentioned he would be heading to Irkutsk about the same time so we'd exchanged emails and he rocked up outside the hotel for a coffee and chat. After so long on the road through Russia, it was magic to just chat crap with someone in English and not have to worry about language barriers, cultural differences etc. Andrew had spent almost a month riding across the North of Russia, across the real wilds, mixing with local village folk, truckers and road workers. Like me, he looked 'weathered' but was having the time of his life. It soon became clear that we were both heading in roughly the same direction around the southern end of Lake Baikal, so I offered him a place on the floor for the evening and a welcome shower. He disappeared for an hour to get his chain and sprockets replaced, then returned armed with beer. Got to love the Kiwis.

After an evening of setting the world to rights, we both awoke at a 'sociable' hour the next morning and set off for Lake Baikal, about an hours ride East of Irkutsk. Containing over 20% of the worlds freshwater, Lake Baikal is immense. The world's oldest and deepest freshwater lake, it falls to over 1,637m deep and is crystal clear.

Andrew had managed to find a side road that led down to the actual shore of the lake. Despite being so big and having a main road running along almost the entire southern shoreline, you couldn't actually get 'to' the lake a lot of the time due to the railway line, and the fact that the road was often high above the actual lake itself.

Bruce SMART

After a short ride down some muddy, potholed-filled tracks, we arrived on the pebble shoreline of the lake. It was stunningly serene and well worth the effort of manhandling the gixxer through the mud. After an hour or so, we made our way back to the main road and went our separate ways. Andrew was heading back to Irkutsk then up the West coast of the lake to meet a Russian friend he'd met on the road. I was heading to Ulan-Ude, then South to Mongolia. Or so I thought.

I should have known better, it'd been a terrific day so far. The roads around Southern Lake Baikal are unlike anywhere else in Russia I'd experienced, more akin to the Black Forest in Germany and Austria, than the usual mind numbingly boring, straight line ruler I was used to. We'd had a blast twisting through the forest all morning, finally getting to lean the bike over, it must have been the first time I'd done this in over 5,000 miles!

But soon enough I was reminded of exactly where I was. Just after this pic was taken I hit another almighty series of holes in the road. There was no escaping it, no way around, I could only brake as hard as I could to take the speed off, then plow head first across the rubble. I didn't feel it straight away, but knew something wasn't quite right. The back end hadn't fallen away suddenly like it normally does when the subframe goes, so I just kept on going. I was soon crossing another 30km off-road stretch of gravel, rock and earth awaiting the works that would soon turn it into a silky smooth highway. As I slowly trudged my way through, another Russian biker pulled up alongside, smiled and shouted, "I wait for you at other side". With that he was gone.

A good 45 mins later I finally reached the end of the works, and there sat at the side of the road was the biker. It turns out he too was heading to Vladivostok, a young lad called Michael. We chatted for about half an hour and he gave me numerous points of contact for the journey ahead. He seemed petrified for me, horrified at the thought of camping out wild in Russia. All you ever hear from Russian's is, 'it's dangerous to camp, people are killed every year camping along the roads, the village people are crazy and will kill you as soon as look at you!'

I'd only every found the complete opposite, and liked the freedom camping wild gave me. I took his number and we parted ways, agreeing to meet up in Vladivostok in a few weeks time. It's a good job I did as not long after I was filling up with fuel and noticed the familiar gaps appearing in the rear fairing sections. As the subframe drops, it causes the fairings to splay, a tell-tale sign something was amiss. Looking at the seat section it was apparent that the frame had gone again, I stripped off the side fairings and the all too familiar sight was there for all to see. Bollocks.

So, what to do? Now accustomed to this, I decided I could limp the bike the 150km to Ulan-Ude and try to meet up with Michael at his motel. I gave him a bell, got the gps co-ordinates and set off. It was agony, I've had to do this more times than I care to remember now, squatting on the footpegs, leaning as far forward over the tank as I could, the idea being to take as much weight off the subframe as possible. You can only do it for about 30mins tops before you have to get off the bike and stretch, it's like being in a stress position whilst on the bike.

It took me hours to cover the 150kms but eventually I arrived at the motel and met up with Michael. He'd already rung around his contacts and sourced a mechanic for us to see in the morning. For now, we just got some grub and rested.

Whilst in the cafe I met 2 lads who were riding across Russia, from Vladivostok to St Petersburg, on pedal cycles, all 10,000km! Daniel Moores and Abraham Cohen were cycling TransRussia, aiming to cover at least 200Km each and every day and finish the whole 10,000km in only 46 days, absolutely incredible. We spent a great hour or two just chatting away, comparing notes on our respective journeys so far and ahead.

Early the next morning, Michael and I hit the road to meet the mechanic at a workshop in the centre of Ulan-Ude. He quickly determined he couldn't do the repair but knew a man who could, so we travelled across the city in convoy and I was soon at another garage on the outskirts of the city. I was used to Russian garages now, forget your 'theatre-like' operations we get in Blighty, this was real dirt on the floor, metalwork and bits and pieces lying everywhere, oil and muck on everything, stuff all over the option. The chap who owned the place took one look at the Beast's broken back, said 'Argon', nodded and motioned for me to take all the fairing off and remove the subframe. Easier said than done, despite all the practice I'd now had, but after about an hour of fannying about, I got her stripped off and removed the broken metalwork.

I've never watched the repair before so have nothing to compare this guys handywork to. Rudimentary springs to mind. Grinding the parts back to shiny bare metal, he got someone to wedge a pole of wood against one section whilst he welded it back onto the main frame piece. In about 20mins, both bits were done and we just had to wait for them to cool before putting it back on the bike. Apparently the previous welds had only been on 2 places on each side of the frame. This guy had welded all the way around, hopefully strengthening the repair further. I've got to say, he did an amazing job, and the repair has still held all the way to Japan, where I got it replaced with a heavy duty stunt one.

I also had to make the hard decision to miss out Mongolia. Right from the trip's inception, it had been THE place I was most looking forward to seeing. Ever since seeing it on the 'Long Way Round' it'd held a place in my travel heart, I was so close now but just couldn't risk taking a broken super bike into such a remote land. I was, and still am gutted to have had to miss it out, but one day I'll go there, of that I'm sure. Hmm, 'TeapotTwo' maybe? Or 'Three' or 'Four'?

It was almost 2pm before I was back on the road, but at least I WAS back on the road. Michael and I rode together for about 150Kms before I had to tell him to just carry on without me. I was riding much slower than him now, hovering around the 50-60mph mark as I just couldn't risk hitting more bumps at speed. It was actually a relief to be back on my own again, free to go where I wanted and when. Michael just wanted to go everywhere at 100 miles an hour, and I just couldn't now, not with the beast in the state she was in. Besides, this was MY trip, MY adventure, selfishly I just wanted to experience it on my own now.

A few hours later the rain clouds closed in and a terrific storm enveloped my world. Stopping at the side of a road in a forest section, I hobbled off the bike, knees screaming with pain. As I straightened up and tried to stretch my legs out, I just caught sight of the beast toppling to the side, crashing onto the mud and sand below! I'd parked the bike on her side stand but hadn't noticed the camber of the road was too steep. So as I got off, the bike simply fell to the side!

Distraught at my stranded friend I quickly got to work trying to heave her upright, just as a passing truck approached. Thankfully the 2 lads inside came to my aid, and the 3 of us easily uprighted the beast once again. Thanking the lads with my best 'Rusk-glish', they were soon back in their truck and away out of sight. I checked her over, expecting a cracked fairing and bent lever at the very least, but nothing, not even a scratch. I stripped the rear side fairings off to inspect the subframe too, expecting the fall to have fractured the welds, but nope, they were fine.

However, it was a good job I did take the fairings off as one of the mounting bolts that hold the subframe to the main frame fell out! This is what they think caused the frame to go the 2nd time, a bolt fell out causing increased load on the remaining bolt holes which consequently catastrophically failed. From that point on I made it part of my daily checks to ensure all the bolts were nice and secure before I commenced a days ride.

Before I left Blighty, Mike Dawson at MD-Racing had told me to loosen off the headsets on the bars – the bolts that hold the levers etc in position on your handlebars. He said it was a racing trick and that, should I come off, the levers and control systems would hopefully just turn on the handlebar, rather than snap off. That's exactly what they did, what a great tip, cheers Mike! I simply twisted everything back to where it should've been, hit the ignition and we were off once more. Lovely job.

By 9pm I still had 400km to go before Chita, it was going to be a hell of a long night. What's more, a storm was closing in all around, but I just had to keep going. Luckily, the farther East I went, the clearer the skies became. It actually turned into a beautiful evening, with the sun staying high until almost 1am.

It took me until after 4am to finally arrive in Chita, I was absolutely done. My knees were past being painful, I was completely numb. I found the first hotel I came to in the city centre, but they were full. Apparently almost every hotel in the city was fully booked due to some holiday happening that week. Not what I wanted to hear really. To be honest I could have just laid down on the floor right there in the reception and gone to sleep, I was hanging. To be fair I must have looked a right sight, a fat, bearded white guy in full mucky white leathers, covered head to toe in muck and insect-roadkill, and stinking to high heaven. No wonder they didn't want me in their hotel.

But the lassie at the counter seemed to take pity on me and asked what I was doing in the city. When I told her I was riding around the world, she was more intrigued by the fact I'd ridden across Russia than anything else. She called over the security guard and babbled in Russian, and he too couldn't believe I'd ridden the beast from Moscow. She set to work phoning around all the hotels and found me a room in a place just outside the centre of town. She warned me it was nothing special, but I didn't care, I just wanted a shower and bed. Thanking them both I hobbled back to the bike, set the Garmin, and headed off into the night. 10 minutes later I was booking in to a motel just on the southside of the city, the beast was safely tucked away in a locked compound, and I was soon in a glorious shower. Then sleep, beautiful sleep!

Life's a funny old game, you never know quite what's around the next corner in your own wee journey. It was now day 66 and I was in Chita, still almost 2,000 miles from Vladivostok. The next stage, from Chita to Khabarovsk, was the biggie, the one everyone whispers about. The once infamous 'Zilov Gap', a 600km wide section of nothing, no roads, just swampland, forest, river crossings and mud. It's halted many an expedition and was used as a natural defence barrier by Russia in the past. Armies could not cross this hostile stretch of land, until Austin Vince and his mates successfully crossed it on their motorbikes in 2000 during their famous 'Terra Circa' expedition.

Now however, it hosts one of the best roads in Russia, beautifully flat, smooth tarmac stretching for almost 1,000km from outside Chita to the junction with the M56 motorway, which heads north to Yakutsk and then Magadan. I should be glad of this development, as without it, there's no way I could cross on the beast, but you can't help feel a sense of loss to this once legendary natural phenomenon.

But this new road doesn't quite start from Chita, oh no. As you leave the city you're faced with a slight predicament, as the turn off to the main motorway appeared blocked, yet cars simply drove around the blockade and continued down the slip road. I'd been in Russia long enough now to know you just go with the flow, so I did a U-turn, rode in between the blocks and set off down the road.

Soon enough I was faced with an ocean of sand, everywhere I looked it was just sand. They were constructing a new road here, but I was a tad early. I plowed my way through, sand up to the axles in places, but the Bridgestone BATTLAX tyres just kept on going as long as the revs were kept low. I pulled up next to some road workers who didn't bat an eyelid to all the cars and trucks that were driving straight through their work. Asking them if this was the right way to the motorway, they just nodded and pointed down the road. Oh well, in for a penny.

After a short 5km section I was back on Terra-firma, but now faced the next sticking point. Fuel. There are a couple of stretches of road in Russia where there is no fuel for up to 220 miles. Two such stretches run from Chita to the junction with the M56, the first coming just 60km outside Chita and lasting over 190 miles. Thanks to Kriega, I had two spare 3.8 litre rotopax cannisters that extended my range from around 160 miles to about 230 miles. So, I set off along this beautifully smooth road and out into the unknown once more.

This stretch is also known for bandits, a place certainly not to camp in or hang about on. I couldn't believe it of such a place, it was beautiful, easily one of the most picturesque I'd seen in Russia. Riding along I kept my eyes peeled for anything out the ordinary, conscious of the news that a Japanese biker had been stabbed to death along this very road a few years previously. But as usual, I didn't experience a single drop of hostility at any point in Russia. I guess you just take your ticket and take your chance.

After fuelling up once more, I was soon on the second stretch of almost 220 miles without fuel stops. I'd been told that it was about 400km's so was getting nervous as I didn't actually know just how far my fuel reserves would take me. At 219 miles I spotted a fuel stop tucked away off the road, behind a couple of trucks. Pulling in I wasn't sure if it was open, or even if it was still in use. Thankfully it was, and a quick whiff of the nozzle revealed the fuel was not too bad, so in it went.

By almost midnight I still had another 1,000km to cover before I hit Khabarovsk. Conscious of the stories of bandits, I nervously looked around for somewhere to camp for the night, but there was nowhere. It sounds farcical to say, being that I was in the middle of Siberia, but it's true. The surrounding land is all swamp or thick forest. To get to it would require some serious off-roading, something I just can't do on the beast. So with the light fading I reached desperation point and found a deserted layby way off the road, which had one of the many inspection ramps found all over Russia tucked away at it's northernmost end. I parked up right behind the ramp, set the tent up using the ramp as a visual barrier to the road, and camped down right on the tarmac. Maybe not the most comfortable of places I've camped in, but I was so knackered I fell straight to sleep, waking early in the morning.

The next morning I still had over 1,000 miles to go before reaching my next planned city stop of Khabarovsk. This stretch of road is probably the most remote you'll find along the main roads in Russia, there is NOTHING for hundreds of miles around, nothing.

So you can imagine my surprise when I found a petrol station that had an actual forecourt and shop, and inside that shop I found IRN-BRU! Yep, the archetypal Scottish sugar-rich drink, right there in deepest, darkest Siberia. Sipping it down, taste-buds now in shock after the 'borscht' fest they'd endured through Russia, it was truly the nectar of the Gods. I savoured each and every drop, making the tiny bottle last.

Not long into the day I reached the junction of the M58 (the road I was on to Khabarovsk, then Vladivostok) and the M56 (which heads north to Yakutsk and eventually Magadan.) It was a strange feeling to stand there looking at the possibilities that lay before me. My plan had always been to head to Vladivostok, but now I found myself looking at this road to the north, suddenly contemplating a change of direction. The famous 'Road of Bones' lay up there, a real challenge to the adventure motorcyclist. Yakutsk and all it's wonders lay just over 1,000km to the north, with Magadan another 2,000km north after that. Could I change it all now? Could I make it?

I soon came to my senses and got back on the road to Khabarovsk, still another 1174Km to the east. Luckily the road was perfect, no bumps, no cracks, just freshly laid tarmac. I stepped up the pace and was soon knocking my way through the miles, merrily enjoying myself on the beast. But all too soon the familiar roadworks loomed on the horizon.

One thing I've learned in Russia is to obey the road signs, if they say it's bumpy then it generally is! Knocking down through the gears I was soon down to 2nd and crawling along at 10-15mph, over loose rock and sand. It was a baking hot day, sitting at about 34 degrees as it had been for most of my trip across Russia. The dust thrown up by the cars and trucks around me just swamped my ears and nose. I had to put the visor down to see, but then it'd become unbearably humid and hard to breath. Oh well, nobody said it would be easy eh!

Late into the day I was still about 160 miles from Khabarovsk, but I decided to try and ride into the night and make the city. As the sun began to set I was having to stop more and more frequently as the pain in my knees was just becoming too much to bear from having to squat on the pegs all the time. I went from stopping every 45mins, to every 30, and then eventually I was lucky to make 15mins before I was screaming in pain.

Bruce SMART

Soon enough I was back on some offroad sections, it was madness to try and get through these in the dark, so I started hunting for a camping spot. My saviour came in the form of a tele-comms tower just off the road in a forest section. Locating the access path I followed it into the woods and found a clearing around the base of the tower, that'll do nicely. I'd set the Vango Chinook 200 tent up in minutes, chucked my sleeping bag inside and slumped in, leaving most of my bags out on the beast. I was asleep in seconds.

At about 1am I was awoken by the shaking of the very ground I was lying on! In my deep sleep I'd no idea what was going on, but as soon as I heard the numerous male Russian voices I was wide-awake. Several torch beams scanned across the tent and onto the beast. I could hear a massive engine booming around me and excited calls from men outside my tent. I've got to admit, I could hear banjo's and pigs screaming, this may not be good.

I stuck my head out the tent and was caught in torchlight. Squinting I stuck my thumb up and pointed at the tent, "It's OK?" A voice said, "Yes, it's ok my friend. We build road here. English?" Thank f^&* for that thought I, replying, "No, Scottish!" Thankfully the lads laughed and urged me to go back in the tent and sleep. Although slightly wary of my surroundings, I was soon unconscious, oblivious to the heavy machinery manoeuvring around me.

Early the next morning I stepped out the tent and couldn't believe my eyes. The beautiful forest that I'd camped in was nowhere to be seen, replaced by a muddied clearing stretching off into the distance. I quickly packed up my kit, eager to hit the road once more, now only about 160 miles short of Khabarovsk. As I got back on the Beast the lads began to crowd around, slapping me on the back and smiling from ear to ear like excited school kids. As I said goodbye, the lads asked me to wheelie, but the thought of trying that on sand on the gixxer wasn't exactly appealing.

I arrived in the city at lunchtime and quickly found a decent, but cheap motel to stay in for 2 nights. My body was in tatters, knees now constantly screaming in pain, I just wanted to get off the bike, shower, and rest! I'd planned on doing the blog and the next vid episode whilst there, but to be honest I wasn't fit for anything. I just slept and veg'd for 2 nights straight, catching up on the social media for the trip. I can't tell you how great it was to read all the messages of support each time I logged on. It really was like having a team along with me, without it, it would be a long, lonely journey. Thanks very much to you all, I really did, and still do, appreciate your support.

I'd been told that the final 600 mile stretch of road from Khabarovsk to Vladivostok was the worst in terms of road surface condition. Reports varied from mixed road works, to no road at all for 100's of miles! By this point I just wanted to get to Vladivostok, I'd been on the road for 71 days, almost 5 weeks of that had been crossing Russia, it was time to get there now.

As luck would have it, there is a hell of a lot of work going on in Russia to develop their roads. Construction work takes place practically 24hrs a day, re-surfacing existing roads and making brand new ones in some places. I appeared to have timed it right for a change as the vast majority of the 600km ride was on beautifully smooth, brand new asphalt. It was a welcome relief to the constant battering the beast and I had taken over the last 10,000 kms. In a few stretches I even stretched her legs again, enjoying the incredible performance this bike can offer, but you can never totally relax here, the road can just change like that. I'd say all in all, out of the 600km, maybe about 100km in total was 'off-road', where there was roadwork's taking place, or sometimes the road had just been left to ruin. It wasn't too bad at all to be honest, no worse than anything I'd experienced before. But then the rain came down, turning the sand and grit in the roadwork sections into a quagmire of red mud. Once you were in it you couldn't stop, just keep the wheels turning as slowly as possible to allow the Bridgestone BATTLAX tyres to grip. They did an amazing job, I never lost it once on the whole journey. Even crossing the jaggy rocks and stones, for mile upon mile, the carcass held where other tyres failed.

I caught up with a large group of Russian bikers just before one section of mud and rocks. They were the usual gaggle of GS, Goldwing, Bandits and Harleys. Passing the tail

GS and Harley, they gave me a double take then huge thumbs up. At that point the front wheel went deep into the mud and I thought I was done for. Keeping the throttle on just enough to stay above idle, the rear wheel kept pushing me through and I ploughed a channel through the muck. After about 10 minutes I was eventually out and back onto solid road once more. The Russian bikers gave me a toot and biker salute, and we went our separate ways.

That final ride was fairly uneventful, arriving in Vladivostok about 8:30pm I made my way to one of the 2 hostels in the city. The 'SeeYou Hostel' is basic to say the least, set in a typical soviet tower block, it's basically a young lads apartment that he has adapted to cram in as many bunks as possible. But it's the people you meet in these places that really make it for me.

Phil Krixx is an Ozzy who had arrived in the city to ship his bike to Magadan. From there he was going to ride the famous 'Road of Bones' down the M56, and on to the M58 to Moscow – the same route I'd just ridden. He was heading to London for a work conference and doing the whole trip on his faithful MZ.

Carlos Ojeda is a Cuban chap who arrived at the hostel at the same time as me. He too was riding around the world but he was on the last section of his mammoth 2yr, 60,000Km trip. He'd put his Aprilia on the train in Moscow and was waiting for it to arrive in Vladivostok, before he shipped it back to Canada. From there he'd ride it the last section to his home in Miami.

The three of us hit it off right away, meeting these lads really made my stay in Vladivostok, and I'd be meeting up with Phil in Oz later in the trip, and hopefully Carlos back in the UK, depending on timescales and schedules.

The hostel was a great place to stay and I recommend anyone to do similar. You meet such great folk in these places, and it's a quick way to get up to speed with what's what in the city. You in turn can pass this info on to the next new arrival before you leave, great system. I met such great guys there, Alex, Yuri, Jack, Charles, Ben, Rowan, the list goes on and on.

I spent a total of 6 days in Vladivostok, ample time to get the blog piece, Fastbikes article and next vid episode done, but I didn't do any of it. I sat down numerous times to get to work on the blog, but I just couldn't concentrate. The last 5 weeks suddenly caught up with me and I found myself absolutely shattered all of the time. I ventured out a few times into the city with Phil and Carlos to do some sightseeing and blow the cobwebs away, but I still couldn't get the work done. No excuses, I just lacked moral fibre!

My original plan had always been to ship to Japan, then South Korea to see my dad, then ship to India. From there I'd ride around India, up into Nepal, then Bangladesh, Myanmar and into Thailand. However there'd been a few developments since my planning days.

Firstly the ferry from Vladivostok had changed and the new route now went to South Korea before Japan. Not a problem, but the costs involved had almost tripled since last year! I was right at the end of my first stage budget so couldn't afford to ship to South Korea, then ship across to Japan, so made the decision to leave the beast in Vladivostok whilst I went to Korea. It'd then be put on the ferry 2 weeks later and I'd meet her in Japan. I used Yuri Melnikov of Links Ltd to sort all the shipping, he and Sveta are great people who know the shipping business inside and out. They are THE people to use, I thoroughly recommend their services. Their contact details are +7-902-524-3447, ymelnik@links-ltd.com

I left Vladivostok on the 3pm ferry to Donghae, South Korea on Wednesday the 24th July 2013. I was sad to leave Phil, Carlos, Alex and the lads I'd met, they'd all been such great people. Hopefully our paths will cross once more in the future. I left the beast wrapped up on the dockside of the quay, watched over by security 24hrs a day. She'd meet me again when I got the ferry from Donghae to Japan in 2 weeks time. Hopefully.

Bruce SMART

So that was Russia done! 7,000 miles crossed in just under 5 weeks, 2 sub-frame fractures and multiple mozzie bites. I'd loved the place, the people, and my first proper taste of adventure. Russia is a land of extremes, weather, conditions, lifestyles and cultures. The folk I met were genuinely the most welcoming and giving I'd ever experienced, they'd literally give you the shirt off their back if you needed it. My time here will stay with me forever.

RUSSIA

A CHINA

KOREA JAPAN

NA

HINA

TAIWAN

VIETNAM PHILI

LAOS

PAP
NEW

CHAPTER 18
SOUTH KOREA & JAPAN

This leg of the trip was really only meant as a filler, a quick 3-4 weeks break between Russia and South East Asia down to Oz. What it turned out to be was one of the most memorable, rich in welcomes, scenery, culture and warmth – in every sense. I'm sad to have left Japan in particular, there are things that frustrated me about this place, but over all it is a superb country, full of the most welcoming and respectful people I've met. On top of that I crashed twice, had an argument with a taxi, and ended up making friends with the old bill. But more of that later…

Boarding the 'Eastern Dream' ferry at Vladivostok, I was full of anticipation of what lay ahead. Russia had been brilliant, it really had, but I was ready to experience a bit of 'normality' now, you know, things like shops with things in them, prices on stuff, colour and brightness! Don't get me wrong, Russia is incredible, but you're very conscious of the fact you're in the Eastern block when there, it's hard to explain!

The ferry to Donghae in South Korea takes 23hrs but is painless, especially when you consider I'd spent the last 5 and a half weeks crossing Russia on a Superbike! There are a few things to entertain you onboard like a bar, restaurant and night club, but I was absolutely cream crackered so just slept. Well that and the fact I now seem to suffer from sea-sickness which, despite there being hardly any swell, meant I felt a tad queasy every time I sat upright.

Arriving in the port of Donghae early the next afternoon, I said goodbye to Carlos who'd come with me on the same ferry as he was continuing on to Japan. My plan was to make my way down to the city of Ulsan where my dad lived and worked. I'd spend a few days here catching up with the old boy, before heading North to Seoul for the rest of the week, then get the same ferry over to Japan. As usual, my plans seem to be fluid at best.

Boarding a bus to Ulsan it was a real culture shock now being in Korea. The colours seemed brighter, the smiles wider, and the noise louder. I loved it and just sat back, letting someone else take the strain of the journey for a change.

It took a few hours to ride the bus down to Ulsan but it was no hardship, I slept most of the way. Once in Ulsan my old boy picked me up, it was such a good feeling to see my Dad again, and this time I was there in his back yard in South Korea. After a hearty meal at his local Korean BBQ place, we headed back to his swanky apartment on the outskirts of the city. For an old boy, he's not done too bad at all with his pad. He works for HHI (Hyundai Heavy Industries) as a quantity surveyor in the oil and gas. For years I've heard him talk about guys he works with, projects he's working on, and now here I was, right there in amongst it all. HHI is a major employer here, literally ten's of thousands of people are employed in the various yards, swarming all over the place on mopeds like busy bees around a nest.

My dad's a good lad, he'd been telling the folks around his office all about my escapades, and many of them had been following the trip through the blog, facebook and YouTube. One of the guys there was called Alex Teasdale, and Alex was the founding member of a bike club called – 'Bang-Go Bikers'. Having heard about a lunatic riding a gixxer around the world, Alex was keen to meet up and confirm his suspicions. So after a few beers with the lads from Dad's work, I found myself the next morning astride a new BMW K1300S, flying around some of the best twisty roads I'd been on since leaving way back in May. The bike was courtesy of one of the club members, Trond Wiik, who was back in Norway on leave and left his bike, gear, and even his apartment free for me to use! An absolutely incredible guy, and I'm glad I just managed to catch him before I left to say thanks. Trond, if you're reading this mate, you're one in a million and I thank you again for such kindness. I hope I looked after her ok for you, she's some weapon.

I'd originally only meant to stay the weekend at my dad's, but to be honest I just wanted to stay and spend a bit of time with him. My dad's always worked away from home, apart from a few stints back in the UK, my whole life was spent with dad working abroad somewhere, arriving home for short periods of time before heading off. He's a great dad, the traditional provider for the family, but ALWAYS there to offer advice and guidance, whether I knew I needed it at the time or not. I remember he took me away fishing when I was wee, a long weekend just me and him, away down to the borders of Scotland as there weren't many places in Scotland you could fish for 'coarse' fish then. It was awesome, I remember it vividly to this day and loved the time we spent together. I don't think I've ever really thanked him for that time, I hope he's reading this now. Thanks Dad X.

Dad's had a rough time dealing with the passing of my mum these last 6 years. I miss her incredibly, I can't imagine how hard it must be for him to deal with. But life goes on regardless of what we do, or don't do, and I hope he finds happiness again along the way.

So for the next 10 days I'd spend the days entertaining myself either doing the next blog piece, writing the next update for Fast Bikes, or breaking my external hard drive and losing ALL the trip files! I'd also go out on the bike with Alex, Roberto and some other lads from the 'Bang-Go Bikers'. The roads in South Korea are incredible, you just venture off the highways and a whole world of glorious mountain twisties opens up. The surface is flawless, the roads are reasonably wide, even the mountain ones, and the traffic light – most of the time. We'd fly around the tarmac skies, stopping in the most unbelievable places to grab a quick drink and admire the scenery. I could easily settle in this place, and it's defo on the list of places I want to go back to.

In the evenings I'd spend time with dad, not doing much really, just spending time together in Korea. My dad's no Gordon Ramsay, his idea of cooking is to heat up a pizza or boil the kettle for some noodles, so we ate out – a lot. I've developed a taste for Kimchi and Bibimbap now, as well as rekindled a love for pizza and burgers. Cheers dad, I know I don't say it often enough, but thank you, and I love you loads ya old fart!

Bruce SMART

After my wee rest it was time to hit the road once more and head North to the capital city of Seoul. I'd heard so many great things about this place and I wasn't to be disappointed, it's mega. I took the KTX, Korea's version of the Japanese bullet train, all the way from Ulsan direct to Seoul. You couldn't get further from the shambles we have in the UK. The train departs and arrives at exactly the time stated in the timetable, each and every time. The platforms and trains are spotless, the staff bow as they enter and leave each carriage, and service is always with a smile. Sound familiar? Take note South Eastern, GWR etc.

In only a few hours I'd arrived in the centre of Seoul and was lounging at the hostel I'd pre-booked. The metro system is fairly straight forward, based on different coloured lines like almost everywhere else. The stations are also in English as well as Korean, and they're numbered too, so you have to go some to get it wrong. That said, when you first go through the turnstiles it can be a bit tricky knowing which steps to go down for your selected line, North or South, East or West, but things soon become apparent.

No trip to Seoul can be complete without a wee trek to the De-Militarised Zone (DMZ), separating North and South Korea. Following the war between the two countries, which lasted from 1950-1953, a treaty was signed by both leaders agreeing to an armistice. Now that's NOT a ceasefire, meaning effectively that both sides are still at war. This 2.5 mile wide strip of land runs along the 38th parallel, effectively splitting Korea in two. It's allegedly the most heavily armed border in the world, and possibly one of the most hostile. Guided tours come here each and every day from the South, so I popped a long for a look.

It really is worth coming to see this place, it almost has a theme park feel as you arrive at the main car park area, just short of the tunnels and observatory roads. First off is 'Freedom Bridge', where POW's from both sides were exchanged following the armistice between countries. There are also a number of shrines and monuments here, all suggesting a desire for reunification, particularly from the South. Maybe one day.

Next were the infamous tunnels. The story told by the guide goes like this. Each time a defector from the North arrives in the South, they are taken for a wee spot of questioning. You know, the type were it's really not a good idea to lie. One such defector came forth with the revelation that the North had dug a number of tunnels leading from the North all the way under the DMZ and into the South. Some were even said to have reached Seoul! Although the defector could not identify exactly where these tunnels were, he was adamant there were over 40 of them, so the South devised a 'cunning plan my Lord'.

Holes were bored deep into the ground all along the 160 mile long border, into which clear plastic pipes were placed. Each pipe was then filled with water and entire Brigades of soldiers were tasked to patrol each pipe, day and night, to monitor any movement in the water. For 3 years absolutely nothing happened, then one day a private noticed that the water level in one piped had gone. After further exploration into this area, the first tunnel was located, with no sign of any North Korean military within it. After this a further 3 tunnels were found, but as yet nothing seems to have been mentioned of the other 37 or so still outstanding?

To begin with the North said they had nothing to do with the tunnels. However, and here's were the Civil Engineer in me comes out again, they were dug sloping back to the North. You see if you were to dig a tunnel in those days, you'd ensure you dug uphill, meaning the water in the ground would run back away from you as you dug. Also the blast and tool marks all indicated the direction of travel was from the North to the South. As the South cottoned on to the tourist trap money making idea of the tunnels, the North suddenly wanted a piece of the action and stated the tunnels belonged to them and they were digging for coal. Infact they'd gone as far as painting the walls of the tunnel black and spreading coal dust during their retreat back down the tunnels when initially discovered. Trouble was they were dug through solid granite, there's no coal for hundred of miles around these parts!

As we surfaced out the tunnel a huge thunder storm struck. I've never seen rain like it, almost as if you were swimming in the open air, drenching you in mere seconds. The claps of thunder were God like, almost shaking the very ground we stood on. Boarding the tour coach our next stop was to be the observatory, where you can look out over the DMZ and actually watch the North Korean army patrol their border side through binoculars. Unfortunately due to the weather, the military had closed the access road as they were worried the heavy rain could wash landmines off the surrounding mountains onto the road! Different world.

We later heard that we'd had a lucky escape in the tunnels. The group after us were still down there when all the power went out, leaving them in complete darkness hundreds of feet underground, whilst the huge thunderstorm echoed massive 'booms' of thunder above. Your imagination would run riot down there!

So it was then on to the 'Dorasan Peace Park', an area right in the middle of the DMZ, in which was built an industrial park. Between 2005 - 2008 relations between the North and South improved under a new liberal government in the South. They improved to such an extent that trade began between the two nations, which led to South Korea building plants in the DMZ. Goods from these were then exported to the North and South, with profits mostly going North. Thousands of workers were delivered each day by train, things were looking good.

But then there was a change in government in the South in 2008, back to the more conservative party and relations once again expired. The park was decommissioned and vacated, the purposely built Dorasan Train station now lying abandoned, bar the arrival of daily tourists. It's like a modern day ghost town walking around this station, the dreams of reunification are plain to see as there's a map high on the wall of the 'Trans Eurasian Railway Network', clearly showing a rail track running right through the South to the North, and beyond all the way to London, amongst other cities. Maybe one day this will be possible, I for one would love to take that journey.

An indication of how much the people of the South want a reunification can be seen in a monument just outside the station. People would donate money to fund the building of the park and station, with the name of each donator now on display along a wall. At the foot of the wall stands a section of the actual railway track which once linked North and South.

For my last day in Seoul I took myself off on a whistle stop tour of the actual city. Like most cities around the world, there are hop-on/off tour buses available, so what better way to see the sights when constrained by time. They start at Gwanghwamun Square right in the heart of the city. The square itself is fairly breathtaking with statues of King Sejon the Great and Admiral Yi Sunshin dominating the skyline.

You can't help but notice Namdaemun, or the Great South Gate, when traveling through the centre of Seoul. It's considered the most important historical and cultural treasure in South Korea for its 600-year-old history, as well as its symbolic role as protector of the King and capital, which was why it was given the official title of the number one national treasure. It was burned to the ground in 2008 during an arson attack, but restored to it's former glory, costing $23 million.

The tour takes you on through some of the iconic sites of Seoul, the various massive malls – each specialising in various items such as fashion, technology, food etc, the National Korean War Memorial, the famous Seoul Tower with its staggering panoramic views, hotels of the highest standard, and historic shrines and temples.

If you ever plan on going to Seoul, and I heartily recommend you do, make sure you give yourself more than two and a half days to explore the city! What a mug I was to think that'd be long enough, but I managed a whistle stop tour of the main sites so that would have to do. Korea is a great country, full of polite people who are only to happy to help if asked. I remember an old boy down in the metro, he saw I was standing in front of the subway map with a confused look on my face. He came over, pointed at the map then me, motioning for me to tell him where I wanted to go. I pointed at a name on my phone and he took me all the way to the right platform. He waited for me to get on the train, bowed and walked off. Brilliant stuff.

So on day 92 I boarded a bus at the famous Gangnam bus station (no I didn't do the dance, although I now wish I had), and went back to the port of Donghae where I entered South Korea two weeks previously. Boarding the ferry I made my way straight to the car deck and there she was, the Beast was back………. and breathe. All was right with the world once again.

Back on deck I watched the evening sun settle onto the horizon as we pulled slowly out of port. I was sorry to leave this place, but eager to get back on the road again, reunited with my faithful steede. The ferry across to Sakaiminato in Japan was just an overnighter, so after grabbing some grub I settled into my bunk and drifted off to sleep.

The next morning I awoke bright and early, ready to whisk through customs and hit the road. Oh the naivety of it all. My first lesson about Japan began right at the gate, the border gate at the terminal. They took one look at me and I was invited into the wee room with a few officers, who began to put on rubber gloves. Uh-huh, now that's DEFINITELY not going to happen here. Thankfully it was only to search my bags so I warned them of the smell and began to unpack. Out came a huge knife, my camping tool and best friend in parts of Russia. But here it took a far more sinister appearance. Next came a small bag of white powder – my washing powder for cleaning clothes in motel sinks. It wasn't going well. Thankfully the next question they asked was my profession, you can imagine their surprise when I told them. Thankfully the mood changed, they saw the funny side, and that was that. For now.

Once I'd gone through customs it was now time for the bike. We started the whole process at 11:30am, first off we had to visit the JAF office over in Matsua and get the Carnet certified. I'd already emailed them to notify of my arrival, so hopefully this would only take an hour tops. The staff at the port kindly took me and a German biker called Karl over to the JAF office, for a small fee of course. True to their word, we were in and out in about 15 minutes, all going well so far. We had been chatting with the chap from the port about SIM cards in Japan. Both Karl and I needed a local SIM card so we could access the internet on our phones and make cheap local calls etc. But it seems that it's not possible to buy a pay-as-you-go SIM card in Japan, not if you are 'Gaijin' – a foreigner.

The chap took us all over Matsua, into telecom centres, malls, just about everywhere he could think of. He even phoned his sister up in Tokyo, but it seems that outside of Tokyo and a few airports, it just isn't possible. So back to the port we went. It was now about 3pm. The next few hours were taken up with obtaining insurance, again organised by the staff at the port – 5,000 YEN for one month 3rd party. But be careful as this is the most basic you can get, only covering death of another party, not your bike or other vehicles involved. Be warned.

Eventually we got through, everything stamped where it should be, docs copied in triplicate, sometimes even more, and I changed into my riding leathers in the staggering heat of Japan. It was still 36 degrees at almost 5pm, I was leaking. I said goodbye to Karl the German, and just as I was about to leave a staff member came running out and asked for our carnets once again, they'd forgotten to make a 15th copy for whatever reason. Digging it out my recently packed bag, I handed it over and sat inside the air conditioned building waiting for its return. A short time later he came running back, apologetically handing it over before whisking away. Packed up again I hit the ignition on the Beast and although sounding a bit throaty to begin with, she was back in the room. My destination for tonight was to be Hiroshima, some 130 miles away. It was going to be a long night.

The expressways in Japan are all toll roads costing on average about $1 per Km, making it a fairly expensive way to travel. So I hit the normal roads that would take me through and over the mountain ranges between Matsua on the North coast and Hiroshima on the South coast. It was brilliant to be back in the saddle, feeling the wind in my hair (?) and the road rushing by beneath me. God I loved my life on the road.

My first lesson about riding in Japan came soon enough. As I approached a set of lights on the outskirts of a town, I filtered my way to the front, like you do everywhere else in the world. As I reached the front the lights changed and I accelerated in front of the truck at the front of the queue, pulling back into my lane and continuing onwards. That's when the skies lit up behind me and an official barking-like voice echoed over a loudhailer behind me. Here comes the fuzz!

Pulling over I took off my lid and got off the bike. Two of the skinniest and shortest grown men I'd ever seen approached, neither with a face that looked like it hid a sense of humour. They barked something in foreign and pointed at the bike and a bit of paper in their hands. Getting the docs out my folder I handed them over and pointed at the map on the back of my lid, trying to signal what I was doing. Their mood changed quickly and one began to speak slowly in English, telling me there was a problem as I had crossed the solid line at the junction. I tried to say I was just going to the front of the queue, but was told I must not do this under any circumstance.

Apparently this is the worst thing you can do on the roads in Japan. You can drive on the phone, text, play games on your ipad, even be pissed as a fart, that's all fine. But cross a solid line and it's instant justice from this lot? Staggering. Things started to go South as they said there was a problem with my papers and invited me back to their station, what choice did I have. Following them back to the nik I wandered if this would be my 'room' for the evening, it was now dark and gone 8pm. Once at the nik a new batch of officers went over my paperwork, a new batch of voices went, "Awwww, Ahhhhhh, Hi, HI!" like some Russ Abbott sketch, I nearly laughed at my predicament but luckily held out.

I was told there was a problem with my insurance as it didn't show on the system. I said I'd got it that day at the port after arriving from Korea. "Awwwwwww, Ahhhhhh, Hi, HI!" came the reply in unison from everyone in the office. That explained it I guess. Next they asked my profession and literally took a step back when I told them. From then on it was laughter and hand shakes, they even got me to stand with their station Inspector and took pics on their phones. I wish I'd got one myself, but stupidly I didn't.

I was soon back on the bike and got an escort back to the main road before I waved goodbye and headed off into the night. I finally arrived in Hiroshima at almost 11pm that night. I was knackered, hot and I stunk to high heaven. Luckily they let me into the hotel I'd pre-booked so I was soon showered and unpacking my bags. A carnet de passage is only valid for one year and I knew mine would expire in the next few months. I'd planned to get my replacement sent to my Mrs, and she would bring it out to me when we met in Thailand a few months later. I pulled out the carnet to check the date and saw that it was Jul 2014? That's weird, I got mine in Sep 2012. Then it hit me when I saw the name at the top, 'Karl EBERL'. Bollocks, we'd been given back the wrong carnets at the port before I left!

Luckily whilst waiting throughout the day, Karl and I had swapped emails as we were both heading to Thailand next. Unfortunately Karl didn't speak English and my German is as good as my Russian, Japanese etc. I quickly sent him an email via google translate and hit the sack. The next morning I had a reply from Karl so we arranged to meet at a BMW dealership in Osaka in a few days, so for now it was sightseeing time.

It was hot, incredibly hot. By 10am it was already 38 degrees and I was suffering in my leathers. In this heat it was almost unbearable riding through the busy city streets, constantly stopping and starting at the lights. The bike was frequently over heating, often hitting over 114 degrees on the dash computer. I assumed it was blocked filters from the battering she'd taken through Russia, but she was due a big service in a weeks time up in Tokyo, so I just dealt with it for now.

First stop, Itsukushima. It's mostly known by the name Miyajima, meaning "Shrine Island". It's a sacred place in the Buddhist religion in Japan. Women were not allowed on the island up until fairly recently, pregnant women are taken off the island near to their due time, and old people are taken elsewhere to die, so as not to spoil the ritual purity of the island!

I arrived at the ferry port across to the island and parked up the bike. I had all the tell tale signs, I'd been here a few times now, I had the beginnings of heat stroke once again. Luckily Japan is littered with roadside drinks vending machines so I armed myself with several bottles of water and lemon juice, found some shade, stripped off and lay down to cool off. I must have slept for a few hours there on the ground in the shade, but when I woke I felt alive once more. Refreshed from more liquids I boarded the short ferry over to the island, then slowly walked along the boardwalk to the sacred Tori shrine of Miyajima. It's a stunning sight, plain as day and there for all to wonder at. The view is certainly better when the tide is in and either at dusk or dawn, but in true TeapotOne style, the tide was out and it was the middle of the day. Yet still, the magic of the moment was still maintained.

The Tori Shrine is an incredible sight. It sits in the bay, and is known as the gate to the island. It's not actually secured to the sea bed, just relies on perfect symmetry and balance in its construction. The area receives some of the strongest tides in Japan, it's amazing how the thing isn't effected at all.

The five-storied Pagoda (Gojunoto) was originally built in 1407 to enshrine the deity, Buddha of medicine. It's only 1 of 5 examples in Japan and is 'earthquake proof' due to its construction, based around a central pillar system. (The Civil Engineer in me came out there, I'm sorry).

There are wild deer and monkeys roaming the island too. Deer are believed to be gifts from the Gods and as such are sacred. They do what they like on the island and are incredibly tame. I spent a few hours on the island just wandering around and cooling off in the shade.

Once back on the mainland I headed back into Hiroshima to visit the 'Peace Park' at the nuclear holocaust site of August 6th 1945. The area of the attack was chosen because of the important Atoi Bridge in Hiroshima. Unfortunately the bomb slightly missed it's target, instead exploding directly above the now famous 'Genbaku Dome' or 'Atomic Bomb Dome'. It's the only structure left standing in the area of the blast, yet every single person inside died instantly, along with up to 166,000 others over the next few months.

The Peace Park sits right in the centre of the blast, now a tranquil park area and museum. It's a weird feeling to walk through the park, in the distance sits the Dome, a distinct memorial to the horrors that once befell this place.

Within the park sit a number of memorials, one such is the The Memorial Cenotaph. It holds the names of everyone killed by the blast, whether directly or indirectly. It also has the epitaph "please rest in peace, for [we/they] shall not repeat the error."

The Children's Peace Monument is dedicated to all the children killed by the bomb, it's a statue of a little girl with outstretched arms, holding a paper crane above her head. There's a real poignant story behind this. It represents a real little girl who died from radiation from the blast. Her name was Sadako Sasaki and she believed that if she folded 1,000 paper cranes she would be cured. To this day, people from all over the world send paper cranes to the memorial, and a fresh supply is replenished daily.

My visit to the Peace Park was actually a lot more moving than I thought it'd be, the site of such carnage and horror, now a serene and tranquil place. But if you think about it, what better way to mark such a horrendous part of history than for it to become the complete opposite of what it once was. All those people died as a result of that bomb, but that bomb brought about the end of the 2nd World War, and no doubt saved just as many, if not more, lives in the process. It's a funny old world eh.

After meeting up with Karl to exchange our carnets, I headed North and stopped for the evening in Okayama. I didn't know anything about the place, except I'd found a really cheap motel practically in the centre of the city. I stopped there for the evening and whilst out walking around looking for somewhere to eat, I found an incredible castle. I don't know much about the place, but got some good pics.

From Okayama I headed up to Lake Biwa, the largest freshwater lake in Japan. The Western shore line is certainly the better one to ride along, far less developed and more accessible than the Eastern shore. The place is huge and the roads up in the Northern end of the lake are excellent to ride, just watch out for monkeys in the forest sections, I nearly had a pillion at one point!

I found a place to pitch the tent right on the shoreline, and in a moment of madness I fell asleep with the tent sides open. I'd not seen any Mosquitos since arriving in Japan so thought I'd be safe to sleep with the breeze coming off the lake. In the morning I awoke to find I'd been eaten alive by my old mates, I was on fire! My neighbour in the tent along must've though I was mad as I dashed out the tent, straight into the freezing cold water in the early hours, swatting away my guests who were royally gorging away!

First stop for day 97 was to be the Suzuka circuit. Although not one of the motoGP circuits, I still wanted to visit this iconic track so set off in the extreme heat of the developing day. It had hit over 40 degrees a few times since I'd been in Japan, and today was no exception, it was scorching. After a few hours I arrived at the track, parked up, paid my entrance fee and walked through the amusement park area, across the fabled footbridge, and down to the main grandstand area.

The circuit was being used by the go-karts that day, not the 140mph ones, but the duel seated, parent and child type that mosey along at about 10mph. I sat in the grandstand and watched the crowds of people queue up for over an hour in the soaring 40+ degree heat, then roll painfully slowly around the 3.6 mile circuit. I had a few hours to waste here so fell asleep in the grandstand, safely tucked away in the shade.

I'd recently sent a message out on a bikers forum called, www.gaijinriders.com (Foreign Riders) saying I was in Japan and looking to meet up with any bikers out there to see the good roads. The first chap to get in touch was Shaun Poole, an expat now living in Toyota, who invited me stay at his place, then ride some way the next day. After arriving at his home up in the hills and settling in, we had a great night chatting with his Japanese neighbours, themselves avid bikers, who could not believe I had ridden all the way there from the UK on a gixxer 1000! At that moment, neither could I.

The next morning Shaun and I headed off along the route 153 up into the mountains, as I was heading for Yamanashi by the end of the day. As we got higher into the hills, the temperature dropped to a more civil 34-35 degrees and I felt like I could breathe once more. We stopped at the Japanese version of 'Rykas Cafe', and had a wee chat with some local bikers.

Soon enough I had to say goodbye to Shaun and make my way north along the 153, heading up to Lake Suwa, before turning East for Yamanashi. Another chap from the Gaijin Riders, John Gavin, had got in touch offering a place to stay with him and his family there. He'd told me that the club were having their annual family camping event that weekend and invited me along. How could I say no to that, a chance to catch up on a few bits and bobs at John's, then meet some folks over a camp fire, before riding up through the mountains with some of the lads, on route to motegi and Tokyo. Sounded perfect.

Arriving at John's place he immediately made me at home with his wife Saori and their two daughters. Over the next few days I got a chance to do some maintenance on the Beast and give her a long awaited wash.

A quick chat about the tyres if I may. Yes I was supported by Bridgestone and got the tyres mostly for free, and I can only give you my word that I'd tell you if they were crap. Those BATTLAX BT-023's I'd used since the start of the trip were simply incredible. The abuse they'd put up with included, potholes severe enough to break my subframe – four times, constant changes in road surface, including holes, cracks, bumps, humps, mud, sand, gravel, and rocks sharp enough to shred other biker's tyres. The 23's never skipped a beat, not once. The latest set had almost 7,000 miles on them and still had loads of tread left. A truly awesome tyre.

So back to the journey and come Friday we were all getting ready to head up to Lake Motosu, one of a series of lakes at the base of Mount Fuji. The road up there, the glorious 358, is an incredible ribbon of tarmac guaranteed to bring a smile to your face. The twists and turns along this road are out of this world and I arrived at the Lake beaming from

Bruce SMART

ear to ear. Unfortunately, Johns van had broken down just outside the town so he'd had to go back and get his other car, making them fairly late up to the Lake. Once at the site, folks introduced themselves and I set up camp for the evening, beer was drank around a big roaring fire, food was eaten and great conversations had. I was made to feel incredibly welcome, the atmosphere relaxed and family like. Life was good in Japan.

Morning broke early in the camp site, kids screaming and running around, free as the birds and living it loud. You can't argue with that out in the country, so it was time to be up and packing. I soon had the kit stowed away on the beast and began saying goodbye to all my new friends. Craig McCracker and James Klauzner were going to show me some of the twisty roads around this area of Japan, before I split off and headed up to the Motegi circuit, then down to Tokyo. I still planned on shipping the bike out to Thailand the following week, from the 23rd Aug onwards, but as yet I still hadn't had any agents get back to me with set dates and schedule. It was insanely frustrating not getting any replies from these people at times.

So here's where things took a wee bit of a turn, initially for the worst, but it turned out being one of the best things to happen so far on the trip. We'd had a brilliant morning out on the bikes, Craig taking the lead along the incredibly fun Toge's (twisty mountains roads that connect the principalities around Japan). After filling up with fuel I took the lead so Craig could film me for a bit. The road was awesome, full of beautiful twists and turns through a cracking forest section up a mountain. It was all going well but I could tell the brakes weren't great, the 7,000 miles from Moscow had worn the pads and filled them with crud, and the front discs were getting pretty anorexic now. But I pushed on as she was getting a big service the next week, relishing the new found biker's bliss that Japan was becoming. My quest was to touch a knee on Japanese soil so I was pushing hard, and then it went wrong.

As I came down a straight towards a right hander there was a slight bump in the road, right at my braking point. As I braked the front lifted in the air, locking the front wheel. As it came down it skidded so I came off the brakes, forcing me wide into some debris at the side of the road. I was heading right for the armco barrier now and had a real case of 'target fixation' as I tried to brake again. The front just slipped in the dirt and that was that, down we went. The Beast crashed head first straight into the barrier, immediately destroying the mudguard and most of the front plastic. The front forks were also blown out so the bike was pretty much unrideable, for now. I was less than impressed, well that's an understatement. Unfortunately my GoPro decided it would work on this occasion so I captured the whole thing on film, you can watch it on the YouTube channel - 'TeaPotOneVids'.

Luckily I had Craig and James with me and they were quickly on their phones to the lads back at the camp. As it turned out there was a guy in the group called Pete Wilkinson who I'd not yet met properly. Pete and John (who I'd stayed with previously) had just set up a business together called 'ApexMoto'. Believe it or not it was a motorcycle business specialising in everything from sales to servicing, to custom paint and vinyl work. I couldn't have picked better company to crash in really!

It took a few hours for the lads to turn up but when they did the cavalry certainly arrived. Pete, John and Sam all came to my rescue and it was a huge relief to have them there. Once the initial piss-taking had commenced, it was instantly like being with old mates. The guys from 'Gaijin Riders' are such a great bunch, I urge any bikers coming to Japan to drop them a line. (www.gaijinriders.com)

We loaded the Beast onto the back of Pete's truck and all headed back to the campsite, waving goodbye to Craig and James as they continued on their days ride. I spent the next few hours getting to know Pete in his truck and I've got to say it was like we were old mates straight away. He's an Ozzy who's lived in Japan for 16 years and is now married to a Japanese woman called Akiko, with two kids. He's got an English teaching school called 'People' with another Ozzy chap called Paul. They're all a great bunch and it was great to get to know them.

Back at the campsite I was welcomed into the fold once more, I felt a right tit to be honest, the great biker who was riding around the world, can't even go around a corner in

Japan! But I needn't have worried, the lads took the piss obviously, but it was all good natured banter and I started to feel at home. We stayed at the campsite for another few days, it was excellent getting to know everybody now I had time to just relax there. I've got to admit, the whole time my mind was racing with thoughts about the trip, what was I going to do now, how the hell would I pay for these repairs, how was I going to get the shipping organised to Thailand, and how was I going to pay for that!

Money was becoming a factor now, I was about half way through the sponsorship fund and reckoned I could get to Oz on what was left, possibly maybe even to South America. I always knew I'd need more, 'Delta Energy Services' very kindly stumped up a hell of a lot to get me going again, but I've always been around £16K short of what I'd predicted I'd need. So I was back on the sponsorship recruitment campaign once more, but more of that later.

Come Monday morning it was time to pack up and head back to Pete's place in Kofu, and I've got to hand it to him, the man's got a knack when it comes to packing. We got all his camping stuff, tools, food, everything for his family of four for a weeks camping, plus the beast and his sons wee scrambler, all on the back of his wee Suzuki truck. We got some looks on the way home right enough, but that wee van did a sterling job.

Once back at Pete's we wasted no time getting the Beast up on the stand in his garage, setting to work stripping her down to assess the damage. Thankfully it didn't seem too bad. The front forks were blown so would need replacing, they would be the most expensive part to replace, but Craig had already found a set on a Japanese auction website (like ebay) for only £350! I needed a new front plastic grill, left wing mirror, front fender, front bearings, and plastic under-tray. All in it was about £460 so thankfully nowhere near the probable £2K it would have cost to get her repaired in a shop. It took us about a week to get everything off the bike, assessed, cleaned, ordered and put back together. Pete did a cracking job and he and his family made me feel very, very welcome in their home. I'll never be able to repay those guys the kindness and generosity they showed me, but I hope one day they take me up on my offer to stay with Nikki and I if they ever come to Blighty.

Remember Pete, "Live your life" and make sure you make your dream of travelling with Akiko a reality

Part of my sponsorship deal with Bridgestone was that I would visit their global HQ in Tokyo when in Japan. Originally I was supposed to visit the Monday after the crash, but obviously I couldn't do that. They very kindly rearranged the meet for the following week, so once all repaired I set off on the morning of day 112, destination Tokyo city centre. The journey went swimmingly, although I could definitely notice a lot of vibration through the handle bars? She tracked straight though if I took my hands off the bars, but it got worse the quicker you went. I'd taken the expressway to Tokyo to save time so the pace was good, but no real twists and turns to speak of.

Coming into the city centre I was following the directions on the garmin when I approached a fork in the road. It was one of them where you're not quite sure what the sat-nav is telling you to do, and as I'd turned off the volume I couldn't hear what the lane-assist directions were saying. At the last minute I swapped lanes, crossing a solid white line. Would you believe it, a copper literally jumped out into the road ahead, blew his whistle and pointed to an area ahead where about 6 of his colleagues were waiting. Great stuff.

The usual chorus of, "Awwwww, Ahhhhhh, Ohhhhhh, Hi, HI!" followed as my documents were passed from one Copper to the next to the next. It was plainly obvious they'd no idea what to do with a foreign bike, I was hot, and now had 5 minutes to get to Bridgestone, just around the corner. After an infuriatingly long 15 minute wait, I was given a ticking off and sent on my way. I'd called Bridgestone to say I'd be 10 mins late, so all was not lost.

I checked to my right and there was a nice space in front of a bus coming my way. I signalled and pulled out into the lane, gone no more than about 10 metres when a taxi decided he wanted to be in my lane and just pulled into me from the lane to my right! His rear wheel arch connected with my knee slider and right crash bung, making a lovely scrape into his car, adding to the war wounds of my bike and kit. I was less than happy I have to admit, and voiced my concerns to the oblivious driver, who only realised he'd hit something when his passenger tapped him on the shoulder. Poor bloke in the back, he had some fat, sweaty Scotsman in leathers screaming at him in a language anyone but a drunken Scot could understand. Looking back I should've just ridden on, the taxi was oblivious, the old bill hadn't even noticed. But in my naivety I pulled to the side of the road and gestured for him to follow. Next thing we are surrounded by old bill and so it began.

In the UK this kind of thing would be done and dusted in a matter of minutes, particulars exchanged by both parties and on your way – providing no one was injured. But here, once again the very same officers who had just checked, double checked, triple checked, quadruple checked, then phoned their superiors for them to check, all my documents, repeated the whole process once again not five minutes later. It took over an hour for them to make a decision, then asked me to accompany them to their station as they needed an interpreter because there was a problem with my insurance apparently. It just gets better eh. I phoned Bridgestone once again to say I was now going to the police station after being in an accident. They must've thought I was right wombat, first I crash and can't make the original meeting, then I get stopped by the police and am late, then I get involved in an accident and am taken to the police station. What a great ambassador eh!

Once at the nik I was put on the phone to a lady who spoke English. She explained that my insurance was the most basic you can get in Japan and only covered the death of another party if I was involved in an accident. I explained that this is what I was given when I entered the country, and anyway the accident wasn't my fault, the taxi had driven into me. She then relayed that the police were appointing full blame to me! I wasn't happy, I'd asked them at the scene if they'd seen it and each of them had said no, so how can they now say it was my fault. Welcome to Japan folks, if you're the foreigner and involved in an accident it's your fault. Period. Luckily they asked my occupation so I told them, and again things went a lot smoother after that. I dread to think what may have happened if this hadn't been the case.

In the end, I was allowed to go on the condition that I provided Pete's telephone number once I got home that evening so they could converse with a Japanese speaker on my behalf. It was all smiles and laughter now, they even wanted a picture with me, their station Chief Inspector getting in on the action as he had been a motorcycle student who visited Hendon many years ago for training apparently!

I eventually arrived at the Bridgestone HQ 2 hours late but they were great. A quick pic in front of the main reception with the boss, then it was off to the 'TODAY' museum on the outskirts of Tokyo. This is a public exhibit centre next to the main Bridgestone factory that showcases its products and involvement in motor sports, industry and the world in general.

Did you know that Bridgestone helped allow a dolphin to swim again? Neither did I. About 5 years ago a dolphin lost it's tail, I never did find out how, so Bridgestone stepped up and developed a state-of-the-art artificial rubber tail for it, incredible!

Unfortunately the actual factory where they make the bike tyres was shut, so after visiting the museum for an hour or so, it was time to head back home to Pete and Akiko's. As the day was still fairly young I decided to take the twisty route and see how the bike felt. This is when I started to notice her just not feeling quite right under braking, she constantly felt like she was going to tuck the front when braking into a right hand corner. The left wasn't too bad, but I really had to muscle her in to the right at speed. To be honest I just thought it was in my head after the crash, so just persevered and got on with it.

Over the next few days I spent as much time on the bike as I could, just trying to settle, and get my confidence in her once again. What I've always loved about the gixxers is that they are fast, insanely fast, but are easy to ride fast as they instil confidence in you. I've felt 100% at home on them since I first sat on the saddle, I love these animals, no it's more than that, they feel part of me now. But after the crash, the Beast just didn't feel right, something was wrong there and I'd no idea what. All I knew was that she wasn't the same bike I'd ridden over 55,000 miles to Japan, and she wasn't like my others Gixxers I'd had before her. It was driving me nuts and continued to do so for the rest of the trip!

Bruce SMART

I was after an interesting backdrop to some piece to camera shots for the videos, so plotted a wee route to Mount Fuji via google maps. I transferred it over to my garmin then hit the road. Unfortunately, I must have taken the wrong turning, or I just followed the directions blindly, and ended up riding up a dirt track. Assuming this would get better I carried on, with the track eventually becoming tarmac once again. However no sooner had I gone 100 yards and followed the hairpin bend in the road, it became a stone and rubble track once more, but now in an ever increasing gradient. The 'road' kept going up and up, getting steeper and steeper. I started seeing signs for bears, the stone gave way to loose rubble and dirt, that then gave way to sand and mud. This was getting a tad daft now, and if it didn't go anywhere at the end, I'd need to come down this lot!

I rode for about an hour up the track, eventually reaching a workers site, complete with dump trucks, excavators and 4X4's. It was a dead end, the road simply stopping into a cut out in the mountain, time to turn around and go back down. I pretty much had the back break locked down all the way, sometimes dragging the rear tyre along as gravity tried to accelerate me down the mountain side. I was bricking it, sweating like a pig and swearing like a frightened Scotsman. If a bear had popped out I reckon I would've stood a good chance against him, the testosterone was pumping like crazy as I readied myself to ditch her once again at any second. Thankfully I finally reached some solid ground, easing off the rear brake as the gradient levelled out and I popped back out onto the main roadway. I stopped at the first drinks vending machine I came to and demolished about three bottles of juice, sweat dripping off me in the morning sun, already it was 38 degrees. The lady at the stall alongside the machine gave me one of those looks your Mrs often gives you when they can't quite believe their life has led them to end up with you?

I managed to get a wee days riding out with the lads too before I left. Pete, Sam, Adam and James all came out for a blat out around Mount Fuji. It was yet another scorcher, meaning the roads were dry and tyres sticky. The pace was phenomenal, memories of my balls to the wall blats around the South East with Jimbo and Dave came flooding back. But this time it was different, I was the painfully slow new boy at the back, unsure of every bend, braking in the wrong place, making everyone nervous. Things just weren't right, for the first time ever I wasn't enjoying being on the bike. In all honesty, if I could have pressed a button and been beamed back to Pete's place, I'd have happily gone.

Thinking it was just me lacking moral fibre, I kept at it, putting the miles on the bike and trying to get used to her once again. I visited the Kai Zenkoji temple in Kofu one day, looking for some decent backdrops for a sponsor promo vid I was trying to do. The place was incredible, just on the outskirts of the city and only a matter of minutes from Pete's place. The whole Yamanashi prefecture (like our districts or counties in the UK) is steeped in Samurai heritage. It was the stomping ground of some of Japans fiercest and most noble Samurai warriors. One such bloke was Takeda Shinge, and in 1565 he established the Kai Zenkoji temple. Stunning, simply stunning.

I'd been contacted on the facebook page by a French chap called Yan Giovanni, who was also riding his motorbike around the world. Yan had been knocked off his bike by a taxi in Tokyo, where his bike and he had taken quite a battering. He'd now been in Japan for a year, but with his bike back up and running he was looking at heading to Korea next. Yan had also met Pete and some of the lads from Gaijin Riders when he first passed through, so we arranged to go for a ride with James and Craig, the guys I crashed with, the first time.

Well, it was going ok to begin with, I still wasn't feeling right on the bike so decided to sit at the back of the convoy of bikes. We made our way up through some stunning twisty mountain roads, tighter than tight in places, but surrounded by incredible scenery. As we rode through yet another tunnel, you could see that the road surface was different, shiny and wet concrete with strips cut into the surface, this wasn't going to be good. I saw Craig at the front drift with his feet down stabilising him, then James slide the back wheel as he touched his rear brake. Yan was next and unfortunately as soon as he touched his brakes he went down, sliding the bike across the road as he slid directly in front of me. I'd no other option, I either carried on going and rode over Yan, or laid the bike down and push it away from us. Down we went for a second time in Japan. Bollocks.

Luckily only I hit Yan after sliding slowly along our lane. I watched the Beast slide on her other side this time, slowly scraping along the petrol covered concrete. She came to rest in the other carriageway, luckily behind an oncoming car. I was fuming, but what else could we have done. We picked up the bikes and slowly rode them through the tunnel to a clearing on the other side to asses the damage. Luckily, the R&G crash protection had done an incredible job. the bar end bung and engine case protector had taken a hell of a scraping but that was what they were designed to do. The rest of the bike was pretty much untouched, just some scrapes down the edge of the left main fairing. My old girl was looking the part now, a real world adventure Beast!

For the rest of the day, Yan and I tottered away behind James and Craig. Those guys knew these roads like the back of their hands, impressively carving their way along the mountain roads, effortlessly gliding along on their machines. I however felt like I was riding on ice, like Bambi on fresh new legs, I just wasn't enjoying it. Yan went down once more on a tight bend where he grounded out his base plate, that was enough for me, time to head home.

I'd started to make headway with the shipping of the bike now. James Cargo in the UK had put me in touch with their Japanese agents (3ways) a month previously, but I'd never had a reply to my email enquiry with them. Turns out they had replied, it had just gone to my spam folder. I normally check this before I delete it, but must have missed it this time? Anyway I got in touch with them directly and was told they could sort out the freighting of the bike, no worries. As my bike insurance was due to run out on the 8th Sep, time was of the essence so I got this jacked up double time with the shipping agents. I decided I'd go up to the North of the mainland to a place called Mount Osorezan, as recommended by Yan. This was quite a trip, about 950km there and the same to get back, but I'd wanted to see the Pacific Coastline area in the Fukushima prefecture, the area most effected by the earthquake and Tsunami in 2011. Sam and Adam decided they wanted to come along too, so we set off on a lads road trip North.

With a departure time of 08:30hrs set, it was almost 11:00hrs by the time we finally left Pete's place, thanks to Sam's time keeping. I think he had to do his hair and nails? This put us back somewhat, so by late afternoon we still had a hell of a way to go. We decided on heading to the city of Sendai for the night, we could grab some beers and grub, have a good night out, then I'd continue up North whilst the lads headed home. I don't think they were quite used to the miles like the Beast and I were, so it suited us all. Sendai is right on the edge of the nuclear exclusion zone, so hotel prices were nice and cheap – result.

Arriving at a reasonable hour, we checked in and did the three S's. Next it was out on the town, in search of beer, food and……. well we needed something to look at! We managed two out of the three at least, and went home drunk and fed.

The next morning we parted ways at the entrance to the expressway, the lads heading South to Tokyo, me heading North up to Amori and Mount Osore. After a long day on the road I eventually wound my way along some twisty, damp back roads and pulled up at Mount Osorezan. This place is known as 'the gateway to hell' and is believed to be the gateway to the afterlife for the departed. It's surrounded by an active voclano, set in a mountainous cauldron with a lake and river as company. Water boils and steam rises, the air reeks of sulphur, it has an incredibly emotive feeling to the place. It is said to be guarded by Jizo, the bodhisattva of Hell and guardian of children. The place is littered with little children's toy windmills, toys and clothing, as the parents of deceased children place offerings to Jizo, to ease their kids passing into the afterlife. A red bridge crosses the river, said to ease the crossing of those chosen to use it. The others must pass through the snake infested waters. A place that sparks legend, you MUST see this place if you ever come to Japan.

Over the next few days I rode back down the North of Japan, visiting Lake Towada, then riding along the Pacific coastline through the areas devastated by the Tsunami. If I'm honest, the place seems to be coping incredibly well with the scale of the disaster a few years ago. There's works going on everywhere to increase the defences against a future event, you can even still see the evidence of what once occurred as steel railings along the

Bruce SMART

board walks lie twisted by an unfathomable power of nature.

The rain began to fall as I reached the coastline so I continued on my journey South, hoping to outrun the storm, stop and get some pictures without damaging the camera. Unfortunately, it only increased in intensity and in no time it was dark. I found somewhere to stay the night and planned on carrying on along the coast in the morning, where I'd get those pics. Once more, best laid plans and all that.

That night I picked up some wifi at a 7eleven store and got the message from the Japanese shipping agent that would change my plans. They had a flight in mind for the bike next week, and wanted me to stop by their office in Tokyo the next day to finalise things. As I also had to go to the Motegi Circuit, this would mean I'd need to forgo the rest of the trip down the coast, and instead use the expensive expressways to eat up the miles, ensuring I made both locations. I was gutted not to get the footage I wanted, but I needed to get this shipping sorted, so that was that.

The run to Motegi was wet, very, very wet. Sitting on the expressway the vibration through the handle bars was unmistakable. This wasn't in my head, I could hardly read the satnav screen it was shaking so much! Eventually I pulled up to the gates of motegi and did my best to blag my way in to get a pic in front of the circuit. I was told it was a private members only day and access was impossible. I was getting a wee bit fed up of riding to all these circuits, only to get a simple pic at the gate. But this was my doing, nobody had asked me to do it, I just thought I would since I was 'passing'. So with a quick pic and piece to camera done, I was back on the bike and Tokyo bound. Later that night I found out that none other than Casey Stoner had been at the track that day to do some testing. Even he hadn't gone out in the rain we had, so I can now say I ride when Stoner doesn't. That'll do me.

After a few hours I got to the '3ways' office in Tokyo and met Tokio Kamimura who was to arrange the air freighting of the Beast to Thailand. The meeting lasted about 30 minutes, during which time he ran through the two options. Ship by sea or air, sea costing

£1,400 and taking 15 days, air costing £1,500 and taking 2. The choice was easy.

I should've known nothing is ever that easy, but in his limited English, Tokio explained the process and we parted ways. Job done, or so I thought. Arriving back at Pete's place I noticed the mileage was now 56,293 miles. I started the trip with 23,003 miles on the clock making the total trip mileage so far 33,290 miles in 22 countries. Not bad, only about another 40,000 to go or so.

I'd been assured that the bike would fly on the Tuesday, if not the Wednesday, so Tokio asked me to leave my flight until Thursday to ensure I was in the country should there be any problems. No worries, I booked my flight to Thailand for Thursday 12th Sep and started packing. Back at Pete's I'd told him about the problems I was having with the bike and despite the fact the guy has a number of schools to run, a new business to blossom, and a family to care for, he still made time to take her out for a spin and get her back up on his operating table.

Bridgestone had given me a new set of their BATTLAX T30 tyres, to replace the old BT-023s I'd had to use from Moscow (remember the T30's sent over from the UK had gotten 'lost' in the Russian post!) So we'd have to remove the wheels anyway to put the new rubber on. We stripped the front callipers off and spun the wheel, bang, there it was straight away. The actual wheel was buckled, unmistakable, but we'd somehow missed it in the initial checks after the accident. Bollocks, but auch well, at least I now knew it wasn't in my head and could get it fixed somewhere down the road.

The process of actually removing the old tyres was not quite as simple as we'd hoped. Pete didn't have any of the kit yet that your normal garage has for changing tyres, so it would all have to be done by hand. Having changed a Bridgestone by hand before, I knew the effort this would take. We broke the bead no probs, but next comes taking the actual tyre off the rims. With a machine this is simple, but by hand you have to use levers, lots of levers, and elbow grease. The tyre walls on the Bridgestone tyre are the toughest around. This is what allowed me to ride the Beast over thousands of miles across Russia without a single puncture, over ragged rocks that shredded other tyres ahead of me.

After half an hour Pete decided it was time to stop mucking around and we'd cut them off. Starting with a Stanley knife, it soon blunted the blade. Next we went to an angle grinder and it quickly blunted that as well. We ended up using a set of industrial bolt cutters to slowly snip our way through the rubber and integral metal reinforcement. The strength of these things is incredible, no wonder they've got such a good reputation for puncture resistance! But thankfully we eventually got the old rubber off and the spanking new T30's mounted, balanced and ready to go once more.

Next we prepared her for shipping. The local Suzuki dealership had given me one of their metal crates the bikes are delivered in from Suzuki, it was for a Hayabusa so would give me a little extra room for some kit too. On my last day at Pete's we set to work building the crate around the Beast, draining out the fluids and disconnecting the battery as requested by the shippers. Finally we wrapped the entire package in cling film and packed in the kit around her. By tea time that night it was job done.

That night was to be my last night at Pete's place so we went out for a family dinner down in Kofu. Pete, Akiko and their kids had become like a family to me in the 3 weeks I'd been allowed into their lives. They'd looked after me, fed me, entertained me and loved me like one of their own. I was sad to leave these guys, Pete especially had become a really good mate and I'll miss them loads. Sam and Adam too had become good mates as we'd spent a fair bit of time together fixing our bikes and hitting the town. It was weird as for the first time I had somewhere that felt like home again since leaving over four months previously. I'll miss that place and one day I'd love to go back with the Mrs and show her the sights and introduce her to my Japanese family.

We all rose early the next morning, the truck to pick up the bike was arriving at 11am. With breakfast done, the truck arrived and with a bit of pushing and shoving, we soon had her in the back, strapped down and ready to go. With that, the truck disappeared down the hill from Pete's and out of sight. I was alone on my journey once more.

After saying goodbye to Akiko and the kids, Pete and Sam took me down to the station in Kofu, where I'd catch a train to Tokyo. I was genuinely sad to be leaving these folks and this place, I'll never be able to thank them enough for all they, and everyone else I'd met over the last few weeks, had done to help. I'm a lucky man to call them my friends, and our paths will cross again one day I'm sure. Stay safe brothers.

I was heading to Tokyo to meet an old mate from Uni, Andy Chalmers, and his wife Joanna. They'd recently moved out to Tokyo for the year with Joanna's work, and had very kindly invited me to stay with them for a few days. Arriving at the main station in Tokyo, we ran into the first problem, it's bloody massive and like a rabbit warren. Over 3,000 trains move through here each and every day. There are at least three floors of platforms, maybe more actually, and on each floor there are a multitude of exits and entrances, none of which lead to the other. Thankfully we had each others mobile numbers so eventually met up and headed back to Andy's place for the evening.

You hear about property in Tokyo being tiny, everyone living on top of each other and in their pockets, but this place was fantastic, a brand new development right in the heart of the business district. This was to be their home for the year courtesy of Joanna's work, what a tremendous opportunity to have, and they were determined to make the most of it. The views from the roof of the building were outstanding, giving full panoramic access to the cities skyline. Wow, wow, wow!

Over the next couple of days Andy and I toured around the city doing the tourist thing, visiting various temples, riding the metro, sampling local cuisines and sipping a few ales. Life was good. I loved the city of Tokyo, it's such a mix of old and new. Huge beautiful temples nestle themselves serenely amongst a bustling metropolis, crowded, manic market streets give way to open, green parks without even a blink.

It struck me how different South Korea was to Japan after my short spell in both. Prior to visiting, I had the opinion that Japan was the epicentre of technology, state of the art lifestyle with an eye to the cutting edge. But Japan to me now is the ageing relative who struggles to grasp the 'newfangled' latest gadgets its young niece or nephew embraces with emphatic ease. Technology is everywhere in South Korea, everyone is festooned with it, industry and commerce stretches forward to the future in a continual effort towards the next 'big thing'. In Japan, it felt like people were more inclined to hold onto their cultural past, reluctant to change from how it's always been done. But that said, I loved the traditional values of Japan, her history, style and culture.

So that was Tokyo in around two days. There are countless other things to see and do, but with the limited time I had, this was the best I could do. I wish Andy and Joanna all the best for their incredible life ahead of them in Japan, and beyond. They're both beautiful folks with hearts of gold. I hope we meet again, and I meant what I said, you're more than welcome at the Smart household when/if you come back to the UK. But bring a sleeping bag, it looks like it's going to get busy!

On Thursday the 12th September 2013 I left Japan, bound for Bangkok and the next stage of my journey. A wee piece of me will stay there in that land, it's a special place and I urge you to go and experience it for yourself if you get the opportunity.

CHAPTER 19
THAILAND, MALAYSIA & LAOS

In all honesty I'd no idea what to expect from these countries, no idea of the infrastructure, the people, the customs, and no idea what awaited me as I stepped off the plane from Japan into Bangkok. Some 8 weeks later, I'd fallen for South East Asia and it's people. The 'Land of Smiles' couldn't be more apt a description.

If you've never been to Bangkok, as I hadn't, the place hits your senses like an enraged bull on crack! The airport is great, no issues at all there, and the travel into the city is first rate via the 'Skylink' train. 35 baht (75p) for the Thai version of our Heathrow Express, not bad eh.

But the second you step off the train into the city, your senses are hit from every angle. First is sight, there's just stuff happening everywhere. People sitting around, people walking in every direction, cars, mopeds, tuk-tuk's, all competing for 3 lanes of traffic space whilst making their own 5 lane highway! Your ears are festooned with a cacophony of noise, stunning you momentarily in place. Horns, whistles, engines, voices, an urban symphony awaits. It's amazing how quickly you just adapt to it all, soon you hardly even notice and settle into the way of things. Crossing roads no longer seems to be a game of noughts and crosses with the traffic, you just look for other people who look like they're going to try, then use them as shields and go for it. Simples.

I arrived ahead of the bike on the Thursday evening so had until Monday morning before the Beast would be available for collection. It suited me though as I had a ton of work to do with the latest vid, blog and Fast Bikes article. So I booked myself into a cheap

Bruce SMART

wee guesthouse and set to work.

By Saturday night I was going slightly mad and thankfully an old mate from school, Gerrie Rhind, had contacted me on Facebook to say his brother Gordon now lived in Bangkok. After a quick exchange online, I was soon sitting in an Irish bar catching up on old times with Gordon. I'd vague memories of him from school as he was around my brother's year, but it was like we were old friends straight away. Sinking a few beers we moved on to the infamous 'Cowboy Soi' where they filmed Hangover Part 2. This place is the stereotypical Bangkok. Bright lights, girl lined bars and a feeling that absolutely anything is possible here if you've got the buck to go with it.

Any of my mates will tell you I have a thing about being touched. Unless I'm in the right frame of mind, just don't do it. I mean really don't do it. Shake my hand, slap on the back, fine. Just don't paw me. This place is not the place to come if you're like me. I swear I'd get nicked back home if I approached women at bars and did what these lassies try here! (Ok, now that the Mrs is satisfied I was a good boy, COME HERE IT's GRRRRR- REAT!!!!)

It's a place you have to experience if you come to Bangkok, you don't need to stay long, but it's part of the city and just harmless fun. Waking up a tad delicate in the morning, it was back to work for the next few days to clear the decks ready for the month's adventures ahead. Monday morning arrived and I set off for the airport to meet the shipping agent from Bangkok who was going to help me clear the Beast through customs.

You may remember this was proving a Royal pain in the rectum in Japan as the agent there turned the whole thing into a cluster. But it couldn't be more different in Bangkok. A quick 5 minute phone conversation clarified what needed done, and the agent agreed to take the morning off work so we could meet and take me through the whole process. That way she could still act officially as an agent, but I paid her directly and not the company, so it was a whole lot cheaper. 500 baht (£10) to be exact and 200 baht (£4) to the warehouse guys for moving the crate. The agent in Japan was trying to charge almost £500!

The whole process of clearing the bike took about 4 hours in total, but that included about an hour and a half for lunch as everyone disappeared. Soon enough I was unwrapping the crate on the warehouse dock like a kid at Crimbo, the place seemingly coming to a standstill as everyone waited to see what the 'Felang' (foreigner) was doing. As she came into view from under the plastic wrapping, people clapped their hands together and eyes widened. I know how they feel, it still does it to me each time I lay eyes on the Beast, she's a stonker!

You have to disconnect the battery and drain the oil and fuel when you ship your bike by air. Thankfully they tend not to be too strict about the fuel funnily enough, as long as it's no more than about a quarter full. After refilling the oil and connecting all the wiring back up to the battery, I found a place to stay for the night and hit the road first thing the next morning.

The Beast still had a buckled front wheel from crossing Russia, and notably the argument with the bend in Japan hadn't helped matters either. So I stopped at 'Red Barons' outside Bangkok to see if they could help. Unfortunately they didn't have a spare wheel in stock so I carried on heading North, destination Chiang Mai.

Another chap from Facebook, John Irvine, had been following the Teapot page and offered me a place to stay if I was heading up that way. I gladly took him up on the offer and after a full day in the saddle, I arrived at his beautiful home to meet him, his partner Pumi, and their gorgeous Rotty 'Aisla'. Now I'm a dog man, I love them and thankfully they seem to like me – except my best mate Russ's old police dog. She just loved toying with me that one, I never knew where I stood with her. One day I patted her on the head and she ripped the shirt clean off me in one swoop! I've met some women like that. Ah the memories ;-)) Sorry dear.

I spent a couple of days up in Chiang Mai with John and Pumi, mostly just getting my phone working in Thailand and finishing off bits of work. I'd be back up this way again in a month or so, so said farewell and hit the road heading out into the North West.

I'd always wanted to do the legendary Mae Hong Song Loop, almost 2,000 curves along some incredible roads with the sights to match. Unfortunately, there'd been a few landslides on some of the more minor roads I'd need to use. That and the buckled front wheel and resulting shocking handling of the Beast, meant I decided against the full route, electing to cut up to the North West to Doi Ang Khang, then make my way to the Myanmar border at Mai Sai. The full Mae Hong Song Loop is without doubt one of the greatest motorcycle routes in the world and I urge you to try it if you're ever in this part of he world.

There's incredible scenery on offer up there in Northern Thailand, it's a fantastic part of the world. The folk are as friendly as I've encountered, the surroundings majestic, and it's cheap as chips. Winner in my book!

19.1 - Day 135: Myanmar Border

Arriving in the wee border town of Mai Sai, I found somewhere to stay for the night just outside of town. Awaking early the next morning, I was full of anticipation about what lay ahead.

Myanmar, or Burma as it used to be known, is slowly beginning to open up to tourists and the West. It's easy enough to fly in and backpack around, even crossing the land borders as a backpacker is now possible. But it still lies as somewhat of a HolyGrail to the overland traveller who wish to drive or ride their own transport in and around this beautiful country. There are now a few select groups of people who have managed to ride into the country, tour and then ride out. However this has required months of organisation through a select tour operator, plenty of buck, and negotiations with various embassies in order for it to take place. It's a blossoming business though, and no doubt in the next few years it'll open up for everyone.

But for now, I'd heard on the grape vine that there was an option at the border at Mai Sai. Here they'd let you ride in to Myanmar, but only as far as a 5km radius, whereupon you'd have to turn around and come back out via the same point. This'll do me though, I just needed the stamp in the passport to say I got the bike in there, I could always come back and do the whole tourist thing another time.

So I rocked up to the border, much to the delight of the locals who flocked around me as I got off the Beast. A policeman met me before I even got to the kiosk and shook his head. "No bike now, no, too much fighting, no good." Ah bollocks.

Turns out the fighting over in Myanmar had just escalated North of the border post, so they'd stopped letting foreign bikes in until it all calmed down. It was still ok to walk over, or jump in a taxi and pop over, but I didn't fancy leaving the Beast there with all the attention she was drawing. Plus I'd need to change out my leathers and unpack my clothes from the bike.

I'd planned to be back up this way in a month or so anyway so thought I'd give it a go then. Turning around, I waved goodbye to everyone standing around and set off South through Thailand, destination Krabi to meet the Mrs. It's a fair old ride from the top of Thailand down to Krabi, about 1,000 miles or so on a variety of roads, so I gave myself 5 days to do it comfortably. I also wanted to get the next vid episode, blog and FastBikes article done before I met Nikki, then we could just enjoy our time together.

Setting off I quickly came across a sign for a restaurant chain I'd been told about by John Irvine in Chiang Mai. Got to say, I'm not convinced about the name - 'Cabbages & Condoms'. Further down the road I came across a stunning looking temple. I've no idea what it's called, it just seemed to be there with a small collection of stalls to one side. There were no groups of tourists clambering around so I was free to just wonder at its' beauty. The place was stunning.

For the next few days I just rode South, stopping only to fuel up and spend each night tucked away in a cheap hostel or guesthouse I found on the way. It was right at the end of the rainy season in Thailand and I was lucky to only experience a wee bit of rain in my

Bruce SMART

journey down the country. But when it did rain, it was impressive.

Unfortunately I also saw the negative side of our sport as a young lad on a moped pulled out on a truck ahead of me. There was no competition, the truck made short work of the lad, he didn't have a chance. I stopped to try and help, but unfortunately the important bit of him wasn't where it should be, and he was gone. Sleep well brother.

I arrived a few days ahead of Nikki in Krabi, so found a great wee guesthouse down near the beach. We were staying in the town of Ao Nang near Krabi, so whilst it was still touristy and busy, it was nowhere near as commercialised, and had a stunning beach to boot. After 3 days there I'd got all my work done, so packed up and moved across to the nice hotel where Nikki had kindly booked us a room for a week or so.

She'd already arrived when I got to the hotel, meeting me in our room with the words, "Right get that off!" Lovely job I thought, but before I could get too excited, she made it clear she meant the suit as it stunk. Some things don't change, even if I had been away for 5 months!

We had a great week together, doing a few of the usual tourist tours like kayaking to Phi Phi Islands, a long-tail boat ride to James Bond Island, and Monkey Temple amongst others. I loved just spending time with her, not having to worry about the trip for a change, if even only for a short while, was bliss.

Since the day we met, Nikki and I have always had TeapotOne as part of our relationship. She was aware I'd be going away for nearly 2 years from our first date, yet she's stood by me through thick and thin. We even split up a couple of times in the last months before I left back in October 2012. The pressure on us both was immense, but we got through it and are stronger for it. I love this woman with all I have, and she reminds me frequently that I don't actually have anything as I sold it all to do this trip! I love her anyway.

Unfortunately towards the end of our time together, my main sponsor Delta, dropped a bit of a bombshell. Delta have been incredible for TeapotOne, without their faith and support of the project, it would have died when I got back after Africa. They offered me a lifeline and gave me a 2nd bite at it, and for that I'll always be thankful to Bob and Martin for their help and coming on board.

Delta were using the trip as a promotional PR vehicle for their new office in Houston, U.S.A. This is where they'd get the most benefit from the project, and also where the PR for the trip in general would be maximised. The UK just hadn't got hold of it, I tried – as many others had, but the media (apart from Fast Bikes and a few others) just didn't seem bothered for whatever reason.

The problem arose that I was now almost halfway through the trip, but had had over ¾'s of the agreed sponsorship funds from Delta. At this rate I would reach Australia and the money would run out. When we agreed the deal, I told Delta that I could get to Oz on the money they were putting forward, and we both assumed it would be a lot easier than it ended up being, to secure the remaining funds. We tried every avenue we could think of, exhausted all our contacts, but was still a long way short of funding the trip.

So I was hit with the email from them that, should I not be able to guarantee I'd reach the States, they'd no longer be able to finance any further part of the trip. It sounds harsh but this is a business unfortunately, and I'd signed a contract to that effect. My last few days with Nikki saw me mulling this over in my head, I could feel me drifting away once again, but as ever she was my rock.

We spent our last evening together down on the beach, watching a breath-taking sunset over the Andaman Sea. I really didn't want to leave her again, my heart and soul a tug of war once more. Holding each other that night, Nikki reminded me of why I was doing all this, of what it meant to us, to our families, friends, and now to so many of you who had been following. The trip had grown from simply being about a promise I made, to me living the dreams of so many, and I'll never forget how lucky I was to be able to do this.

Bruce SMART

Saying goodbye the next morning, I was full of the drive to get going again, envigoured and motivated as ever to succeed. This was the last time I'd see Nikki until I reached New York in 2014, or sooner if I failed to get the required finances onboard. I wanted to get on with our life together, but I had to see this through, if only for my own sanity.

The ride to the border was uneventful and I pulled up at the kiosk on the Thai side, Sadao, around 2pm. Easy as you like, you just present your passport and paperwork at the police and customs kiosk's, they stamp and you move on. Job done.

Getting to the Malaysian side it's almost too relaxed. As a 'felang' (foreigner) and being on a bike, after the first stamp in your passport, you're just waved through. I had to get off the bike and actually wander around the complex to find someone to ask about stamping my carnet. I'd paid a hell of a lot of money for it and strictly speaking I needed it to get the bike into and out of the country. Without the stamp it was illegal and when it came time to leave Malaysia, they could impound her, and that wasn't happening.

Thankfully I found a chap who took me to an office where the lady did the paperwork and stamped me in. No money exchanged hands, no questions, just smiles. I think I was going to like Malaysia!

Arriving in Kuala Lumpur the next day I found a cheap motel fairly near to where I was meeting the guys from 'Malaysian Motorcycle Getaways', who'd kindly invited me on one of their tours. Luckily it was also across the road from a shopping mall so I quickly got myself kitted out with a Malaysian SIM card and got some grub.

In the morning I set off early to be there on time, but the traffic in KL is legendary. Arriving at where the SatNav said it was bang on time, I couldn't see any trace of the office? Asking around the local businesses and shops drew an equally blank response, so I gave Feizal a bell. Turns out they're just down a side street from where I was, so in no time I'd joined the rest of the group for the tour briefing and we were off.

I'd been invited to tag along with one of their 'Northern Tours'. The contact with Feizal had come through Martin of Delta, who's been out there with them many times now and never ceases to fall in love with the place. Having now been on the tour, I can see why. Malaysia is a playground for bikes, particularly the Cameron and Genting Highlands. It's simply stunning and offers every type of biker a plethora of routes to sample.

Every day is full of activity, from simply riding the glorious roads and breathing in the breathtaking scenery, to visiting temples, landmarks, and local 'must-dos'! One such place is in Penang, and is called, 'Bali Hai'. It's a seafood restaurant right on the sea front and has the tagline, 'If it swims, we have it'. They're not kidding, one look at the living 'tanked' buffet along one edge of the floor reveals that. They've got everything you can think of, including Moray Eels and a huge Grouper! I couldn't help but feel sorry for these beautiful buggers, what a way to go. But I can't complain, I eat fish and it's a bit of a double standard for me to cast up just because I was face to face with my dinner!

I didn't eat the fish that night, just stuck to the rice and other bits of seafood. It was funny to watch the chap trying to get a lobster out of one of the tanks. They don't half put up a fight, I found myself routing for them as he tried about 5 before just giving up!

That night after dinner we retired to the hotel where the band were getting in to full swing. I popped to the bathroom and when I returned, none other than Mike, the big Aussie in our group, was now on stage belting out, "Mustang Sally". Good lad! He ended up doing about a half hour set, by which point all but 3 of us where left in the bar. Cracking night, cheers Mike.

The tour was 5 days/4 nights long, and took us almost to the Thai border in the north, over to Penang island in the West, before returning to Kuala Lumpur by late afternoon. Feizal, Kazhed and the lads are excellent guides and hosts, every aspect of the trip is taken care of. You can literally turn up with a rucksack (enough clothes for the 5 days), change into the kit they provide – including lid, then jump on a bike and off you go. Of course if you want to bring your own kit, feel free. The roads they take you along are outstanding for bikes, a mixture of incredibly fast sweeping curves and tight country bends that progress you through all Malaysia has to offer. I heartily recommend them folks, you just can't go wrong. (www.ridemalaysia.com.my for more details.)

19.2 - Day 156: motoGP at Sepang, Malaysia

As I travelled the world, I made it my mission to visit each of the motoGP circuits along my travels. I didn't expect to get into any of them, just turned up and got a pic with vid footage from outside the gates. The previous year I spent my 36th birthday outside the San Marino circuit, now called the 'Misano World Circuit Marco Simoncelli', but this year I'd be in Sepang, Malaysia, for an actual motoGP! The very circuit where such a great talent was sadly taken from us a few years ago. Ciao Marco.

Facebook followers had come up trumps again, in the form of Derek and Cynthia Reed. They'd gotten in touch to offer their spare room whilst I was in Malaysia, what's more Derek had a spare ticket for the GP. My cup runneth over.

I made my way straight to their place after saying goodbye to Zahed and the group at 'Malaysian Motorcycle Getaways'. It should only have taken about 20 minutes tops to get to Derek's place, but I'd spent the last week just following a guide and I have to confess, I'd fallen into the habit of it. I seemed to have lost the ability to follow the SatNav directions, instead just following the flow in front. Put that together with the KL road network, – miss a turn off and you end up miles out your way, and it was about an hour before I finally pulled onto their driveway. Nonetheless the welcome was just as warm and I was met by my very own brolly girl, Derek standing out in the rain!

Over the next 4 days Derek and Cynthia looked after me in their home like the incredibly generous people they are. In the evenings we sampled all manner of local cuisines around their area of the city. During the days I'd go to the circuit at Sepang, watch the practice sessions alone on Friday, then with Derek for qualifying and race day over the weekend.

Arriving at the circuit on the Friday morning, I caused quite a stir, with several people actually thinking I was racing? Personally I can see where the similarity between myself and the 5'4", 45kg Dani Pedrosa lies. Easy mistake.

Even here, I had people coming up to me saying they'd heard about the trip and some were even following on Facebook and YouTube. It was awesome to get such support this far from home, I felt incredible! If any of you are reading this that were there and came to say hello, thank you very much, you made my day.

I popped into the KTM stall to see if they had the new 1290 on display. Unfortunately it wasn't released yet but one of the sales guys came over to shake my hand. Dennis was another chap who'd been following the trip since the early days, all the way over here in Malaysia. Amazing thing the t'interweb eh!. Thanks for saying 'Hi' mate, it was a real pleasure to meet you.

I had a great weekend at the races, I love the atmosphere at the circuits when there's a race on. The sights, the sounds, smells…. Did I mention the sights? WALLOP, WALLOP, WALLOP and WALLOP. Thank you from the bottom of my heart, to whoever invented spandex. Awesome.

The racing itself was immense, from moto 3 to MotoGP it was action packed stuff. Despite not really setting the racing world on fire of late, Valentino Rossi still commands a huge following, with seas of yellow on display around the ground. But young Marquez is not far behind these days, as the red and white '93' flags begin to flood the landscape. What a talent that lad is.

Monday was D-day as I had a conference call with DELTA to try and sort something out regarding funding of the rest of the trip. As luck would have it, Cynthia is a marketing 'guru' so set to work on a plan for World Domination. Cynthia I can't thank you enough for your help and support here. You're one in a million XX.

The meeting went well and I've got to give Bob and Martin a huge thank you once again, for showing such commitment to the trip. It would have been very easy to just pull out there and then, but they stuck by me, giving the last sponsorship payment of the year. This meant I had to raise enough funds to get to Central America at the very least, then once they were assured I'd get to the States, I could access the last segment of sponsorship funds. This left me with an £18K shortfall to complete the trip, of which I needed about £8K to get to Central America. I had financial commitments at home which must be met each month, so unfortunately time was not on my side. I couldn't just stay in one place and get a job to earn some money for the next section, as any money I'd make from casual work, wouldn't even cover my overheads at home.

With that all in mind, I set myself a deadline of the 22nd December to raise the needed £8K. With that I could fly to Chile then ride North, aiming to arrive in Texas by early March 2014. If I didn't raise this, then the trip would be over and I'd need to figure out a way to get home.

I set up a 'SponsuMe' page to help raise the funds, where folks could buy any number of rewards, from wristbands, badges and lanyards, to signed copies of the book & DVD I'd produce on my return. I never wanted your public money to go to funding the trip folks, that was always meant to go to the charities. But unfortunately I had no other choice now. Without your help the dream would end, and with it would go the opportunity to raise another £60K for my chosen charities.

The response was absolutely staggering, within 3 weeks it had raised over £8K and I could now almost get to the USA! Incredible, absolutely incredible, I can never thank each of you enough.

19.3 - Day 160: Back to Thailand

I was sad to leave Derek and Cynthia, they'd both been so incredibly kind and welcoming, already feeling like old friends even after a few days. But the show must go on and it was time to head back North into Thailand, then Laos and Cambodia, before coming back down through Thailand and Malaysia, to cross over to Indonesia in a month or so. Best get a move on then.

We said our goodbyes for now, their beautiful dogs seeing me off at the gate, and soon I was on the road once more. The roads in Malaysia and Thailand are great so progress was nice and swift. In a matter of hours I was up at the border and sailed straight through? I got my passport stamped out of Malaysia, but there was nowhere obvious to get the carnet stamped? I took a gamble here as I knew I'd be back in Malaysia soon anyway and if I didn't get it stamped out, then I wouldn't need to bother getting it stamped back in again when I re-entered in a few weeks. Fingers crossed eh.

The Thai side was equally as relaxed. They didn't even stamp my passport IN to the country, let alone bother about the bike? I knew this couldn't be right so got off the bike and went and found an office with some 'official' looking folks in it. I explained that I was coming in to the country and would be heading to Laos and Cambodia, before coming back in to Thailand and coming back out this way. Maybe I confused them, maybe they didn't understand, maybe it's a plan to get more money out you later on, or maybe they just didn't feel like doing any work. Either way, they just smiled, shook their heads, and waived me on saying, "You felang, it's ok, it's ok". Getting back on the Beast and riding up the road, I knew this would bite me in the arse, and it very nearly did later on.

My plan was to ride north to Chiang Mai and meet John and Pumi Irvine once more. I'd stay a few nights with them whilst the Beast got a much needed service. I'd had to cancel any thoughts of trying Myanmar again as the budget simply couldn't allow it, which I was gutted about but it couldn't be helped. From there I'd ride into Laos, down to Cambodia, across Thailand, into Malaysia to Penang, then across to Indonesia. Then I'd ride South to Bali and either Island hop to East Timor and put the Beast on a boat to Darwin, or air freight straight from Bali to Perth. That was my loose plan anyway.

On my way north I stopped off at Kanchanaburi, the home of the infamous 'Bridge Over The River Kwai'. Contrary to the film it's not actually made of bamboo, but iron and steel. It's still in use today as a rail road, so be careful as you walk across as the passing trains roll right by. I got there as the light was fading and caused a fair stir as I pulled up on the Beast right in the middle of a market. Loads of people came up for pictures next to the bike, even a young monk! I tried to get him to sit on the bike for a wee pic and vid, but he was too shy.

As darkness fell I walked across the bridge, whistling 'Colonel Bogie' as I did, it had to be done. The river below was lined with beautiful huts, whose lights danced on the surface in the moonlight. It was an incredibly peaceful place to be, the sound of a buskers guitar echoing in the night. Ironic eh, I couldn't help but think of all the souls that were lost here, and in the construction of this very railway.

Asking around, I found a cracking wee place to stay right on the river called, 'Sam's River Rafthouse'. You get a room in one of the floating pontoons down on the river, they're basic but comfortable enough and it's less than a fiver. Perfect. In the morning I woke early to get on the road, but stopped to admire the view from right outside my room. I hadn't noticed in the dark how beautiful the place was. I'll come back here with the Mrs hopefully one day.

As it'd been dark when I got to the bridge, I stopped by once more to get a few pics in the daylight. The place is equally as impressive and emotive.

After posting a pic the previous night on the facebook page, a friend got in touch to say a distant relative had worked on the line as a POW and was buried in the war cemetery in town. I stopped by there that morning and found Gunner A.E. Staples, who now rests in Kanchanaburi War Cemetery, Thailand, after growing up and living in Deptford South East London. One of countless other heroes who lie in peace on foreign soil. I for one believe we should NEVER forget their sacrifice. Lest We forget.

Whilst taking these pics I was approached by a chap who said, "You're not riding around the world are you? Something to do with Fast Bikes and Bridgestone?" Now, anyone who is in the job know's all about 'Wah-ing' or 'Chomping'. It's basically the black art of getting people to point out the obvious. A prime example is to ask a colleague the time when they're standing directly under Big Ben. You get the idea? Yes it's childish and immature, but it's fun.

So, baring in mind I was standing there in a white leather suit, festooned with 'Bridgestone', 'FastBikes' and 'TeapotOne, Around The World 2012' logos, I was a tad unsure how to respond. Nodding my head I was fully expecting the obligatory, "Waaahhh-hhhhhhhh!!" that normally follows the successful conclusion of said game, but instead the chap stuck out his hand to introduce himself.

Mick Newbatt is the Country Director for Thailand of the Commonwealth War Graves Commission. Apparently The Royal British Legion had issued an 'all stations alert' that there was a mad man rampaging around the world on a Superbike, and that I was now somewhere in Thailand. Isn't it great how things just fall into place at times! I love this travel lark, it's a beautiful thing.

Mick kindly invited me to his office where we had a wee chat, before his colleagues took some pics for us. In typical fashion, apparently there was a coach load of models turning up to visit the cemetery later in the day, but I had to make some progress and get up to Chiang Mai in the North of the country. We said our goodbyes and I was soon back on the road. Mick if you're reading this, it was a pleasure and honour to meet you mate. Take care my friend.

After another full days ride I pulled up to another great welcome at the home of John & Pumi Irvine back in Chiang Mai, with the welcome just as warm from their cracking rotty, Aisla. I don't know who was more pleased to see who! My original plan had been to stay with John & Pumi, and hopefully have John join me for a ride around the Golden Traingle. I was also going to try and get into Myanmar again, as well as get the Beast serviced at 'The Piston Shop' in Chiang Mai. Unfortunately, following the discussions with Delta, I now had to shave as much mileage and time off the trip as possible to try and ensure I made it to Houston. So I made the decision to scrap the Myanmar attempt and the hopes of touring North West Thailand, settling to just get the bike serviced and head straight to Laos. From there I could travel down into Cambodia, back through Thailand, Malaysia, then into Indonesia, and down to Oz for Crimbo. Simples eh?

I had a couple of days in Chiang Mai with John & Pumi first, after dropping the Beast off with Nat at The Piston Shop, John took me on a tour of the local sights around the city. Like everywhere else in Thailand, temples (or Wat's as they're known locally) abound throughout the city, with over 300 examples available for your viewing pleasure!

After a wee wander around one of the Wats in the city, we stopped off at the famous 'Riders Corner' for a bite to eat and chat with the staff. If you're a biker and ever in Chiang Mai, this is a must-do stop on your trip. The place breathes bikes, so stop by and inhale it in.

After lunch we headed out of town to the incredibly beautiful Wat Prathat Doi Suthep. Set atop the Doi Suthep mountain, it was first founded way back in 1383, with the first road leading to it only being constructed as late as 1935.

It's origins are surrounded in legend and mystery, but this one caught my favour.

It's said that a monk had a dream where he was told to go to an area and look for a relic. When he went, he found a bone that is said to be one of Buddha's shoulder bones. It possessed magical powers and could vanish, glow, multiply and move all by itself. The monk took it to the ruling King of their provence, but the bone did absolutely nothing so the King told the monk to keep it. A neighbouring King heard of the mystical bone and asked the monk to bring it to him, which he did. This time the bone put on a full show, splitting in two. The King enshrined one bit and strapped the other to the back of a white elephant which he set free in the jungle. Legend has it that the elephant climbed Doi Suthep and on reaching the top, trumpeted three times before dying on the spot. The King took this as a sign and ordered a temple be built there.

The temple itself is reached by 309 steps, formed by two serpents that guide the way to the top. For the less physical, you can catch a tram all the way to the top. John and I went for the steps, narrowly escaping simultaneous heart attacks by the time we reached the top!

The views of the surrounding country are breathtaking, or so I am told. It was peeing down with rain when we were there, the whole place enveloped in a shroud of low-lying cloud. However, the temple itself is breathtaking. Even on an overcast day, the golden enshrined temple was mystical in appearance. I can only wonder at what this place is like in the brightness of a sun filled day!

That evening I'd been invited to the Chiang Mai branch of The Royal British Legion for a few beers at their new HQ in town, the 'Basic Line' hotel. It was a cracking night with great company, one of which was Keith McVeighty, a former Isle of Man TT racer and travelling marshall. Keith is now a bit of a local guru regarding the roads around Northern Thailand, so if you're ever up this way, head to the Basic Line and ask for him. Say hello from me too if you meet him, top bloke.

After a top quality service at 'The Piston Shop' by Nat and his team, the Beast was once again ready to hit the road. If you find yourself up this way and need any work done on your bike, these are the fella's to come and see. Excellent service by guys who really know what they're doing around big sports bikes. It was a pleasure to meet you Nat.

Having stayed with John and Pumi on two occasions now, they already felt like old friends. So it was with a bit of a heavy heart that I packed up the kit once again and got ready to hit the road to Laos. As usual I'd meant to get a good early start, but with the great hospitality and comfy bed, I struggled to get my fat ass ready by 9am. Nonetheless, John and Pumi were there to see me off once again, my very own TeapotOne brolly dollys!

The road to the Laos border at Chiang Khong was a beauty, seeing me merrily twist and flow along the great tarmac, arriving by about 1pm that afternoon. As I rolled down the hill to the border port I'd no idea what to expect. It was a hive of activity, queues of trucks lined the steep descent down to the river pontoon, and crowds of people were hurriedly scrambling up and down the hill. I parked up the bike and just sat for a minute or two, trying to suss out what the score was here, where did I go, and what did I have to do. I should know by now that it's simply impossible to remain undetected in this get-up, so I was soon surrounded by dozens of Chinese tourists, all clambering around me for a photo, all wanting to touch the bike and my leathers! Brave souls if you ask me. But I made lot's of new friends there, the smiles abound as always and it was a big thumbs up all round.

Waiting my turn in the queue, which only tourists seem to bother about in these parts, I was soon standing in front of the nice policeman, presenting my passport to be stamped out of Thailand. Oh yeah, about that……..

Remember the story when I came back in from Malaysia, where the Thai officials couldn't be bothered to stamp me in? Yep, this is where it bit me in the arse. After a minute or two of puzzled looking, the policeman asked where my entry stamp was. I tried to explain what had happened but he just looked at me like I'm sure I've looked at people a thousand times when they're trying to give me some pony excuse on the street. He just tutted, took a sharp intake of breath and said, "big problem Mr, no good". Bollocks.

Sitting for about an hour, a Senior officer eventually rocked up on the back of a moped and told me to step into his office. More than a little apprehensive, I did as he asked and found myself in a little room behind the main counter. Once again I regaled my story and the Chief just looked at me in that same fashion. On finishing he simply said that that couldn't have happened, no way. Several times I had to point out on a map where I crossed in to Thailand and repeat the date of entry time and time again. Sensing that this was likely to result in me being the star of a future episode of 'Brits Banged Up Abroad', I played my trump card. On the paperwork they asked my occupation, so I told them. I even showed the faithful pic of me in front of number 10, fully loaded up with weaponry. They seemed impressed, the Chief even shook my hand. He disappeared for a bit, eventually returning with some paper and a pen, asking me to write down exactly what had happened, adding a wee apology at the bottom stating I'd never meant to enter illegally. Simple as that, it was sorted. Well, that and 500 baht for 'paperwork' necessities. In the circumstances, that would do me nicely ta, job done.

As the bike had never been stamped in to Thailand, there was no need to get her stamped out, so next step was down to the ferry. By the way, I wouldn't recommend this route of entering Thailand, I was very lucky not to get nicked there and should I have been, I would have had very little room for argument. Get the required paperwork at every border, even if it means going out your way to find the relevant people. Better safe than sorry.

Anyway, riding down to the bottom of the hill it had started to rain, turning the ground into soft, slimy mud and rock. I found the kiosk to buy my ticket across the River MeKhong, another 500 baht (£10) and waited in line behind a big truck.

Soon enough the barge zipped passed us in the rapid current, then struggled to make its' way back to dock. It was a simple flat barge, towed by a tug boat, and wasn't quite what you see at Dover and Calais. But this is an adventure, so in for a penny…..

The first obstacle was just getting on the thing through the mud and rock that lined the river bank. The lads had obviously seen this a million times before as they quickly constructed a make shift ramp and roadway out of the rocks that were scattered around. I followed a big truck up the ramp and onboard, finding my spot right at the front. Within about 10 minutes we were all loaded up, water visibly seeping over the top we were that laden. I wondered if we'd make it across, but 30 minutes later we docked at the other side in Laos. It was a memorable crossing for me, I've done loads of different border crossings in the 54 countries I visited in this trip, but this one will always remain in my memory, I loved it.

Arriving in Huay Xai on the Laos side of the river, it was now 1730hrs and I just managed to get my customs paperwork done before the place shut. Not fancying a repeat performance by not getting my passport stamped into Laos, I found a wee guesthouse in the town and bedded down for the night. Venturing out that evening for some grub, I found a great wee café down the road, got some good scran, then returned to my mozzy infested abode for some kip.

Awaking early and having been eaten alive once more, I was soon at the police kiosk to get my passport stamped and visa for Laos. The cost of the visa depends on what your nationality is, so for a Brit it was $35. It was all written up in a table Sellotaped to the window, so it must be official.

Whilst there I met loads of backpackers who had just arrived themselves, they were heading off all over the country, but it was great to chat with them and hear some familiar accents. Hitting the road about 10am I had about 300 miles to cover to reach my next stop, Luang Prabang. I'd no idea what to expect of the roads here, I didn't even know if they had roads to be honest, but riding out of Huay Xai along 'Highway 3', I needn't have worried. It was awesome, in fact I'd go as far as to say it was epic, probably one of the greatest motorcycling roads I've ever had the joy to ride. Even with a buckled front wheel, it was still a joy to glide along this pristine tarmac, twisting and turning my way up into the mountains and across deep, lush, green valleys. Progress was great, I should be in Luang Prabang by about 3pm at this rate, life was great!

I'd learnt to never count my chickens on this trip, always assume that the worst may still happen. If at all possible, NEVER tie yourself down to a definite long-term schedule as it's almost impossible to keep to on a trip like this, and that's exactly what happened here as I turned off highway 3 and headed South along highway 13. About 30 miles down the road from this point, the once glorious freshly laid tarmac, slowly begins to dishevel as spots of broken up gravel strewn roadway appear. These are generally right on tight bends and at the bottom of steep hills where the heavy trucks have struggled for grip. This occurs more and more until the road is basically potholed gravel for the next 140 miles. Progress went from a brisk and smile inducing 45mph average speed through biking heaven, to a painful and laborious 5-15mph pain infested crawl. As darkness descended I was still way up in the mountains, the only civilisation the odd villages that would appear, clinging to the side of the mountains at the roadside.

One good thing about being in such a remote place is that when it gets dark, you get the most intense view of the night sky. It literally comes alive above you, stars twinkling in the deepest, darkest canvas I've ever seen. If I hadn't been so knackered, I'd have probably just pitched the tent up and slept under it. But as it was I'd already pre-booked a place in a hostel in Luang Prabang, the thought of a shower and some hot grub pulling me on through the night. It was foolish to ride on such roads in the dark, but I pushed on and eventually rolled into the city, finding the hostel by about 9pm that night. I was FUBAR'd.

I'd planned to stay in Luang Prabang for 3 days, 2 of which I'd use to get the next vid episode finished and uploaded, then a day to sightsee around the place. As luck would have it, as I switched on my MacbookPro to begin work, I was met with a continual beeping sound and a computer that point blank refused to load up? Using my phone to search google for possible causes revealed that it was likely my RAM drives that were faulty. They'd probably been shaken loose as I kept the laptop in one of my tailbags on the bike. It would be easy enough to fix, but I didn't have a screwdriver small enough to fit the tiny screws apple uses on these things. Hacked off, I put up a wee status update on the Facebook page and went out for some grub.

Yet again you folks on 'faceache' (facebook) came up trumps as a chap called Davie McCurry got in touch to say not only did he have a suitable toolset, but that he also lived in Luang Prabang and passed by my hostel every morning on his way to work! I've no idea how these things kept happening to me on this trip, but whoever was sorting it all out, thank you X.

After a quick message on facebook, I met Davie first thing the following morning, picked up the toolset and arranged to meet for a beer that evening. I quickly set to work on the macbook and in no time she was back up and running. The day was spent working away on episode 10, and in the evening I met up with Davie and his Mrs Julie-Ann for some beer and grub. Turns out they were a Scottish couple who were now in Luang Prabang teaching English in the local schools. We had a great night chatting about my trip, their trip here, and life in general. Davie and Julie-Ann, if you're readings this, it was an absolute pleasure to meet you both and I thank you wholeheartedly for spending the evening with me.

19.4 - Day 170: Plain of Jars, Laos

Destination for today was to be Phonsavan, about 160 miles South East of Luang Prabang and home to the incredible Site 1 of the Plain of Jars. I'd never heard of these before and only found out about them after googling 'What to do in Laos'. The road there along Highway 13 was superb for the most part, once more I was delighted to see fresh unblemished tarmac for the majority of the way, and sampled one of the most glorious sections of twisty road you could wish to ride.

I arrived in Phonsavan by late afternoon, checking into one of the few hotels I could find. It was expensive compared to Thailand, around $25 for a room for the night, but I needed a good wash and it was just down the road from Site 1 of the Plain of Jars, meaning I could get a nice early start the following day.

The Plain of Jars are a megalithic archaeological landscape, dating back to around 500BC. They can be found all over the Xieng Khouang plateau, and there are literally thousands of these stone jars scattered all over the countryside. They range from a few feet tall to well over six feet, sometimes standing alone or in small numbers, sometimes in huge groups of a hundred or more. Nobody is exactly sure of their purpose, but it's believed they were some form of ancient burial tomb as remains have been found in some, along with burial trophies such as crockery and weapons. Others believe they were an ancient form of storing rice or whisky.

Although found all over this provence, there are currently only 3 sites cleared for public viewing. You see Laos is the most heavily bombed country in the world, having been routinely bombed throughout the Vietnam War. As a result it has the largest number of unexploded ordnance found anywhere, making wild camping extra exciting should you brave the countryside!

Early the next morning I went straight to Site 1 and spent an hour or so wandering around the site, marvelling at these mystical structures. Soon enough it was time to hit the road once more, my destination set for Savannakhet some 370 miles away. A big ride through such twisty roads, but I was up for the challenge and it was a joy to eat up the miles on these roads.

You know how I said I'd learnt not to count my chickens too soon? Yep, fate had other ideas in store for me here as I turned off the beautiful highway 13 and began to trudge my way along the 'route 1D'. The name should have warned me, but I'd seen this type of road many times before, it starts with a bit of gravel and muck, but soon enough you're flying along lovely fresh unspoilt asphalt.

Only this time, I wasn't. The gravel gave way to mud, which gave way to rocks and earth. I kept slogging on thinking that just around the next bend would be my saviour. My average speed was now down to around 5mph, it was 1st and 2nd gear most of the way. Progress was painfully slow, and painfully painful too. Due to the slow speed, all the weight was on my wrists and knees where I had to stand on the pegs for large sections to get the bike over the various obstacles. It was sheer hell and torture. By late afternoon I was delirious with pain, I'd run out of food and was on my last litre of water. In the baking heat the Beast was cooking, running at a steady 110 degrees or more as she just couldn't get enough air through the radiator at such slow speeds. I'd had to do water crossings, mud and wooden bridge crossings, I even had to dig my own way through a recent mudslide to carry on. There was a section of loose rocks that just looked like the side of the mountain, so I followed a track the other way. 30 minutes later I was back at the rocky mountain, the other route coming to a dead end over a cliff?

Stupidly I didn't even take a walk up the rocky path to see where it went. Had I got to the top and it been a dead end, I would be stuck as there was no way of turning the bike around, and anyway I couldn't have ridden it back down such large loose rocks.

Fatigue had taken its' toll, I just wanted to get where I was going now and had slipped into auto pilot. I took a run up at the rocks and slowly but surely scrambled my way up, the rear tyre spinning furiously at times across the jagged underlying rocks. Any minute I expected to hear the 'Bang' as the rubber gave way, torn to pieces on the outcrops below. But these Bridgestone BATTLAX T30's are superb, they held their own out there in the wilderness and got me up and over this rocky summit.

I saw some incredible sights that day, remote villages deep in the Annamese Mountains that had never seen a sight like me before. The look on their faces as I trundled into, then out of, their domains is something that will stay with me forever. Never any malice from them, always the eventual smile being returned and a wave goodbye as I disappeared down the track. Awesome.

As darkness began to fall I was deep in the mountains, the climbs and descents had become savage, the 'road' no more than a cart track of rocks and mud. At one stage I was having to lock the back brake up and drag the rear wheel as I slid down the steep hills along loose rocks and boulders. I'd done well up to now, always managing to keep some semblance of control in the situation. But then it happened.

In an instant the front wheel dug into a crevice, momentum sending me and the bike to the side. Although low speed, I still fell about 10 feet down the hill from the Beast, looking on helplessly as she ground down the hill on her side. I was so tired I could have cried, to be honest I almost did. Sitting on the ground in the middle of nowhere, I looked around for some help. Nothing. I listened to hear if anything was likely to come by soon, but I hadn't seen anyone in over an hour. Only the occasional tractor machine, tractor engines steered by long reigns from a cart about 10 feet behind, had been my company throughout the day.

The bike weighed 200kg and had another 20kg of kit strapped to her. She was lying on her side the wrong way, meaning I'd have to lift against gravity to right her. What's more, it was about a 1 in 3 hill and it was all loose rock. I was shattered, hardly able to keep my eyes open let alone lift the Beast. I sat for about 20 minutes, part hoping someone would come and rescue me, part hoping I'd wake up from this nightmare. It didn't happen.

I remembered at this point some advice I'd been given from other travellers regarding filming. Always, when you're at your lowest, when you least want to be on film, when you least want to even get the camera out, THAT's when you have to get it on film. With gritted teeth I set the camera up and hit record. I'm glad I did.

A few years previously I'd been to the HUBB UK meet with Horizons Unlimited and watched a demonstration on how to pick your bike up by yourself. Believe it or not there is an art to it, and it works! You need to pick up by the handle bar on the front brake side. That way you can engage the front brake as the bike begins to rise, the front wheel then can't turn so all your effort causes the bike to rise up, not run along the ground on the front wheel. The problem I had was that the ground was just loose rocks, so even with the front brake jammed on, the wheel just slid along the ground anyway. I solved this by jamming some rocks under the tyre, and eventually, after much sweating, puffing, and swearing, the Beast was back upright. I however, was flat on my arse panting like a dog. At that point, a tractor engine came around the bend at the bottom of the hill, it's occupants all off and pushing from the rear. I got it all on film so you'll see for yourself in the DVD.

Over the next hour I dropped the bike another 4 times, and as darkness settled in for the night I was nowhere near anywhere. I'd covered maybe 100 miles that day, in about 14 hours of riding. I was shagged.

I'd finished the last of my water after picking up the bike yet again, so now had nothing. I was absolutely gasping, sweat dripping from my leathers, my mouth dry as.... a dry thing. At that point I crossed a fast flowing stream, in desperation I did what you should never do in foreign lands. I figured that it was fast flowing and didn't smell, so it should be fairly safe to drink. Holding my bottle in the flow, I soon had 2 litres of beautifully clear, cold mountain water. I downed about a litre in an instant, the taste amongst the finest

Bruce SMART

I'd ever sampled. Refilling once again, I rode a little further down the track then decided to set up camp for the night, there by the 'roadside'. I'd not seen a soul for hours, and as I finished putting up the tent I noticed some lights in the distance heading my way. I was apprehensive, as I'd been told to watch out for the mountain bandits, something you're told in just about every country I'd been to. As I went to get in the tent some voices called out in foreign. Looking up the lights were now just down the road from me and running my way.

Soon I was surrounded by 5 lads, all with head torches shining directly in my face, and all with some kind of rifle that I could see. They pointed at me, at the bike, at the tent, and I could hear one of them saying, 'passport, ID'. Well I was buggered if I was going to hand over any of that out here, so just played dumb (I know, difficult for me). After what seemed like forever, one of the lads pointed at my tent, shook his head and said, "No!" Pointing along the road in the direction I was heading, I realised I was not going to be able to sleep here tonight, so packed up in the dark, muttering affectionate Glasgow sayings under my breath. I'm glad they didn't speak Scottish!

I soon overtook the lads as I trundled along the rocky path and could see them running behind me in my peripheral vision. Memories of Africa came flooding back and I was buggered if I was going to stop for them and their guns again. As I rounded a bend and began to drop down into a small valley, I could see a whole load more lights all dancing through the darkness, coming at me like the horns of the buffalo ahead. "A shite, I'm buggered" were my exact thoughts at this point, as a rope was dragged across the path ahead, effectively blocking me from going any further. In an instant I was surrounded by around two dozen rifle clad lads, all excitedly shouting amongst themselves, like they'd just caught a big prize. Again they began shouting at me in foreign, again I could hear the word passport etc, but there was no way I was getting that out here. We had ourselves a stand off there in the darkness, in the middle of nowhere. Me and the Beast verses the world once more.

It seemed like hours that I was standing there in the dark, nervously glancing all around me, waiting for the first punch or kick to come, or the first shot to ring out. Instead came a voice in English, "My friend, you can not go on tonight, it is very dangerous on this road, many bad men. You must stay with us until morning." Looking round, I saw a young lad holding out his hand, his face warm with friendship. I could have kissed the wee shite!

So it was that I spent the evening sleeping on the ground next to the Beast, outside a wooden shed in the middle of a village atop the Annamese Mountains. They wake early in these parts, up with the sun to get out to the fields for a days work. So by about 0530hrs I found myself being licked in the face by a pot bellied pig, not the best way to wake up, but not the first time either. Ahh, fond memories of days on the door in Glasgow!

As I stood up and began to straighten out my kit, that's when it hit me. The sudden cramp in the stomach, the gurgle from deep down below, and the instant urgency to get somewhere quiet! But I was in the middle of this village, there was nowhere private, so I hurriedly got on the bike and headed off up the rocky path. Within about 5 minutes I was surrounded by forest, I didn't care if there were bears in there or bandits, I just had to go. Unfortunately, I wasn't quite quick enough. Some days you're the bear, other days you're the woods. That's enough said about that.

I dropped the bike another 2 times that morning, each time I had to quickly drop her again as the urge to relieve myself hit once again. It was miserable, I was in tatters, if I could have flicked a switch and been home in an instant, I'd have done it there and then. But you've no other option, you just have to keep slogging on, the pain and misery would have to end at some point surely!

My saviour came a few hours later as the path slowly descended from the mountains down into the lush green valley below. The rocks and mud gave way to gravel and dirt, which in turn gave way to compacted rocks and dirt as I saw signs of civilisation up ahead. As I trundled into the village I instantly recognised this was different to what I'd been used to up in the hills. For a start this place had a shop with stuff for sale lying on the planks of wood. There was the odd jeep scattered around and the road began to look like it was actually used from time to time. I rounded a bend and there up ahead was a t-junction, but not just any t-junction. This one had a proper road running across it, an actual tarmac, flat, well made, no rocks, no mud, no gravel, bonafide asphalt road! I actually parked up the Beast, got off and kissed the ground. I rarely get emotional but confess I wiped my nose.

After fueling up, I hit the throttle and still had another 170 miles to cover to reach Savannakhet before nightfall. It was a painful ride, my body in tatters from the hammering we'd taken the last few days. But eventually I rolled into town and found a guesthouse for the night. Not too bad a place, it had a bucket of cold water to use as a shower, and a wee shop over the road where I could buy a pot noodle and some crisps for scran. Luxury.

As knackered as I was, I still had to get the next episode of the series done, so switched on the MacBook to get going once more. 'BEEP, BEEP, BEEP...... BEEP, BEEP, BEEP!' Ah bollocks, looks like I hadn't fixed it after all. I was pretty much knackered without my Macbook, I needed it to do the HD video editing as a normal laptop just doesn't cope with that level of processing, they tend to fall over. As well as the vids, I had a monthly commitment to Fast Bikes to produce content for them, as well as my 'monthly' blog for the website, all the social media stuff, and an increasing amount of media interest from back home and around the world. So I was a fairly busy chap on the road, especially now the race was on to try and secure further corporate backing to fund the remainder of the trip. This couldn't have come at a worse time to be honest.

Sitting there in that crappy room, I was feeling pretty sorry for myself I must admit. I had about 9 days to get to Penang in Malaysia where I was putting the Beast on a boat to Indonesia. In that time I still had to ride the rest of Laos, in and around Cambodia, through Thailand and into Malaysia. I knew I could do the Thailand/Malaysia bit in about 3 solid days, but I'd no idea what the rest of Laos and Cambodia would present in terms of road quality. If progress was as slow as some of Laos had been, there was no way I'd make it, and now the computer was knackered so I'd need to find somewhere to get that fixed too, adding to the timeframe.

So I made the decision to cut out Cambodia and head straight to the border with Thailand, then head straight to Bangkok where I knew there was an apple repair place. So that's what I did.

This time I used the 'Friendship Bridge No.2' to cross from Laos back into Thailand. There are now 3 such bridges to cross from the countries, and they are definitely the more civilised way to go. Everything is there on site, you're directed through the various stages you need to go through, you can't go wrong. But I must confess, I did like the river crossing and the real 'adventure' style of the Huay Xai border more.

Within 2 days I was back in Bangkok and had found a great hostel right in the centre of town called the 'Boxpackers Hostel'. It was literally across the road from the famous electrical playground that is 'Pantip Plaza' where I hoped to get the Macbook sorted. It couldn't have worked out better really, I booked myself in there for 4 nights and it cost a little over $50. Not bad for central Bangkok, and the place was stunning. If you're ever in Bangkok and are looking for a budget place to stay, you won't beat this place, it's clean as a whistle, quiet, has laundry facilities, there's even an onsite restaurant and bar. The wifi is great too, fast as broadband and free. Not often you get that in any hotels now. Check them out at www.boxpackershostel.com

First things first I went straight over to Pantip Plaza to hunt down the apple guru who would fix the macbook. I found their repair centre on the 4th floor and found a lad and lassie lying behind their desks, heads on hands, staring into their Samsung phones? The bloke at least looked up and acknowledged my existence. I explained my problem and he said straight away that it would be my drives or logic board. Excellent thought I, this guy knows his stuff, but then he proceeded to go back to watching his phone, without so much as looking at my mac. I asked him if he wanted me to leave it or could he fix it here. He just replied, "No" without even looking up.

To be honest that was enough for me, I wasn't going to try any harder to give them my money so left the shop on the hunt for another technical wizard. Unfortunately it seemed that everywhere I went, they just directed me back to the same shop with the Thai 'Kevin & Perry'. Not a chance.

That night I met up with Gordon Rhind again for a few beers with his mates from the local football team. We had another great night down in Cowboy Soi, but I had to make my excuses and leave fairly early on as the belly still hadn't quite calmed down after the Laos 'water' experience. Whilst out that night I met one of Gordon's mates, Andrew Thomas, who just happens to know of a place that fixes his company Mac's. Don't you just love the way things seem to work at times.

So the next day I met Andrew and he took me to 'unlimit:mac' (http://www.unlimit-mac.com/) where they spent the afternoon sorting the mac out. Turns out it was the RAM, so it needed replacing and now worked like a charm. Back at the hostel I spent the next 2 days solid working on episode 10, before finally getting it uploaded and live.

19.5 - Day 179: Return to Malaysia

After leaving Bangkok, it took another 2 days to ride to the border with Malaysia, once again crossing without incident. I quickly made my way to the island of Penang where I was to be staying at a hostel in George Town, close to the shipping agents I'd be using to get the Beast over to Indonesia.

Arriving in good time I was soon housed in 'Kimberley House' a relatively new hostel located bang in the centre of 'Little India' district of the town. Weird really as it's actually the Chinese district, but ours is not to reason why and all that?

The hostel is conveniently located about 5 minutes walk from Prangin Mall where you'll find most things you could need. 10 minutes walk takes you to the nightlife hotspots where you'll find western friendly pubs, full of backpackers all eager for beer!

I was using 'Cakra Enterprise' to ship the bike over to Indonesia. There used to be a ferry which ran between the two countries, but this was no longer allowing vehicles, leaving somewhat of a gap in the market. Mr Lim has stepped up to the plate here and now arranges the shipping of bikes from Penang to Belawan, using a local vegetable boat. You learn not to ask to many questions once you're on the road, just go with the flow, so that's what I did.

Originally Mr Lim had told me to be at his office for 10am on Monday 4th November. That's what caused the major rush through Laos, meaning I missed out Cambodia to ensure I was there on time. On the Saturday before this, I got an email from him saying there had been a mistake and he was now taking the Monday and Tuesday off work, so could I meet him on Wednesday the 6th at 10am. It's just the way things are done here, there's no point in getting worked up, so that was that. Wednesday morning I rocked up at his office and paid the money, arranging to meet him again the following day to take the Beast over to the mainland where she'd be loaded on the boat.

Thursday morning saw me standing outside his office, met by 2 other groups of bikers also using Mr Lim for their shipping needs. Almudena Teulon and her other half were 2 Spaniards travelling the world on their KTM 990 Adventure. They were a few weeks behind me, but should have been following on down to Australia, so we hoped to meet up along the way, but unfortunately it didn't work out that way as they missed their boat from Dilli to Oz.

The other chap was Chris Bowen, who'd been riding a Triumph Tiger he bought in Miami, all the way from there back to London, the wrong way round. He'd already ridden across the States using the Pan American trails, then shipped to New Zealand, then Oz, and had just worked his way up from East Timor to Penang. He was doing it in stages, so travelled for a bit then went back to his job as a contractor to earn enough to do the next stage. A great way of doing it if you can, and he was having a ball.

He'd shipped his bike over from Belawan with Mr Lim and had it in storage at the port for a month whilst he went back to work. Arriving at the port we had a few hours to wait whilst they unloaded the boat of it's cargo, ready to reload with the Beast. Whilst there Chris got his bike out of storage but unfortunately the months wait hadn't been kind. The poor fuel he'd got in Indonesia had been sitting stationary in his tank, meaning all the crap settled to the bottom, effectively clogging up the filter. Try as we might we couldn't get the fuel pump to suck any fuel through to the engine. We tried bump starting it up and down the warehouse, both dripping with sweat in 5 minutes flat, much to the amusement of the workers, who offered us their wee mopeds in exchange!

Eventually Chris had the idea of just giving the thing a damn good shake, so with two of us it was easy to just lay it down on either side a few times, effectively dislodging all the sediment. It worked a treat and up she fired. Lovely job.

Unfortunately the front brake discs had seized solid, locking the front wheel in place. We removed the calipers and pads, but the pistons were all out of shape. A wee hunt on the trip facebook page got a resounding reply from all you guys once again, and it was diagnosed that moisture had gotten in to the brake lines, requiring a bleed of the brakes. It was hot, we both didn't really have the tools or knowledge for the job, and we just wanted back to our respective digs, ready for beers that night.

But now came my turn to get the Beast loaded onto the fruit & veg boat, and it's as basic as you like here. Health and safety officials the world over would have a cumulative coronary, they just wrap a rope around the bike, hoist her up with an old crane, then swing her onboard amongst all the fruit and veg. Basic, but it does the job and the Beast and I were once again temporarily parted. Once loaded, I jumped on the back of Chris' bike, and we rode back to George Town. Well, he had a back brake at least!

That night we met up for beers and exchanged tales from the road. It was great to hear of his adventures and also get advice for my trip ahead as I'd effectively be retracing his steps back to Darwin. In return I could give him a few tips for the trip onwards he was about to take. Top night with a top lad, cheers Chris if you're reading this.

Having boarded the Beast on the vegetable boat to Belawan, I caught a flight from Penang to Medan and spent a few days there awaiting her arrival. It really was crunch time for the trip. I now no longer had a budget, what was left in the bank was all I had and was hopefully enough to get me to Sydney. After that there was no more so I'd have no other option but to return home.

I started a 'Sponsume' (crowd funding) page to see if the remaining £16,000 could be raised, but I didn't just want people to donate their money for nothing. So, as a series of different rewards, I offered everything from wristbands and t-shirts, through to pre-ordering this book and DVD, even personal talks and a replica of the trip helmet, and the response was incredible.

I'd never intended to have you folks pay for me to go on a jolly around the world, that was never my intention, your money was to go to the charities. But unfortunately the way it worked out meant that in order to carry on the trip, and in order to carry on fundraising for the charities, I needed your help more than ever.

And help you did, raising £8K in about 5 weeks, I was utterly blown away! Thank you from the bottom of my heart, it really does mean the world and there was no way the trip could be completed without your help. A huge thank you goes out to the two huge mystery donators, your generosity was truly humbling and I can only hope you enjoyed the rest of the trip anywhere near as much as I did.

Thank you, thank you, thank you.

CHAPTER 20
INDONESIA & EAST TIMOR

20.1 - Day 185: Medan, Indonesia

Arriving at Medan's new international airport, Kuala Namu, I'd no idea what to expect. Unlike what the name suggests, it's no Heathrow, think London City's smaller country cousin. When you arrive in Indonesia you get your visa on arrival at the airport, right at the passport checking station. It costs $30 for a month's visa and is as simple as filling in a wee form. No dramas, and once you've got the visa, you can even skip the long passport queues and go straight to baggage collection. Happy days.

Unfortunately the carousel broke down just as they started to load the bags on, so after about a 45 minute wait, we were back in business and I was soon walking out into the arrivals hall.

In order to keep your hunger for 'Teapot' news fed, I made it a point of sourcing a local prepaid SIM card a.s.a.p. when entering a new country. That way I could festoon you with info in a daily Facebook barrage, as well as find out what the hell's going on via the wonder of Google.

However it appeared there was nowhere to get a local SIM card in the airport, despite what a few fellow travellers had said online. I even asked at the info desk and at the 'newsagents' in the airport, they just looked at me like I'd asked for a bacon sarnie!

The airport is only about 15 miles outside the city of Medan so I thought I'd grab a taxi to the hotel I'd booked online. The 'Grand Sirao' sounded regal, the reviews seemed great and the price, well the price should have forewarned me what to expect. £10/night, which by Indonesian standards is mega cheap, and when I finally arrived I found out why. But more about that in a sec.

That taxi ride from the airport was my introduction to the joys of Indonesian road travel. With over 238 million people inhabiting it's 17,500 islands, the majority of which reside in Sumatra and Java, Indonesia is the world's 4th most populated country. Combine this with a fledgling road system and a rapidly increasing public personal wealth, and you get an insane amount of vehicles all competing for not much road space, all going to the same places. It's hell on wheels, whether you have 2, 4, 10 or more.

The initial 15-mile taxi ride took me almost 2 hours as we crawled our way through potholed streets, horns blaring continuously, the air thick with traffic fumes and incredibly humid equatorial heat. The air felt oppressive to breathe, your eyes stung as the sweat collected the fumes off your face and ran into your eyes. First impressions…….. Next!

Arriving at the 'Grand Sirao' hotel, to be honest, I thought there'd been a mistake. The pics on booking.com showed a modern, glass fronted building, pretty much identical to most 'corporate' hotels you get round the globe. But this had the look of somewhere that had recently survived a hurricane or natural disaster! The streets around it reminded me very much of Northern Africa, litter festooned everywhere, the roads more potholed minefields than traffic thoroughfares.

There wasn't really any other alternative as the few other hotels in town were incredibly expensive compared to what I'd been used to. The Grand Sirao was £10 per night, double what I'd been paying in some places around Thailand and Malaysia, but the others here were £50 and above! Indonesia is not a cheap place to stay in most cities, be warned.

In general the hotels and guesthouses aren't quite what you'd expect in terms of facilities either. Bed bugs are fairly common in the cheaper places, don't expect hot water, even in the 'power showers', and be prepared for the South East Asian toilet to prevail. Often I found that my ensuite room came equipped with a toilet, shower, sink and bath, all in the form of an open hole in the floor with a large vat of mosquito infested water sat to the side. Just what you need after a day in the saddle in near 40 degree heat!

Ok, so I wasn't off to a very good start in Indonesia. I was grumpy, tired, hot and hungry. Not a good combination for me, DON'T POKE THE BEAR!

Arriving on Saturday, I had until Monday before the Beast would be ready for me to pick up from the port in Belawan, just north of Medan. I'd intended to work on the next vid and blog, but the advertised internet at the hotel was pretty much non-existent, and my Macbook Pro decided it didn't want to play. I spent the rest of Saturday killing mozzies in my room, a game I was now fairly proficient at, and on Sunday I went for a walk around Baghdad...... I mean Medan.

Actually I'm glad I did as it got me out there amongst the Indonesian people, who are amongst the friendliest folk I've met. They really go out of their way to introduce themselves to you, ask about where you're from, why you're here and what you'll be doing and seeing. They take a pride in their country that is a delight to experience, making you feel at ease in such an initially bewildering environment.

As I wandered around the city of Medan, I found a Telkomsel office where I could get a prepaid SIM, so in no time was back in the game. There are two main mobile service providers in Indonesia, Telkomsel and XLAxiata. Apparently XL has the better coverage, but there were only a few places in Java and Lombok where I couldn't get a signal with Telkomsel. I don't use calls or texts, just data for the t'interweb as I can do everything I need with Skype, WhatsApp and email. I got 3GB of data for the month for 130,000 Indonesian Rupee's – about £6.50. Not too bad I thought.

Monday arrived and I made my way to Belawan to the office of Mr Adnan. He has no email, or at least never replies to any, so you literally turn up and go from there.

The details are:

Bruce SMART

Mr Adnan
PT MELDA JAYA
JL. BANGKA TIMUR
NO. 49, BELAWAN, INDONESIA.
TEL : 06177908505 & 081376510927

It's a bit of a shock when you first turn up there, the place just looks like a residential street in a bit of a shanty town, but this is the right place. Mr Adnan is a nice guy and, like Mr Lim in Georgetown, he takes care of everything. You just follow him around like a puppydog, signing whatever and smiling at whomever he introduces you to.

There were a few delays along the way, due to various 'links' in the chain being AWOL, but by about 2pm I was done and dusted and back on the Beast heading South out of Belawan.

So here's the first hurdle when biking in Indonesia, the roads. Unlike Malaysia you can't ride a motorbike of any size on the toll roads. You can try, but the police at the gates will just turn you around again. This means you have to use the national routes, along with everyone else in the entire planet it seems! I've never ridden in India, and everyone who has, tells me that it's worse. If this is the case, I NEVER want to ride in India!

Traffic in Sumatra is horrendous, at least along the Northern A25 route I took down through the island of Sumatra. Right from Belawan and through Medan, it's just a trundling roadblock of vehicles, all trying to compete for the same square foot of empty road to progress that bit further. Combine that with the intense heat and humidity, then the air thick with fumes and pollution, and it makes for a fairly unpleasant experience.

I started most days at around 6-7am and would ride non-stop, bar fuel, until it got dark at the end of the day, around 6pm. I'd still be lucky to cover more than 150 miles in a day on average, the traffic was just a disaster. Trucks and buses fill the roads, taking up entire lanes in both directions, making overtakes almost an impossibility. Every now and then I could work my way to the front of traffic, then experience a brief 5 minute respite where I could open up the throttle once again to take the strain off my wrists. Soon enough I'd catch up with yet another tailback, and it was back to trudging along at 5-10mph, absolute murder!

It was the wet-season here in Indonesia and I experienced the full effects as I tried to ride the 280 miles from Pekanbaru to Jambi. I'd had a few messages from local Indonesian followers on facebook who were all warning me of this road. Apparently the mountain section between Pangkalankasai and Seberida along the AH25 (Asian Highway 25) was alive with bandits after sunset and was a terrible road. I should have known by now not to listen too much to such comments, as more often than not, they would be proven exaggerated at worst.

I set off at 5am that morning, determined to try and ride the 280 miles to Jambi in one hit. The first 60 miles were fairly swift, I was out the city before the really heavy traffic built up, and was cruising along moderately busy roads through some beautiful countryside. I'd also started to pick up new roads with freshly laid, unpotholed tarmac in evidence. Life was good at this point, I started to think that maybe I would do this. Yeah you guessed it.

As the road descended into a valley and spread ahead of me through great flat plains of fields, it began to get fairly damp. Well damp is an understatement, it was sodden. Great lakes lingered in fields at the roadside and stretches of roadway slipped quietly underwater in places. I'd done maybe three water crossings by the time I hit the biggie. Queues of cars sat at each bank of a huge lake, which had devoured our only path. I pulled up and watched to see what the other mopeds and trucks were doing. I could see a truck make it to the other side, and behind it were 3 mopeds, all coping with the water. It didn't look too deep, maybe coming halfway up their wheels as I watched. In a hurry to keep going, I worked my way to the front of the queue and rode down the slipway into the muddy water.

Bruce SMART

So far so good, I kept the revs high, feathering the clutch and just pointed her nose down the middle of where I thought the road was. Staring ahead I suddenly noticed that the mopeds in front were now alarmingly submerged with water high up on their engines. In a second they'd stalled at which point I just caught sight of a tidal wave coming straight for me. I'd failed to notice a big truck coming the other way on the opposite carriageway. He wasn't hanging about, storming through the water and causing a huge surge to spread across the lake, directly over to where I was. If I'd had my brain in gear, I could have switched off the engine and just pushed the Beast the rest of the way, but hindsight is a wonderful thing. As the wave hit, the water went straight up and over the front of the bike, swamping the air intakes as murky water flooded into the engine. With a cough, the Beast died on me and that was that.

With water so deep it came up to my thighs, I pushed the bike through to the other side, then struggled to get her up the incline and back onto dry land. The other mopeds were being picked up and shaken by their crew, (you often see mopeds that are 2-5 people up in Asia), water cascading from their innards. That wasn't an option open to me, so I carried on pushing her up to the top of the hill.

I remembered hearing that you could sometimes tow a drowned bike and this could force out the water from the pistons. As I didn't have anything to tow it with, I tried to bump start her down the hill. It didn't work, so I had to push her back up the hill again.

By this time a policeman had arrived on his wee moped and was now standing next to me, smiling broadly. In my best Indo-glish I tried to ask where the nearest mechanic was, and to my surprise he seemed to understand. Two minutes later I was back on the Beast being pushed along by a policeman on a moped, as he headed the 1.5Km to the next village. Soon enough I found myself being deposited at a roadside garage and quickly becoming the epicenter of village conversation.

The young lad at the garage looked inundated with similarly flooded mopeds, but he quickly got to work, showing me what he was doing on the them so I could copy on the

Beast. I stripped off the fairings and air box to get access to the plugs, and we set to work. In no time the plugs where out and the air filter cleaned/cleared. Replacing the plugs, she still wouldn't start so we drained the oil and found water in there too. Changing the oil did the trick and the Beast was soon roaring back into life.

I'd attracted quite a crowd by this time and was soon chatting to a lad who spoke good English. I asked him about the road to Jambi but unfortunately he didn't know. Translating for me, he asked around in the garage and I was again told it was a very bad road, lots of bandits and bad people. I'd be far better to get a truck and put the bike in the back. Guess what, they just happened to know a truck driver who'd do the job. I knew I'd pay way over the odds, but to be honest, by this point I'd had enough and just wanted off of Sumatra, so that did me.

Waiting for the truck to arrive, I sat at a roadside café hut, village life continuing all around me. It was one of those moments you have on a trip like this, where what you're actually doing strikes you in the face, the dawn of realisation a slap of sudden consciousness. Here I was, a fat lad from Blighty, riding a Superbike around the world. Alone but for the folk I met along the way, not a care in the world except the most primitive such as where and when would I eat next and where was I going next. I absolutely loved it, I felt at home there in that world, I felt alive.

About 4 hours later I was sitting in the cab of a truck, the Beast unceremoniously lying on her side atop some canvas sacks in the trailer, and we were slowly trundling our way South to Jambi. As we reached the section of road I'd been warned about, the surface became beautifully smooth with fresh tarmac sweeping its way through some gorgeous hilly forests. The same roadblocks I'd seen throughout Sumatra were in evidence, staffed by people wearing scarves over their faces and holding out buckets or nets to catch the money being given to them by passing traffic. Whether the scarves were worn to hide their identity, or simply to block out all the dust and fumes from the traffic, I'd no idea but not once did any of these people ever try to get money from me. They only seemed to approach cars, vans, trucks and buses, bikes were never targeted.

As night fell, we were still a long way from Jambi and I'd been told it would be at least a ten-hour drive from where I'd been picked up. The driver, Harry, spoke very limited English so the conversation was soon exhausted and he just told me to sleep and get some rest. As I tried to doze off in the cab, every bump in the road reminded me of my baby in the back, lying on her side, scraping across the metal floor of the trailer. I winced with every sound, imagining a sorry state of affairs when it came time to finally get her off the truck. By 3am we'd arrived in Jambi and I'd found a cheap place to stay just on the outskirts of the town. The Beast was in great shape thankfully, and we soon had her lifted down off the truck.

The rest of the journey South through Sumatra was fairly incident free but equally as tough. I don't know why I found Sumatra so hard, the roads weren't bad apart from a few potholes, the heat and humidity no worse than the Sahara or Japan in summer. But I don't think I've felt so unwell or drained as I did travelling through Indonesia. Each and every minute was a chore, and I doubt I'll ever go back. Shame as the people are great and there is so much more to see of the place, but it's just not my cup of tea.

(As it's turned out, it seems I developed a heart condition during my trip. I've not felt particularly well for a long time, always feeling tired and sickly, but I just put it down to life on the road. But once I got home it didn't get better but worse, resulting in a trip to the Doc's who referred me to the hospital. A quick ECG revealed it wasn't beating right, so that's where I'm at now, on medication and awaiting the medical wizards to sort my life out.)

20.2 - Days 194-197: Jakarta

Crossing on the ferry from Bakauheni to Merak in Java took only two hours so I was soon riding off the deck onto Java soil for the first time. I was heading straight to Jakarta to meet Glenn Stirling and Terry Burkin from 'Sanctuary'. The lads had very kindly come onboard to sponsor the Indonesian leg of the trip, and Glenn had offered to put me up for a few days in Jakarta. The plan had been to do some PR with the local media, but as it had taken me almost a week longer to get through Sumatra than I'd planned, I now arrived whilst the lads were away on a job. I spent the first night and day just getting on with the next blog and Fast Bikes article. Once done, Glenn had arrived home so we spent the day in the local boozer, chatting about the trip, Sanctuary, and also about a local charity which Sanctuary had recently got involved with.

The 'Gentur Cleft Foundation' (www.genturcleftfoundation.com) was established to help local children with cleft deformities receive the help and treatment they required. Chatting with Glenn about the amazing work this local charity was undertaking, I was chuffed to help raise their profile through the media interview I was given with the Jakarta Globe. You can find out more info about Gentur at their website.

I'd done no sightseeing in Jakarta, I simply didn't have the time, so the lads decided to take me out on my last night to show me the town. Nothing cultural just a top rate bar underneath a luxury hotel, surrounded by beautiful women. It was tough folks, but I struggled through! I even got interviewed on stage with the band, what a top night, cheers lads.

The next morning Glenn had organised for a member of the local constabulary to accompany me through the legendary Jakarta traffic out to the city limits. I'd not normally bother to be honest, but Jakarta traffic is insane so every little advantage is welcomed. Unfortunately, this morning I discovered I'd got the only puncture of the trip, a hulking great nail lodged in the rear tyre. Luckily, there are tyre 'shops' all along the roads in Indonesia, so I only had to travel about 100 metres down the road to get her plugged up and ready to go.

These Bridgestone BATTLAX tyres had been incredible. Right from the BT-023's I used in the first leg through Europe and Africa, to the new T30's, I put this rubber through as extreme a 'road test' as any tyre could be put through. They are designed for the 'Sports Touring' market, for people who want sports performance but more longevity and wet grip from their tyres. I'd taken them across the Sahara Desert, got my knee-down in the Arctic Circle, ridden across Russia and Siberia, and ridden some off-road tracks that most GS owners wouldn't even attempt. In over 74,000 miles, I only ever had 2 punctures – 1 when some disgruntled locals put a machete through the rear in Africa, and the other when I got this nail in Jakarta. They truly are superb tyres and I've said it before, even if Bridgestone weren't giving me tyres for the trip, I'd still spend my own money and use them. In my honest opinion, I still think the older BT-023 is a better all round tyre than the newer T30, but for the Sports rider, the T30 offers the better dry feedback and agility. Do yourself a favour and chuck a set on your bike to test them out for yourself.

All repaired, I set off into the madness that is Jakarta traffic. It truly is biblical, there is no other word for it. Everywhere you look is solid traffic, everyone crawls along, each trying to inch farther forward than the other. No road etiquete prevails here, no highway code applies, it's simply every man for themselves. At each junction, men stand in the midst of the madness taking money from drivers wishing to enter the fray from side streets. Once paid, these guys literally put their lives on the line by standing out in the middle of oncoming traffic, blocking their way to let their customers edge out slowly in the madness. It's just insane, the traffic inevitably edging to a standstill as the sheer volume prevents any further progress.

Local police push their way on foot into the middle of this traffic anarchy, and begin to direct their symphony of control. Mopeds are carried aloft on foot, eventually extricating themselves to freedom. As one by one each vehicle is set free, inch by inch the road is once again revealed and the journey can continue. I'll never complain about London in the rush-hour again.

20.3 - Java

I'd chosen to take the Southern route through Java as I'd been told the Northern route had more trucks and heavy traffic. From Jakarta I headed down to Bandung then along Highway 3 towards Yogyakarta, destination Borobadur. This ancient Buddhist temple is believed to date back to the 9th century, and is probably the most famous landmark in Indonesia.

Located in the wee village of Borobadur, just north west of Yogyakarta, it's easily reached by any means and is continually swamped by visitors. I arrived in the village in the early evening so quickly found a place to stay for the night, and planned to rise early to view the temple at dawn, the best time to view this incredible place.

Well that was the plan, I awoke through the night with the now familiar stomach cramps, nausea and sweats. I spent the night clamped to the bathroom, each time I braved a return to bed, I was quickly sent running for the porcelain throne!

By 5am the following morning I was in a world of hurt, I felt terrible. I managed to get myself dressed into the leathers and pack all my kit, but each time I went to leave I'd have to run back to the bathroom. Before I knew it, it was gone 7:30am and I hadn't even been to the temple yet. Lying on the floor, sweat dripping from my very soul, I made the decision to miss out the temple and just get on the bike and go. There was no way I could visit it like this, even if I got there I'd surely end up having an 'accident' whilst trying to walk up the temple grounds. The thought of puking, or worse, over people was enough to convince me to just go. I was already behind schedule and couldn't afford another day sitting around.

I hit the road again but soon stopped after coming across the Mendut Temple just on the outskirts of Borobadur village. I could get pics of it without straying too far from the bike (and some form of 'stopper' for my leaking innards!)

Back on the bike I kept the visor open and kept a steady stream of water going in to my body, trying to flush whatever this was out. The road started off ok but soon enough it became the familiar mountain twisty track I'd grown used to in Indonesia. Potholes littered the surface, periodic traffic congestion causing tortoise like progress as I twisted my way up, down and around the lush green mountains. At one stage, out of nowhere I projectile vomited whilst riding on the bike. I'd no time to even stop and take my lid off! Thankfully I hadn't eaten anything that day and the previous nights escapades ensured it was only fluid filled. Nonetheless, pleasant it was not and I don't recommend it!

After spending the night in Malang, I'd planned to ride by Mount Bromo the following day for some more pics and vids. But yet again I awoke feeling terrible, I just couldn't settle in Indonesia, the place was really making me work for each and every hour of every day.

20.4 - Days 201–205: Bali

I hit the road again and headed straight for the port to Bali at Banyuwangi. Thankfully the road from Malang up to the northern coast road was great, hardly any potholes and not too much traffic – compared to Sumatra and the west of Java. Leaving Malang at 8am I was at the port by noon, waiting for the next ferry over to Bali.

The crossing over to Bali takes around an hour, with ferries running every hour 24hrs a day. I didn't even bother to leave the hold but chatted away with the locals who were all crowding around the Beast and I.

Arriving in Bali, it was about a 2-hour ride from the port to Legian over in the capital city of Denpasar. The road was superb, almost all freshly laid tarmac with the odd short section of roadworks. As the road clung to the shoreline you were exposed to the most beautiful scenes of glorious blue and white surf caressing incredible stone and sand beaches. I wish I'd stopped to get some pics and vids, but to be honest by this time all I wanted to do was get to Legian, dump my kit, shower and be surrounded by a touch of Western culture.

A friend of the family called Peter Lewis had got in touch through the Teapot facebook page. He now lived and worked in Bali so kindly offered to meet up and show me the ropes there. At the time Pete was the manager of 'Monsoon', a great bar just down the road from where I was staying, so that was to be my HQ for the next few days I was in town. It's a tough life I know.

I'd booked into a fairly decent and cheap place called 'Su's Cottages' where I got my own room with a proper bathroom, no bedbugs and even aircon, all for about 1,800,000 rupees for 5 nights – about £85. Not too bad I thought. The staff were great, really friendly like everyone else in Indonesia, and it was great to have somewhere homely to stay for a few days.

As it had taken longer than I'd planned to get to Bali, I was now unsure if my 1-month visa would suffice and see me through to the land border with East Timor. A quick chat with Gary Leighton, one of Pete's mates in the pub, revealed that he was the very man I needed to speak to, as he owned a company who specialised in visa extensions in Bali. The next day Gary sorted my visa, the quickest service anywhere in Indonesia and thoroughly recommended, great friendly folks. (www.baliexpatservices.com)

Whilst on the road I'd been contacted by some fellow travelers from the UK who were riding their motorbike to New Zealand. Amy & Paul were emigrating to NZ and decided to ride their bike there and see a bit of the world. They'd got in touch after meeting Mr Lim back in Penang, who'd told them about my trip and were now just arriving in Bali. Before long we were all sitting in the bar, gassing about our respective experiences and enjoying the local tipple, 'Bintang' the nectar of the God's. It was a great evening and an absolute pleasure to meet Amy & Paul. Their trip sounded awesome and I found myself jealous of the fact they were nearly 'home', somewhere I was really starting to miss if truth be told.

I spent the next few days just chilling out around Legian in Denpasar. I had all the intention in the world of getting out on the Beast and exploring the island of Bali, but by the time I'd got there, all I wanted to do was get off the bike for a few days and just blend in to the background. I walked around the city, down streets I don't know the name of, into bars and shops I knew nothing about. I strolled along the beach, watching the groups of holidaymakers and locals all having a great time. I was living the dream, doing what everyone would give their back teeth to do, but to be honest I felt a tad lonely. Not for the first time I was witness to the beauty available all around us, but had nobody there to share it with. Sometimes it's a lonely place on the road………. but then I had a beer and all was right once more.

After chatting with some folk in 'Monsoon' I'd discovered there was an apple shop in town that may be able to have a look at my Macbook Pro. It was worse than ever now, often refusing to start up at all for hours at a time, even then eventually crashing with the now familiar 'beep-beep-beep' screaming into the air. A quick visit to the store and a conflab with a technical wizard, soon had the problem isolated down to a faulty RAM slot. Removing the effected slab of RAM solved the issue, although I was now down to 8GB RAM instead of the previous 16GB. But at least the mac now worked and I could get on with my steadily growing backlog.

For the next few days I worked away, slowly eroding the list of jobs to do. In the evenings I'd pop down my new local to meet the lads, it was great to have some normality in life again. Soon enough it was my last night, it was weird to think these relative strangers had now become good friends in only a few days. I was genuinely sad to leave them and move on, but again, that's the life you choose when traveling. Pete, Dietmar, Gary, Matt and the lads, I hope I meet you again some day folks, thank you very much for your kindness and hospitality, take care.

20.5 - The Journey Through the Isles

As the sun came up on day 205 I was already on the road, heading East along the coast of Bali to the ferry port of Padang to catch the boat to Lembar, in Lombok. The ferry is 24hrs a day, leaves every 2 hrs, takes about 4hrs to get there, and costs about 250,000 rupees (about £17 – although this does seem to vary depending on size of bike, who is at the till, phase of the moon……?)

The ferries around most of the islands are fairly standard, the vehicles go on the main deck area, and there is seating available on the upper decks with some form of 'tuckshop' for food/drinks. Sometimes there is a VIP area that offers slightly more comfortable seats and air con for a price – around 30,000 rupees on top of your ticket (about £1.80).

The journey overland from Bali to Australia means you need to island hop your way across to West Timor, where you can then drive/ride to the border with Timor Leste (East Timor) and get to Dili. From here you can pick up a freight ship to get your vehicle across to Darwin, whilst you fly. Most people take anywhere from a few weeks to 2-4 months. I was trying to do it in one week!

My plan had been to be in Oz for the first week of December, tour around and spend NYE in Sydney before shipping over to Chile on or around the 1st or 2nd Jan. Then I'd ride South to Tierra Del Fuego, get a pic at Ushuaia before turning around and riding north all the way up the Pan-American Highway, eventually reaching Texas and Houston by mid March to meet the lads from Delta for a PR push.

Unfortunately I was running a couple of weeks behind meaning I either tried to catch the ship from Dili that was due to leave on the 10th Dec, or I waited for the next one which was scheduled for about the 21st Dec. No contest for me, I hit the road running. It'd mean I'd miss everything the islands were known for, the incredible diving, the beautiful beaches and volcanoes, all the tourist 'must-dos' would simply be ridden by and forgotten. But in all honesty, I was done in now, I just wanted to get to Dili and get to Australia!

Arriving on Lombok by lunchtime, it's a simple ride straight across to the other side of the island to the port of Labuhan where I could catch the ferry over to Sumbawa. At only 65 miles, it should've taken a couple of hours tops to get there, but the skies opened and the only road to follow became a raging torrent in places. The traffic quickly built up and the tailbacks grew. I eventually rolled into town at 9pm, apparently too late for the ferry. Riding around this apparent ghost town I struggled to find anywhere to sleep, until a passing moped stopped to take pity on me. With a smile he led me to a run down building and said, "Hotel Mr", and was gone. The kindness and generosity of most people in Indonesia has to be experienced first hand to be truly appreciated. They're a great bunch of folk.

The 'hotel' itself won't win any stars, but it cost just over £1 for the night so I wasn't arguing. I could have asked for a discount as I was sharing the bed with a swarm of bed bugs, and the room was already occupied by a city of mozzies, but I was too knackered to care. I slept in my leathers after spraying the room with deet. Normally the 95% deet would probably kill me when sprayed in a confined space like that, but the windows were basically wire mesh with huge holes in them, so ventilation wasn't an issue. In a heartbeat I was out like a light.

I awoke by 5am the following morning, eager to hit the road. By 6am I was at the port and soon on the first ferry of the day over to Poto Tano in Sumbawa. It cost somewhere around 200,000 rupees (about £13), takes about 2hrs and there are ferries roughly every 2hrs throughout the day. Arriving on Sumbawa by about 9am I was soon riding straight across the island, my final destination the ferry port of Sape on the very eastern edge of the island. Again the roads were generally in great condition, the fuel in good supply, and thankfully the traffic much, much lighter than it had been in Sumatra and Java.

By about 4:30pm I'd covered the 250 miles and pulled up at the entrance to the port. I was welcomed with open arms by a police man who seemed overjoyed to see me? He shook me by the hand, asking where I was from. 'Scotlandia' came the reply, and his grip instantly got tighter, his smile wider. They love the Scot's over here, in fact they seem to love the Scot's everywhere! The copper waived over another bloke and I was whisked off to a nearby cafe and told the next ferry would leave at 6pm. My new mate was a mute chap, but he understood English and did his best to try and communicate. I bought him a few drinks whilst we sat in the cafe, and before long it was time to buy the ticket and board the ferry.

The ferry from Sape, Sumbawa over to Labuhan Bajo in Flores takes about 8 hrs and leaves twice a day. It cost about 350,000 rupees (about £20) for a big bike and was probably the best ferry in terms of service. I decided to treat myself, the VIP room was actually pretty nice with reclining leather seats, large screen TV's with English movies and your own wee tuck shop, all for 30,000 rupee's!

As the night drew on I got my macbook out to watch a film. The choice on my mac is fairly limited, 'TT Closer to the Edge' or 'Fastest' so I started with the latter. With my headphones in I was engrossed in the motoGP action but soon was aware of a presence around me. Looking up I found that the majority of the room were now all standing around me watching the film over my shoulder. After gaining the consensus of approval, I turned up the volume and we all enjoyed the show. After that it was time for 'TT Closer to the edge', which met with equal approval and adoration. That passed a fair few hours at least!

By 4am we'd docked into Labuhan Bajo in Flores and I was now sitting in the dark trying to find somewhere to stay. I'd been told that this place was akin to Bali, the main place to stay on the island of Flores. I'd booked a place on booking.com but for the life of me couldn't find it. I'd gone way up into the hills, down dirt tracks similar to Laos in the pitch black, following the directions given by google maps. By 5am I'd found a resort tucked down another dirt track and asked the security if they knew of the place I was looking for. As luck would have it, it was right next door but you could only access it by an incredibly steep, muddy track, again in complete darkness. I've got to admit I'd had a sense of humour failure by then so sacked it off and rode through the town, stopping just outside where I found a recogniseable hotel. By now it was Sunday and I had to get to Aimere in Flores by Tuesday morning to catch the twice weekly ferry over to Kupang in West Timor. Still doable, I could afford a stop over here in Labuhan Bajo.

I spent the day doing my laundry then took a wee ride down into the town to see what was about. To be honest it wasn't what I'd expected at all, there was nothing apart from a few shops, a market or two and some tourist info, cruise and dive stores. I don't dive so that was out, I didn't have time or money to go on a cruise, and shopping is possibly my least favourite thing in the world, so all in all not a great success. I went for a stroll along the shore and I've got to say, the place is beautiful.

The next day I tried to meet up with some Welsh ladies I'd been put in touch with whilst in Bali. They run the '2 Dragons Beach Bar' in Labuhan Bajo but unfortunately were away when I got into town. As the rain began to come down I decided to make a move and leave town, but as I pulled up at the only petrol station on the West of the island, I found it was out of petrol! This wasn't good. If it didn't get filled up before tomorrow, I'd be screwed for making the ferry.

Feeling a tad sick I decided I'd book into a decent hotel just outside town, so spent the evening in a clean bed with no bed bugs, sleeping like a baby after a feed of hearty Spag Bol' and garlic bread. Boo-Tee-Full. When I'd checked-in, the receptionist had asked all about my journey, where I'd been and where I was going. As luck would have it her cousin lived in Aimere so she made a quick call to confirm the day and time of the next ferry to Kupang. Luckily for me it was now a day late so wasn't due until Wednesday at 7am. That gave me a bit of time this side, but would really push me for making the ship in Dili. Oh well, nothing I could do now.

Leaving early on Tuesday morning the Gods were smiling as the petrol station had been filled up. The port of Aimere is about 160 miles from Labuhan Bajo, but takes around 5-6hrs to ride. The road is good in most places, but very twisty as it winds it way up, down and around the volcanoes and forests of the island. Progress is slow but fairly enjoyable as the surroundings are stunning. In Flores you also start to see Christian churches replacing the never ending mosques that cover Indonesia. This dates back to the early Portuguese settlers, in fact Portuguese is still the dominant language as you head East over to Timor and Timor Leste. Although not religious in the slightest, I found the presence of the churches strangely reassuring, far less threatening than I find the mosques and their strict ritual of worship. But anyway, let's not get into that debate eh!

December the 3rd, day 210, was also my son's 16th birthday and I wasn't there for him yet again. I'd known I'd be away for this since setting the date of the trip. I'd been careful to talk it over with him for many years to ensure he was ok with me being away for so long. We'd been away on the bike touring Scotland and then Europe, spending a few weeks at a time camping and touring our way around. He'd always backed me on the trip so I'd gone ahead and planned it. But now I was away, the full reality of missing such an iconic moment in your kids life really hit home.

I 'speak' with my boy every few weeks via facebook whilst on the road. He's crap at replying but not in a bad way. He's just a typical teenager, busy with his own life, school and his girlfriend – How can a dad compete with that! He'd always said he didn't want anything special for his 16th and his mum had confirmed it. He's a cracking kid, very mature and considerate for his years. But now I found myself on the other side of the world to him on this special day, a 9hr time difference and with no phone signal to message him. I felt incredibly alone, almost ostracised even, although self-inflicted. I had an overwhelming sense of guilt at not being there for him, something I've felt since leaving his mum many years before, if the truth be told. I'm not looking for sympathy, you live by your decisions in life and deal with what comes your way. Thankfully life has been good, I met Nikki and life had been great, but I'll always feel guilty for denying my boy of what I consider a 'normal' life. Sounds weird I know, but that's me……. a bit weird.

20.6 - Day 211: Aimere, Ferry to Kupang, Flores

I made it to Aimere by about 4:30pm Tuesday afternoon in the pouring rain of the wet season. Drenched through I rode up to the port buildings were there was already a substantial collection of vehicles and people waiting. Some 'Indo-Glish' conversations confirmed that the ferry was due the following morning, anywhere from 5am to 1pm?

I settled down on the ground next to the bike as a crowd gathered around us. I must have knodded off as I awoke to a tap on the head. "Mr, Mr, hotel" as a guy pointed up the road. Five minutes up the road was the 'Go-Go Hotel'. It didn't look too bad compared to some of the places I'd stayed in Indonesia, but it certainly wouldn't bother the Hilton. In fact it wouldn't bother the Red Bull in Peckham, but a bed is a bed.

Unfortunately they were fully booked but the landlady pointed me up a side street to another hotel near a church. A few minutes later I was in an outhouse beside a guys home, it had four walls and some sort of roof, a bed alive with bed bugs, but I didn't care. £1.20 for the night did me, yet again I slept in the leathers and was soon out like a light.

Unfortunately going to bed at 7pm I was wide awake by 1am. I lay there on the bed until 5am when I got back on the Beast and rode to the port. The ferry was due in at 7am now and set to sail at 8am for the 22 hour journey across to Kupang. By 10am we could just see the boat on the horizon as it slowly crawled towards the port. By 10:30 am it had docked and a mad surge of people, vehicles and cargo spilled off onto the dock, frantically surging towards us like an avalanche of life.

Despite the utter chaos, the unloading was completed in about 20 minutes and I was soon beckoned onto the ferry, the Beast tightly packed away behind a few pallet loads of rice. I made my way up to the 1st deck to source the VIP room as found on every other ferry I'd been on, but to no avail, there wasn't one on this service. A 22-hour crossing, overnight with limited seating on plastic chairs you find in any school in the UK. The other options are either to sleep next to everyone else on the metal bunks available in two big rooms, or sleep out on deck in the elements. I sat on a chair for the first hour, chatting with staff and other passengers, but soon enough the small talk was exhausted, and so was I. Crossing into one of the dorms, I found a space on one of the metal bunks, lay down and passed out. For once I was happy to have the stinking leathers, as I got the bunk all to myself for the entire journey!

The journey wasn't too bad actually. The Indonesians are a very social bunch, they like to talk, or more accurately shout, amongst each other until the early hours. They then hit the sack for a few hours before rising early at dawn and starting all over again. Like the rest of South East Asia, they also love karaoke, singing and dancing along to any and every music that's around them. It's not done in an anti-social or malicious manner, it's just their culture, it's the norm. But for someone from Blighty, who's tired, crabby, unwell, hungry and feeling particularly unsociable, it was really starting to grip my doo-dah at 2am when most of the guys in the dorm were pissed as farts and signing away to a screeching women on the telly. Thanks to my mate Lewie from Hear Wave Technology (www.hearwavetechnology.com) I was kitted out with some cracking in-ear moulded ear plugs, of which I made full use of on this ferry.

Come 9am the following morning the port of Kupang was in sight as the crew and passengers all began to prepare for imminent departure. I'd watched as person after person the entire crossing had simply thrown their rubbish overboard into the sea. I'd been meticulous to place all my waste into the bins provided so watched in abhorrent horror as the crew came along, collected all the bins, then threw the rubbish overboard! That's probably the biggest issue for me in Indonesia. Like Africa, it's an incredibly beautiful country that is being decimated by rubbish. There's nobody else to blame here apart from the local people, they just drop and dump their crap wherever they stand. The Indonesian government really need to invest in a mammoth education program to get people to put their crap into bins, and then have those bins disposed of in a suitable manner. The bins are there, I've seen them, they're just not utilised.

Anyway, by 10am I was off the ferry and making my way to the 'Hotel Las Hasienda' near the airport. The English biker I met in Penang, Chris Bowden, had told me all about this place and I made a direct path for it. Owned and run by a German chap called Michael, it was an oasis in a desert of crappy accommodation. Clean, efficient, great value and service, it even offered amazing food. I was sold. Luckily I got the last room available and booked in for a few days. I had to get to the Timor Leste consulate to apply for my 'Letter of Invitation' to cross the land border into Timor Leste. Without this you will be turned away when you get there, so it's essential you have it. Normally it takes 3 days from the time of application, but I explained I had to be in Dili by Saturday to catch the ship. He had it ready the next day, what a star!

After a brief stay at the hotel, I left early on Saturday morning and made my way north east to the border with Timor Leste up on the northern coast, just north of Atambua. I'd been told it would take about 5 hours to cover the 180 miles, but I did it in 4. The road was generally good with only a few short sections of rough track through the earth. The sights along the way were equally as stunning as anywhere else I'd seen in Indonesia. They even made me stop and get off the bike a few times, so they must've been good!

The last 20km or so to the border takes you down what looks like a single track road, up and down some hills towards the coastline. Some sections are littered in potholes, but take it steady and you'll be fine. I was almost out of brakes too, so found myself hard on the rear brake trying to slow my descent in the downhill sections. Soon enough you roll into the border town and face the now familiar process of every border on the planet. Customs and immigration, each border having a slightly different way of going about it, but essentially it's all the same. The Indonesian side is straightforward enough, took me about 40 minutes but I had to wait for someone to come and handle the carnet.

After that I stopped for a quick pic with a border troop, before heading down 'no-mans land' to the Timor Leste border post. For whatever reason, the guard standing outside the building wanted all my kit off the bike before I went inside, so in the near 35 degree heat, I sweated my way through unstrapping/unbuckling each of the bags, then carrying it all inside. You hand over your 'Letter of Invitation' then the all-important $30 US – the official currency of Timor Leste now, and go through to the next section, customs. They pop your luggage through some x-ray machines, stamp your passport and it's job done, you're now in East Timor, lovely job. (Remember to get your Carnet stamped at the little hut on the right just before you leave the complex. There's normally a soldier on duty at the booth, but they're not always switched on to the Carnet issues. Be warned.)

Heading off into the country I'd no idea what to expect really. I'd been told that the road was there but in various states of repair, destruction and construction. My Garmin had given up and couldn't quite believe I was there so I used it simply as a glorified compass to ensure I kept heading North East towards Dili. I needn't have worried as there only is one road. Once you come out of the border complex, follow the road to a junction, turn left over a bridge, and that's it. From then on just follow the road ahead and keep the sea on your left.

As luck would have it, it started to rain just as I entered the country. Not just a wee trickle either, this was a proper tropical, wet season rainstorm. I'd been told it would take about 3 hrs to reach Dili from the border, but with the rain coming down the way it was, I could visibly see the off-road stretches of road before me disappearing under torrents of water rising at an alarming rate. I didn't stop once, just kept her moving all the time, even through some fairly deep-water sections down by the coast. I'd learnt from Indonesia, so took the deep water slowly, ready to cut the engine the instant the water looked like it may reach the air intakes, but thankfully it was never an issue.

The road ascended into the hills, potholes became more frequent until it was just a rocky track up the side of the mountain. Not an issue on an adventure bike, but on a Superbike it's slow and painful going. As long as you keep the tyres turning and the revs low, momentum keeps the bike moving forward through any mud or sand, so I just kept her ticking over and chewed up the road ahead. They've been building the new coastal road for a few years now, so every now and then you come across some major road works in your path. In the dry it's just dusty, but in the wet it becomes a bit of a quagmire. As usual, I found the tried and tested method of following the most recent tracks through the mud ensured I got the firmest ground under the wheels, limiting the amount of slipping and sliding I had to endure.

Finally I reached the outskirts of Dili after about 2 hours or so, as the road once again became good solid tarmac. I came across the first petrol station I'd seen since leaving Indonesia so filled up there and immediately noticed how expensive everything was in Timor Leste. Roughly speaking, everything is about 4 times the price of Indonesia, sometimes more. But this is good preparation for when you reach Darwin, OH MY GOD, this place is pricey, but more of that in the next chapter.

I was ecstatic to reach Dili, it's all I'd been focusing on since arriving in Medan 4 weeks previously. Now I was here I had to get the bike cleaned in preparation for Ozzy quarantine, and ensure it made the next ship to Darwin, due to leave on the 10th of Dec. Today was Saturday the 8th so I had time, just.

I found a place to stay at the Excelsior Resort in Dili, just down the road from the Toll shipping agents yard, and also close to the only place in town to get cash, the Timor Plaza. I won't recommend the Excelsior as somewhere to stay it's fairly expensive, the service isn't great, the food is pretty garbage and unless you have your own transport, it's a bit out the way of anything unless you get a taxi. That said, there were no bed bugs and it was quiet, so it did me for my last few nights.

Bruce SMART

On Sunday I got to work importing all the vid footage into the editing software so I could begin work on episode 11 – Thailand & Laos of the YouTube series. It takes a good few days to do, then another few days to edit and produce the finished article, so I'd finish it later in Darwin. For now, that took care of my Sunday.

Come Monday morning I was up early and sitting in the portacabin at the 'Toll' yard for 9am. Unfortunately nobody there could do anything for me so I had to wait until 10:30am when another lady rocked in to the office. I've got to say, she didn't instill me with a hell of a lot of confidence, fumbling her way around the paperwork and giving me various answers to the questions I had. First things first I needed to get the bike cleaned, and 'Toll' directed me to 'Troys Logistics' just down the road from the hotel I was staying in. Troy is an Ozzy chap who used to work for Ozzy customs and as such is fully aware of the lengths they can go in their quarantine inspections. He and his team do an unbelievable job in cleaning and preparing vehicles, stripping them to their bare chassis, cleaning everything down to the wiring, before putting it all back together. Everything that goes in the container has to be absolutely spotless, as clean as new in order to pass inspection.

So imagine my horror when I rocked up to Troy's only to be told that they were no longer cleaning bikes as they'd had too many problems in the past with people complaining of electrical problems once their bike was put back together! I had the rest of the day to essentially strip the bike and clean her myself. This was not going to be fun. Heading back to the 'Toll' yard I explained the situation and was told that the lads there could do the cleaning for $300 US. This sounds a lot, but it was up to $750 to get it cleaned by Troy, and if you fail inspection, the Ozzy authorities have been known to ship the vehicle straight back to where it has come from and charge you for the pleasure of it!

On a good note, the ship was now delayed to Wed 11th Dec so I now had an extra day to get the cleaning done. We set to work, I stripped the Beast of all her plastics and luggage, disconnected the battery, and stripped off any loose stickers and bits of wrapping. The 'Toll' lads then got to work scrubbing her down whilst I got on with cleaning each and every item of luggage, as well as the actual Kriega bags themselves. Even my tent, rain suit and boots all had to be spotless inside and out. The tools, footpump, you name it, if it was going with the bike then it had to be completely clean. I decided that there wasn't a chance in hell of the helmet or suit passing inspection, so kept these with me to go in the planes' hold as luggage at the airport. I also managed to pack some spares and other none essentials into my rucksack, thus limiting the items that could fail the inspection, as well as the amount of cleaning we'd have to do.

It took all day in the scorching heat, but we eventually got it done. As the lads strapped her down into her own container, the sense of relief was palpable. All that remained now was to see if she'd pass the quarantine inspection in Oz. Fingers crossed, and more about that in the next chapter.

All in the shipping of the bike from Dili to Darwin cost $760 US – this includes the cleaning (they only charged $80 in the end), lashing, and all the other various extra's shipping agents throw in. You have more to pay once in Australia, but I'll cover that in the next chapter too.

I booked my flight to Darwin for the next morning and at 0710hrs on Wednesday the 11th of December 2013 the wheels lifted off the tarmac signaling the end of the South East Asian leg of TeapotOne. I won't lie, I was relieved to be heading to Oz and really looking forward to what lay ahead. Whatever that may be? But I was also sad to be leaving this amazing part of the world. Everything South East Asia has to offer is what makes travel and adventure travel the addictive bug that it is. Anything is possible in this part of the world, the people are incredibly social and friendly – as long as you abide by their social rules and etiquette, and of course money is King. If you want adventure travel on a budget, you'll do a lot worse than to come and explore all around the countries and islands of South East Asia. I will be back.

MALAYSIA
SINGAPORE

INDONESIA

AUSTRALIA
AUSTRALIA
AUSTRALIA AUSTRALIA

AUSTRALIA

CHAPTER 21
AUSTRALIA

Day 228 of the trip and I finally arrived in Darwin in the Northern Territories of Australia. South East Asia was fantastic, the surroundings beautiful and majestic, the people welcoming, smiling and friendly. But 228 days after leaving London for the 2nd time, I was in dire need of some familiar Western surroundings and homegrown craic. Travelling is great, I'll never take for granted how lucky I was to be doing this, but sometimes you just need a bit of what you're used to. Australia, let's be 'aving ya!

After originally leaving London on the 1st October 2012, I finally reached the perceived 'halfway' point of Australia on the 10th December 2013. After 44,000 miles, 39 countries and 217 consecutive days on the road, I was finally there but never would have believed the effect this place would have on me. I'm in love.

After packing the Beast up in an empty container in the 'Toll' yard in Dili, I'd caught the plane the next morning to Darwin. Arriving at 0830hrs I was soon in a taxi heading into the city. Booked into 'Chilli's Backpackers' hostel on Mitchell Street, the epicenter of social life in the town, I can't put into words the feeling I had those first few days. After so long in foreign lands, surrounded by strange places, strange customs and strange languages, I was now back in somewhere I could fairly recognise. Well, cancel the bit about the language, but apart from that, Darwin was like Troon with extreme heat…… and humidity, and crocs, sharks, abbo's…..

The first thing on my list was my stomach, nothing new there. I'd been craving a bacon and egg roll for as long as I could remember, so made a beeline to the first place that looked open and there she was. Heaven.

The 'Tap' is a local institution in Darwin, one of the 'must-dos' in town. It's got an old tree growing right up through the middle of the bar, the staff are really friendly (and easy on the eye too – yes even the girls), and the beer is cold. What more do you want from a drinking establishment?

I spent the first week just slogging through my workload as I had the Indonesian blog to write, the Laos Vid, and the next article for Fast Bikes to do. The ship from Dili had been delayed again so it wouldn't arrive in Darwin until the following Tuesday, and the Beast wouldn't be unloaded and ready for quarantine until the Friday, so I just had to sit and wait. There's a lot to do around Darwin in the form of tours out to the Kakadu National Park, helicopter and fishing trips, bus tours out to the wilderness etc, but to be honest it's an incredibly expensive place to visit. I'm on a really limited budget on this trip, even more so now shipping costs had sky rocketed due to fuel surcharge rises. This meant I couldn't do any of the organized trips, so instead just settled for a walk about town and a wee visit to Crocosaurus Cove, just down the road from the hostel. This place was pretty good, with a fairly large selection of 'salties' on display, from tiny wee 1m ones, to a couple of huge 4m plus beasts. You can even get into a clear Perspex tank and 'swim' with one of the big ones at feeding time? No thanks.

To top it off I went to draw some money out the ATM and it swallowed my card! Many frantic calls later and I was talking with Visa international who very kindly arranged for some emergency cash to be provided. They even allowed me to withdraw more than their usual limit as I explained I would be riding around the country for a month before I could pick up my replacement card from a friends place in Sydney. So I had £3,000 in my sky rocket, enough to cover a bike service, fuel, food, lodgings and hopefully a fair amount of the shipping over to Chile. Or so I thought.

21.1 - Day 225: Quarantine Day!

Finally the day arrived where I'd be reunited with the Beast – hopefully. Quarantine in Australia is the toughest in the world. Your bike has to be as clean as it was when it rolled out the showroom in order to pass. They don't stop with the bike either, every item of kit you have with it is inspected down to the tiniest little seed. It's white glove treatment, and if they find anything at all that they're not happy with, then you have to get a special clean, at your cost, before they inspect it all again. Not only that, but each inspection must be pre-booked, again at your own cost, in half hour sections. You pay for each additional half hour AND any additional inspection bookings that may be required, should you fail one.

So you'll understand why I was slightly apprehensive about this day. The bike has been through every type of terrain you can think of, over a sustained period of time. It's been submersed in water, mud, sand, ridden through fields of crops, fallen down rocky hills in distant lands, to be honest I didn't think I had a hope of getting it through without a further clean. The lads in Dili and I had given her a thorough scrubbing, but if they went as far as removing some of the bolts, as they've been known to do before, then I was Royally fubar'd.

Arriving at the 'Toll' depot I met a couple of other bikers who had also just shipped from Dili. They were on the standard 'GSs' so went first in the queue. Each inspection seemed to take around 30-45 mins, so eventually it was my turn. You know you're back in the '1st world' when you have to wear a hard hat, high-vis and boots when walking onto the shipyard. In Dili I was in flip-flops, shorts, t-shirt and sunnies!

Soon enough I met the lad who was doing the inspection and he seemed in a great mood. A few light questions and I discovered that this was their last day before finishing up for Crimbo, in fact I'd be his last inspection! This could be good. On seeing the Beast I knew I was on to a winner as he started asking questions about the bike, why I was doing the trip, where I'd been etc. We stood and chatted about that for 5 minutes before he began his check.

He gave the fairings a quick look over, shone his torch up the inside of the bike from below, then said, "I'll not go overboard as it's a road bike, it's not like you've been riding through rivers and shit is it!" "Ha, Ha, Ha, no not at all, don't be daft" said I! With that, he had a quick look at the luggage, then that was that! Lovely job.

My plan had been this; Get the bike through quarantine, then ride to the test centre and get the bike technically verified and insured. Then I could ride to 'Cyclone Motorcycles' and put her in for a quick service and set of tyres, before heading off South early the next day. Unfortunately the best laid plans don't usually follow suit. The computer system at 'Toll' is linked up to the customs system, meaning before they can release the bike, it must be processed by the main Australian customs system, and at the moment the computer said, 'No'!

All 3 of the bikes were stuck waiting for their status to switch over to 'cleared'. We all sat in the cabin, chatting about our adventures and where we were going next. One by one, the bikes were cleared and soon just little old me was left. As time ticked by I was getting more and more concerned I would miss the technical inspection, which shut at 5pm, and therefore be stuck in Darwin over the weekend until Monday! Eventually I got the nod that I was free to go at 4:45pm, so rapidly made my way to Goyder Road to the technical centre for the inspection.

Luckily enough, it didn't actually shut until 6pm, but by the time I'd had the inspection, filled out the forms and got my insurance in place, it was 6:10pm and I'd missed getting the bike in to Cyclone for the service.

Getting Your Bike Into Oz
Before I go on, let's detail exactly what's needed to get your bike into Oz, for the sake of those of you coming behind me:-
1. First thing I did was let Toll in Darwin know I'd arrived and that I was waiting for the bike. Give them your email and contact number, if you have one. Try to get a rough idea as to when the ship is arriving and when unloading is to take place. This can vary alarmingly from what you get told in Dili.
2. As soon as you arrive in Darwin you can go to customs house and get your carnet stamped, you don't need to wait for the bike to arrive. You'll need an address of where

you're staying, hotel, hostel, campsite or private address is fine. You'll also need your passport and the Bill of Loading you'd have been given when you shipped your bike. The address in Darwin is 21 Lindsay Street, it's about 5 mins taxi ride from Toll.

3. Contact DAFF (Department of Agriculture) to arrange the quarantine inspection and also to create the entry documents. You need to do the entry docs first in order to be given an entry number. Once you have this you can book the inspection, once you know when the bike will be unloaded that is. You can call them on +61 8 89207007 or I emailed a chap at garry.tucker@daff.gov.au (bear in mind that he may no longer work there, so best to call instead). The cost of this (quarantine inspection booking) was $145 for me at the time, paid over the phone by card, or cash at the DAFF offices at the airport.

4. Next is the actual quarantine inspection. It takes place at the Toll yard, just turn up nice and early and introduce yourself to the staff in the 'International' section of the Toll reception. They're lovely folk and do this all the time. For the actual inspection, bring boots or hard toed shoes, as 'Health & Safety' is now king here. Toll will issue you with a hard hat, high-vis and safety specs. You'll be taken to the quarantine yard where you'll meet the DAFF officer who will carry out the inspection. Stay calm, be polite, and all will be good – as long as you've cleaned your bike and kit! A word of warning, any kit that's on your bike will also be inspected, so if you've got a tent and/or sleeping bag, make sure you clean them out before shipping to Oz.

5. Once you pass the inspection, you then have to wait for the computer system to switch over to 'clear' then all you have to do is pay 'Toll' their fees for handling in Oz. It's about $150 a bike, on top of what you paid in Dili. You can then ride your bike to the technical inspection.

6. Technical Inspection: This is basically a quick MOT of the bike to make sure it's road worthy, so make sure your lights, brakes and horn work, your tyres are pumped up and have sufficient tread, and all should be fine. I had bald tyres and an indicator that didn't work, so strictly speaking they should have failed me. However I had the bike already booked in for a full service and new set of tyres at a local garage, so they were happy to let me go as long as I took it straight there. After the inspection, you just need to get your insurance, which is about $250 for 3 months, you can get as little as 1 months insurance though if you want. You'll also have to register the bike there too, so you'll need

photo ID, proof of where you're staying – such as a receipt from the hotel/hostel, and proof of ownership of the bike. I had the V5 logbook for the bike that is all in my name. Unfortunately it says across the front that this is not proof of ownership, but in the UK we don't have anything else? After some discussion, they accepted it. The place is on Goyder Road, you really can't miss it, open from 8am to 6pm Mon-Fri.

7. That's it, you're free to ride off into the Sunset. Now all you have to worry about are suicidal Roo's, wombats and Emu's! It's an awesome country to ride in, but take care in the bush as there is wildlife everywhere, and it's exactly that….. WILD!

So, once I'd jumped through the hoops, I found myself at 6:30pm on a Friday night with nowhere to stay in Darwin, possibly the most expensive town in Australia! I took a wee ride out to where I was getting the bike serviced, 'Cyclone Motorcycles', and as luck would have it there was a motel practically right next door. I rocked up to 'The Leprechaun Resort' and booked in for Fri/Sat nights, aiming to hit the road early Sunday. It was a cracking wee place with great staff, run by Scotty and his Mrs who were from the UK. I got chatting with Scotty and we had a great long natter about the trip, bikes and life in Oz. Incredibly he stunned me by offering my stay completely free of charge as a way of backing the trip! I was blown away by their generosity and can never thank them enough, absolutely beautiful people.

Early the next morning I dropped the Beast off at the doc's for her service and new boots. I'd had to buy a set of tyres as Bridgestone weren't willing to get a set organised there in Darwin, so a spanking new pair of BT-023s were waiting for me. On top of that she'd be getting a new chain and sprockets, new pads front and rear, and the standard oil and filter change, as well as cleaning out the K&N air filter. They were open to 3pm and were getting started on her right away, so I fully expected to be hitting the road the following morning.

Nope, I got a call about 12:30 to say that everything was done except the rear brake as the pin holding the caliper on was corroded in place. They wouldn't be able to complete the works until Monday, but as that was all that needed doing I could hit the road late morning, not a disaster. So I now had the weekend in Darwin, but I was out of town and without transport, so I just hung around the motel and got the rest of my admin underway. Monday morning came and I was all packed, eager to hit the road South and get as close to Brisbane as I could for Christmas Day – in 2 days time. Aah ignorance is bliss eh.

Come 11:30am I'd still had no word from the garage and was just away to call them when they beat me to it. Apparently they'd managed to free the caliper so now just had to fit the new rear pads, fit the new tyres, change the oil etc and we'd be ready to roll? Basically everything they'd said they'd done on Saturday morning! I was less than happy as they said it wouldn't be done until at least 3pm, yet another day wasted. So come 3:45pm I get a call to say she's ready so wander over to pick her up. I'm presented with the bill, $790 which to be fair is about what I was expecting as the tyres alone were $500. But to my horror the chap then said, "Oh no I've not included labour yet" and proceeded to present the new bill of $1,790!!! For a simple service, new pads and tyres? I was absolutely gobsmacked as this pretty much used up half of my entire budget for Oz!

Unable to really express my astonishment and concern, I just paid, got on the bike and left. My head was spinning, what the hell was I going to do now for cash for the rest of the trip?

21.2 - Day 229: Christmas Eve, out into the Bush

Eager to hit the road once more, I was on the road early doors. The rain had started to creep in the night before, and Scotty had warned that there were big storms forecast for the area. Not wanting to get stuck in Darwin any longer, I pointed the Beast's nose South along the Stuart Highway and gave it some lemons!

It's a long way to the first major turn off at 'Three Ways Roadhouse', about 650 miles to be exact. The roads are in great nick, especially compared to what I'd been riding of late, but they are painfully straight with only the slightest kink every 60-100km to keep you awake. The going was fairly swift if I'm honest, I only stopped for fuel and just grabbed a sarnie on the go for lunch. I rolled up to the Three Ways Roadhouse at about 6:30pm that night, just as they were starting to close up for Christmas, but they very kindly let me pitch my tent outback, and even let me use their showers, all free of charge. I was absolutely shattered and slept like a baby on the warm ground of the outback.

'Ho, Ho, Ho….' I was up and at'em bright and early Christmas Day morning, on the road by 7am and turning East along the Barkly Highway, Australia's own Route 66. I missed home more than ever today, thoughts of Nikki and my boy filling my head more than normal. I wondered what everyone would be doing, thinking of everyone sharing their gifts, enjoying their dinners and watching all the crap we get on the box. For me it was life on the road as usual, I couldn't complain, I was living the dream.

Like parts of Russia, petrol can be fairly scarce in the outback. Generally you have to be able to cover about 250 miles in between fuel stops, way outside my 160 mile maximum of the gixxer. To combat this I carry an additional 8 litres of fuel in two 'Rotopax' fuel containers, kindly provided by 'Kriega'. These are a great bit of kit and have saved my arse on more than one occasion. The first stop along the Barkly Highway from 'Three Ways', is the Barkly Homestead Roadhouse. Affectionately known as the most expensive station in Australia, it lives up to its rep charging almost $2.50 a litre. But what else do you do, they even have a sign up that kindly asks you to use the next services if you think they're too expensive, it's only another 180km down the road!

I'd met an Ozzy couple at the station who were also driving around Australia. They'd just driven right up the middle past Uluru and Alice Springs, and remarked on how little wildlife they'd seen compared to past trips. I too had only seen a few live cattle so far, everything else was just dead at the side of the road, victims of encounters with the numerous 'road trains' which rule these lands. It turns out that the government had recently conducted a wide scale cull of much of the wildlife in the bush. Numbers of kangaroos, wombats, horses, emus and the like had exploded in recent years, causing mayhem with traffic and crops. They'd removed over 12,000 wild horses alone from the outback, and who knows how many of the others. All I can say is that I saw very few wild roo's or likewise during my whole time in Oz.

By lunchtime I was in the mining town of Mt Isa, in the heart of the Australian outback. This place has a reputation as a wild town, the residents are cash rich due to the mining that caused the growth of the town, but it's remoteness and extreme weather seem to send some wild. Pulling into a service station to fill up, I grabbed a sandwich and bottle of 'Yazzoo' for my Crimbo dinner. Sitting on a bin outside in the shade of the sun, I watched life pass me by. The place seemed alive compared to the other ghost towns I'd ridden through the last few days. Campers, trucks and other bikes surrounded the station, all gathering provisions for their own voyages ahead.

After a brief stop I was back on the bike, heading East out of the town when I came across a sign for the hottest place in Australia. Apparently this place has the highest ever-recorded temperature of 53 degrees. The sign next to it showed a current temp of 51! I kept moving.

Riding in this kind of heat is an intense experience, especially in full leathers, full-face lid and aboard a Superbike. I've said it before but the only way I can explain it is like this. Imagine sitting in front of a hairdryer on full power, set at maximum heat. Now imagine doing that whilst sat in an oven, wearing full riding leathers. With the visor down the heat and humidity stifles your every breath, but with the visor up the dry heat cooks your eye balls. Pleasant it is not.

Fairly soon I was leaving the State of the Northern Territories and entering hostile territory for the biker, the State of Queensland. You may have heard that the State government has introduced what seem like draconian laws targeting all bikers. Well, they have and it's all because of the 'Bikies', organised underground bike gangs who had been causing havoc in Brisbane and other cities in the State. They run the drugs and underground world of the country, and had now moved into extortion and protection rackets in Brisbane and the Gold Coast. Rival gangs were trying to assert superiority and it'd escalated to running gun battles in the high street, mass violence and injury to passers by. The public called for something to be done, so the government acted. They'd rushed through a series of laws and legislation which now prevent everything from the wearing of 'prescribed colours or patches', to requiring written permission from the police if you want to ride in a group of three or more.

It sounds horrendous, and I must admit I was fully expecting a grilling from the local old bill as I rode through the State, but I wasn't stopped once, even when riding with other bikers. I actually got the chance to speak with a serving copper from Brisbane about this and he told me what I thought would be the case, they're not looking for your everyday normal biker. They're looking for the trouble makers, the one's who caused all this in the first place. That said, if you're riding like a tool or even a bit fast, they will come down on you like a ton of bricks here. Be warned.

Continuing on along the highway, I was running on fumes with the next petrol station still about 10km away. I limped the Beast there, thankfully arriving before the engine ran dry, but to my dismay the place seemed closed. I could see a table set up in the shop, complete with empty plates recently used for Christmas dinner. A young kid came flying around the corner on a brand new skateboard, eyes wide as he saw me on the forecourt. "MUMMMMMMmmmmmmmmm!"

Within a minute a lady came through the shop and opened up the door. After a brief chat, she said she'd switch the pumps on so I could try and get some fuel. The problem was, as they hadn't been used all day and it was extremely hot, it could take a long time for the pressure to build up and allow the fuel to actually reach the nozzle? True enough, the first couple of pumps we tried brought forth nothing, until we tried the last one and bingo, through it came. Happy days.

As I filled up, a huge rainstorm descended over us, practically flooding the roads instantly. It was an impressive thing to witness flash floods in action, but thankfully in this area at least, the road was high enough to escape. Huge parts of Australia lie on a flood plain, and due to the prolonged periods of extreme heat that bakes the ground solid, when it does rain, the ground acts as a huge catchment area where the water just gathers. Depths of water up to 2m can quickly be reached in areas that you'd never dream would flood.

Heading off into the setting sun I was just deliberating to myself whether I should risk riding into the night and try to reach the East coast by morning. Dawn, Dusk and night time are the most dangerous periods to ride in Oz. Animals frequent the roads at these times, attracted by the roadkill for food, or simply the warm surface to lie on through the night. I passed a layby and just caught sight of a mob of roo's who were heading straight for my path. As they jumped into the road I'd just managed to hit the brakes in time, and they bounced right in front of me, off into the scrub and away. These were the big Red buggers, not the wee grey ones you see feeding out of people's hand at the zoo. Some of these are almost 2m in height and can way over 400lbs, not something you want to connect with on a bike! Previously I'd sat behind a 'roadtrain' as we thundered along at 90mph into the dusk, my logic being that I'd use it as a blocker to any critters that chose to play chicken with us on the road. The only signal I got of an unsuccessful opponent was a 'bursting' 'squidgy' noise followed by a red cloud that completely covered me in what was left of old 'Skippy'! The leathers were kicking up more than ever now.

That pretty much answered my question for me, so I started looking for somewhere to camp up for the night, at which point I came across the outpost town of Richmond. That'll do me nicely, and that's where I lay my head for Christmas Day night 2013.

It's weird, I'd gone without any internet signal on my phone for only about 2 days, but lying in the outback that night, I felt incredibly alone. I just wanted to be able to message my boy, Nikki, family and friends and wish them Merry Christmas, just have a semblance of contact to home at this festive time. But it wasn't to be. Life is tough eh.

The next day I battered my way through the last of the outback before reaching the Bruce Highway, which runs from Cairns to Brisbane, just South of Townsville. I'd decided I would head as far South along the East coast as I could as I was due to meet an old friend in Noosa for a day or two. Firing along the road, I rode with my jacket wide open as the zip was buggered. Suddenly my chest was on fire as sting after sting worked it's way down, nestling on my comfy bouncing belly! Quickly I pulled over and partly stripped off to dislodge the offending item, a wee hard-bodied black beetle-type thing. No idea what it's called, whether it's venomous, or if I'm just a big girl. All I know is it hurt, a lot. I wanted some 'there there' juice, but was fresh out, so I grew a pair. As I was dancing around half naked at the side of the road, a car flew by with the horn tooting. At least I made someone's day eh!

As the early evening sun began to set I was heading for the idyllic wee coastal town of Airlie Beach. The road through the edge of the State Forest was a welcome diversion, full of twists and turns as it sped me out to Pioneer Bay. I'd booked a bed at the 'X-Base hostel' and as I booked in, I was greeted by, "Oh look, it's the naked biker!" Zoe and Sandra were two British lassies who were on a road trip down from Townsville to Brisbane for New Year. They'd been the one's who'd passed by in the car earlier, small world eh!

We were all in the same dorm, along with a Dutch lad called Daan, so hit the pub and had a great night. It was brilliant to socialise with folk from home, people with the same sense of humour and mindset. For a Dutchman, Daan held his own and was a cracking lad. Beers were sunk, stories told and laughs had. Thanks to you all for the great night, awesome times.

The next morning I was back on the road, heading South along the East coast. I eventually got to the beautiful holiday coastline town of Noosa, where I was to meet up with my old mate Finn and his family for a night or two. Finn's an old friend from my days on the door in Glasgow, he'd now emigrated over to Oz, married and had two cracking wee kids, Oonagh and Fearghus.

I'd met them the previous year in London after I got back from Africa, and they'd made me promise I'd come and see them when I got going again. So here I was, descending on their family Christmas! True to form, they wouldn't just let me stay one night and welcomed me into their family for two brilliant nights of relaxation and fun in this beautiful seaside town. We lounged by the pool, wandered along the beach and generally just chilled out. I loved it but had to tear myself away and get on with the trip.

21.3 - Day 235: The Glasshouse Mountains

My destination was the Glasshouse Mountains to meet Andy Reynolds, who'd been following on the trip facebook page. I headed on down to meet with Andy and his Mrs, Linda, as they took me for a great wee ride up through the mountains. Stopping for a brew in a beautiful café, we chatted about the trip and how they'd ended up out there, as both were Brit ex-pats.

It was great to meet them and hear their story. Continuing the ride we stopped off at a view point over the mountains, and they told me the Aboriginal 'Dream Time' story behind them.

- The Glasshouse Mountains, Dream Time

The mountains are of great historical and cultural significance, and are found just North of the town of Caboolture in Queensland. Captain Cook named them during his voyage up the East coast of Oz in 1770, with their names – Beerwah, Tibrogargan, Coonowrin, Tunbubudla, Beerburrum, Ngungun, Tibberoowuccum and Coochin – reflecting the Aboriginal culture surrounding them.

The legend behind the mountains goes like this:

"Now Tibrogargan was the father of all the tribes and Beerwah was his wife, and they had many children.

Coonowrin, the eldest; the twins, Tunbubudla; Miketeebumulgrai; Elimbah whose shoulders were bent because she carried many cares; the little one called Round because she was so fat and small; and the one called Wild Horse since he always strayed away from the others to paddle out to sea. (Ngungun, Beerburrum and Coochin do not seem to be mentioned in the legend).

One day when Tibrogargan was gazing out to sea, he perceived a great rising of the waters. He knew then that there was to be a very great flood and he became worried for

Bruce SMART

Beerwah, who had borne him many children and was again pregnant and would not be able to reach the safety of the mountains in the west without assistance.

So he called to his eldest son, Coonowrin, and told him of the flood which was coming and said, "Take your mother, Beerwah, to the safety of the mountains while I gather your brothers and sisters who are at play and I will bring them along."

When Tibrogargan looked back to see how Coonowrin was tending to his mother he was dismayed to see him running off alone. Now this was a spiritless thing for Coonowrin to do, and as he had shown himself to be a coward he was to be despised.

Tibrogargan became very angry and he picked up his nulla nulla and chased Coonowrin and cracked him over the head with a mighty blow with such force that it dislocated Coonowrin's neck, and he has never been able to straighten it since.

By and by, the floods subsided and, when the plains dried out the family was able to return to the place where they lived before. Then, when the other children saw Coonowrin they teased him and called "How did you get your wry neck – How did you get your wry neck?" and this made Coonowrin feel ashamed.

So Coonowrin went to Tibrogargan and asked for forgiveness, but the law of the tribe would not permit this. And he wept, for his son had disgraced him. Now the shame of this was very great and Tibrogargan's tears were many and, as they trickled down they formed a stream which wended its way to the sea.

So Coonowrin went then to his mother, Beerwah, but she also cried, and her tears became a stream and flowed away to the sea. Then, one by one, he went to his brothers and sisters, but they all cried at their brother's shame.

Then Tibrogargan called to Coonowrin and asked why he had deserted his mother and Coonowrin replied, "She is the biggest of us all and should be able to take care of herself." But Coonowrin did not know that his mother was again with child, which was the reason for her grossness. Then Tibrogargan put his son behind him and vowed he would never look at him again.

Even to this day Tibrogargan gazes far, far out to sea and never looks at Coonowrin. Coonowrin hangs his head in shame and cries, and his tears run off to the sea, and his mother, Beerwah, is still pregnant, for, you see, it takes many years to give birth to a mountain." (taken from www.coolrunning.com.au)

After a blat around the mountains, we headed back to Andy's place where I met his two young daughters, Kelly and Leah. I was made to feel right at home, the kindness and generosity shown to me was just amazing, I can never thank you guys enough.

As we were just up the road from Australia Zoo, I took a wee trip down and had a wander around. It's a great wee place, loads to see and plenty of interaction for the wee ones. I drew quite a crowd myself as I wandered around in the mid-30 degree heat in my scruffy white power ranger suit!

Afterwards Andy took me down the famous Ettamoogah Pub for a few jars, before we retired to his family home for a beautifully cooked roast and great company. It was a cracking night and I was made to feel like one of the family, awesome. Andy, Linda, Kelly & Leah, thank you very much for your kindness and warmth guys, you've really helped to make Oz a stage of the trip that'll stay with me forever.

The next morning, after fighting a life or death battle with the largest spider known to man, I was soon on my way in to Brisbane to meet back up with Finn and his family for New Years.

21.4 - 2014 Let's be 'avin ya!

After a quiet New Years Eve at Finn's place, he and Oonagh took me into Brisbane early on New Years Day for a whistle-stopped tour. Brisbane really is a beautiful city, it's got a great mix of new and old, definitely somewhere I'd like to come back to one day and

Bruce SMART

see more of.

By late morning I'd said my farewells to Finn, Rach, Ferg and Oonagh, and was back on the road South, heading for Byron Bay, the most Easterly point on the Australian mainland. It's a beautiful location, picturesque in every sense of the word. As I rode into town, people were everywhere, in the shops, sitting at café's, running or cycling along the street, carrying surf boards to and from the beach, generally just chilling and having a great time. This place just screams 'RELAX'. Following the road out to the lighthouse, I parked up the bike and began the walk out to the peninsula, once again drawing more than few inquisitive glances in my grubby white suit.

After the obligatory few snaps at the sign, I made my way back to the bike and hit the road once more, this time now heading West inland. Over the next day or so I followed the Gwydir Highway as it twisted and turned through valleys, along rivers, up into beautiful rainforest-like mountains, the views were superb and the roads a welcome surprise to the usual mundane Ozzy 'Roman like' rulers.

As the day progressed the surroundings became more and more barren. The mountains disappeared, the greens gave way to browns then yellows, the skies cleared from the grey and clouds, to beautiful blues. Someone turned the oven up as the temperatures soared.

By the end of the day I'd made my way to a town called Dubbo, the cross-roads of New South Wales. Originally set up as a sheep and cattle station, when the Gold rush of the 1870's hit, the town experienced a population growth and grew to the town it is today.

You may remember I met a Kiwi chap called Andrew Edwards way back in Russia? Andrew was riding around Russia on his way to London, our paths crossed in Irkutsk and we rode to Lake Baikal before going our separate ways. Andrew now lives in Sydney and we'd kept in touch. After a quick email, he'd arranged to meet me in Dubbo for a beer. I've got to admit I didn't realise this would mean him riding over 500kms, but for him it was a breeze.

We had a great night catching up, sharing stories of our adventures since we last met. Andrew kindly invited me to stay with him and his family when I reached Sydney and the next morning we once again went our separate ways.

Riding across the outback I was back in familiar territory, I'd grown to like the remoteness and rawness of it out there. It's an amazing place to experience, you're literally in the middle of nowhere at times, the only sign of human intervention is the road you're on. Occasionally you see a fence line appear alongside the road, leading to a gate. Faint tyre tracks lead off into nowhere, no other sign of life present. The fence line runs away alongside the road, then stops and you are alone once again. Magical.

Reaching Broken Hill on fumes once again, I found myself a motel for the night then took a wander through the town. A mining town from its inception, it really does have the feel of the Wild West to it, the streets and buildings straight out of a John Wayne film. Known as the 'Silver City' due to the silver ore mines it was founded on, it's also known as the capital of the outback. Just North of Broken Hill is Silverton, the location for the Mad Max films, amongst many others. It's also got the home of the Flying Doctor's service at its local airport. But for me, it was to be the home of a delicious Subway sandwich for my tea, then early to bed as I was cream crackered!

Setting off early again the next day, I was soon back in the solitude of the outback as I surged West, destination Adelaide. It was a fair ride, some 350 miles or so, but the going was great. The roads slowly began to develop a few kinks that almost resembled bends, which in turn gave way to twists then actual corners! I could also feel the temperature drop as I neared the coast, I almost felt cold for the first time since the very North of Norway!

Arriving in Adelaide I was to meet up with Adam Baird who'd been following on the facebook page. He'd very kindly offered me somewhere to stay when in town, so I took

Bruce SMART

him up on the offer. Arriving at their place, I met Adam, his beautiful wife Katherine, and their cracking wee lad Josh. What a great wee family they are, it was an absolute joy to spend time with them and they made me feel like a long lost friend. Thanks very much guys, it was a pleasure, I really mean that.

That evening Adam and I went for a quick pint down his local, parking the two bikes up across from the pub. Adam's got a beautiful KTM RC8R, what an incredible looking and sounding machine it is! It defo got me thinking about my next machine once I got home, as I felt like I was due a change after 5 GSX-R's.

The next morning it was freezing and wet. Well ok, it was 13 degrees, but considering I hadn't been in anything less than 25 for the last 6 months, this was a shock to the system! My suit has now shrunk to farcical levels, the sleeves practically come up to my elbows, the front zipper corroded in place so I can't do it up anymore. As a result, it was fairly well ventilated as I also had to ride with it wide open. But I grew a pair and ventured out for a quick squirt around Adelaide, with Adam leading the way.

Heading up to Mount Lofty, I got a quick view over the city, it's genetics plain to see. The Central Business District (CBD) of Adelaide is made up of a square mile where most of the financial and business sectors are located – much like the city of London. There are a few cafes to cater for the office workers there, but apart from that there's not much. This is why people visiting Adelaide often leave thinking there's not much to it, but the city was created to have lots of individual 'boroughs' all around the outside of the CBD. Each borough has it's own set of bars, cafes, shops etc, they are like small towns and this is where the real life of Adelaide is found. I loved the place, yet another to go back to and spend longer in.

We spent the afternoon over at the home of JD, one of Adam's mates from a biker forum he belongs to called, www.bikeme.tv It was a cracking afternoon, chatting with folks about the trip, about bikes, about Oz, about anything and everything really. Good times and yet another huge tick in the box for Oz, the people really are top notch.

21.5 - Day 242: Adelaide to Port Fairy

After yet another great night of conversation and food with Adam and Katherine, it was time to hit the road once again. Wee Josh wanted to join us on his own wee Beast, it even has it's own bike mat, but he'll have to wait a few years yet. Adam was to join me for the first section of the trip, as far as Meningie Bakery, near the Coorong. We started off the morning with a quick tour of Adelaide with JD, before he and I set off South. After a few hours we'd reached the wee town of Meningie, which sits on the South East bank of Lake Albert. It also houses an awesome bakery that serves the greatest iced buns known to man. Adam also introduced me to my new downfall, Farmers Union Iced Coffee, my own personal crack!

After Adam turned around and headed home, I continued on South, my destination for the evening to be the town of Port Fairy in Victoria, right near the start of the Great Ocean Road. Along the way I saw something I never expected to see, a 50ft giant lobster/prawn thing at the side of the road? The Aussies fair love their big models!

I also had an interaction with another of Victoria's predators that evening, the plod. I was merrily making my way along, about 10 minutes from my final destination, when a highway patrol car came over the crest of the road in front of me. As we were going head on I took my time rolling off the throttle as I was under the impression they'd need to be behind in order for the radar to clock your speed. Nope, wrong on that one. Straight away they lit up the lights and did a U-turn behind me. By now I'd come off the juice and was meandering along at a sedate 100km/h, the limit for most roads in the State. They quickly pulled me over and without hesitation, the officer told me he'd got me on their onboard radar doing significantly more than the allowed speed. There was nothing I could say to this chap, so I just accepted my fate and waited. It was bollock freezing at the side of the road. The wind off the ocean was ripping through me as I stood at the roadside, my body now shivering uncontrollably. To give the bloke his due, he asked loads of questions about the bike, where I'd come from and where I was going. When I told him about the trip he seemed genuinely interested and spent time asking all about it. He disappeared for a short time, but when he came back he knocked me for six.

The speed they'd got me at meant I should loose the bike, as well as my licence, in the State of Victoria. It'd also be an incredibly high fine, one I couldn't afford to pay even if I blew the whole budget! They really are Victorian on speeding in Victoria, personally I think it's ridiculous. However, this guy was top class. Let's just say he did me the biggest favour he possibly could, and we'll leave it at that. I owe you one Mr Policeman Sir, thank you. I didn't even have to mention what I do for a living either.

Lesson learned, I continued on far more sedately for the rest of the trip, it just wasn't worth it. Arriving in Port Fairy I found a place to stay for the night and crashed out.

21.6 - Day 243: The Great Ocean Road

What can be said about this road that hasn't already been said? Never has a title been more apt than here, it truly is superb. The actual ride is nothing special, the speed limit is fairly low and the traffic crowded in parts, but it's what goes with it that makes the difference. The scenery all around you is awe-inspiring, breathtaking, spectacular, you name it, it is.

Heading East from Port Fairy I wondered what all the fuss was about, it just seemed like a road through some fields to me? But all of a sudden you break through to the coast and bang, straight away the majestic, yet powerful South Australian coastline captures your heart. The bays created by a meandering coastline draw you in, viewpoints seemingly every few hundred metres compel you to stop and admire. It is an incredible experience to witness, and an even more incredible feeling to actually ride along its length. The pinnacle has to be the famous 12 Apostles, now reduced to about 3, yet still a spectacular vision. Normally I spend a max of maybe half an hour at places, constantly wanting to get back on the Beast and get back to the road. But here I found myself captured by the natural beauty of the place, it just grabs you in, everywhere you look you see something else that takes hold of you. As the tides and light levels change, so too does the view, like a natural cinematic show, you just sit back and watch. Simply beautiful.

Carrying on along the GOR, I made my way to Queenscliff to catch the ferry over

Port Phillip Bay to Sorrento on the Mornington Peninsula. There I was to meet Mick Donoghue, another chap who'd been following on facebook and had very kindly offered me a place to stay whilst in Melbourne.

Mick is a fellow copper and works in Victoria, with his beautiful Mrs, Amber. They have a place in the cracking wee seaside town of Dromana, a beautiful place about an hour from the city of Melbourne, and an hour from the Philip Island circuit. Perfect.

Word must have gotten around about me, as no sooner had I arrived than a beer was in my hand and we were making plans for the pub. I LOVE Oz! We had a top night getting to know each other, Mick and Amber are great folks and a real pleasure to be around. The next day Mick was feeling a tad under the weather, I think it was 'man-flu', so he took the day off work and we headed out on the bikes to try and blow the germs away. It seemed to work.

After some sightseeing on the way to the circuit and a spot of luncheon in Cowes, I'd received a call from the PR staff at Philip Island. I'd emailed them earlier to say I'd be coming along and asked if there was any chance of a pic at the track. Low and behold if they didn't just offer me a guided tour of the place and a drive around the outside of the circuit! Don't mind if I do!

Philip Island has a completely different feel to it than any of the other motoGP circuits I've been to around the world. It has a real homely vibe, almost like our BSB circuits in Blighty, you don't get the sensation of being kept away like so many of the bigger tracks these days. In fact, in every race apart from motoGP, you can actually ride your bike right up to the track fence line, even during race time!

Once at the reception, a chap from the PR team met us and took both Mick and I out onto the famous circuit. He even let me take the Beast onto the hallowed starting grid where I got some pics done under the big old 'Melbourne' sign. I was in my element, beaming from ear to ear. I can't thank the PR staff at Phillip Island Circuit enough for their help and welcome. They are the only track to even acknowledge my enquiry to visit their circuit as I travelled the globe, let alone actually meet me and show me around. What a difference it made, thank you very much.

The 'Nobbies' were next, not what you're thinking, but a natural rocky outcrop right out on the tip of Phillip Island. There's a cracking viewpoint out here that attracts the crowds. Whilst stopped to get some pics, we got chatting with loads of people who enquired about my number plate and what I was doing. It was great to see their faces light up when Mick told them about the trip, and to hear their stories of travels.

Out past the 'Nobbies' lies 'Seal Island', no prizes for guessing why. I remarked that there must be some Great Whites around then and was told that the bay right before my eyes, the one where people were merrily waterskiing and riding their boats over, was the foremost breeding ground for Great Whites in the world. These Aussies are simply insane. I took a step back from the water and I was about 800ft above it!

To finish the day off, Mick took me for a spin around the Mornington Peninsula after a quick drink in the sun. It really is a beautiful place to live, I refuse to believe anyone can get stressed out here, unless of course there's a saltie or shark chewing your arse off. After another top night's hospitality with Mick and Amber, I said my farewells and made my way to the centre of Melbourne were I found a bed in one of the hostels.

I'd met up during the day with another chap who's following on facebook, Craig Stratford. Craig, his Mrs Elsie and mate Ian, all very kindly met up with me in the city for a beer and a bite to eat. It was a pleasure to meet you guys, thanks very much for taking the time to meet up, and thanks also for your incredible support. It really has blown me away how the trip caught the imagination of so many, and how people readily extend their hand of friendship to a complete stranger in a foreign land. Talk about 'Pay it forward', I've a credit line as long as the M6!

Whilst in Melbourne I'd also arranged to meet up with an old friend of mine from my school days. I'd grown up with Ronan Pringle since primary one, we'd gone to the same secondary school together, been in many of the same classes, played rugby together and socialised together. He came to my 21st birthday in Glasgow, and the next day he emigrated to Oz. I hadn't seen him since.

So 16 years later, we were standing in a boozer in Melbourne taking the piss just like when at school. Friendships are funny things, you don't see each other for years, sometimes decades, but it's just like you'd been down the pub last weekend when you meet up. If you're reading this Ronan, it was magic to see you again my friend, and a pleasure to meet your gorgeous wife (no idea how he did that?) and her family. Let's make sure it's not another 16 years before we do it again bud.

Hitting the road once more the following morning, I had to stop off at 'Ramsay Street' for the obligatory photo. Unfortunately Charlene, Bronwyn, Jane or Holly Valance weren't in, so I settled for a pic of one of their houses and headed North East.

I was due to meet up with some more lads who were following on facebook at a place called Bright, in the Snowy Mountains. I'd been told the roads around here were incredible on the bike, so was looking forward to trying them out. Meeting up with Shane, Frank and Mark they took me for a fantastic 6hr blat through some of the greatest roads I've ever ridden. I'm afraid they completely spanked me and left me for dead. Even without my excuse of a buckled front wheel, I think I'd have struggled to keep hold of these lads, they were proper rapid! Back home I'd always been one of the fastest amongst my group, felt completely at home on my bike and in full control. For some reason since that crash in Japan, I seemed to be filled with indecision on a bike, continually feeling like I was going to fall off, that the front wheel was just going to let go and slide us down the road. I had no confidence in her any more and it was killing it for me when the pace heated up and the twists introduced themselves to the ride.

Turn your thoughts back to Russia and you'll have heard me talk about Phil Krixx and Carlos. They were the lads I met in the hostel in Vladivostok whilst waiting for the ferry to Korea. Phil is the one with the ZZTop beard and lives in Canberra, so this was to be my next stop off on the way to Sydney. I arrived fairly late at night due to the incredible day in the saddle with Shane and the lads around the Snowy Mountains. Phil greeted me like family and before long, we were tucking into some beers and great scran. He's quite the wee housewife is Phil, a cracking cook, one of his many hidden talents.

The next day he took me for a whistle stop tour of Canberra, seeing the sights of this capital city. The whole place is completely engineered and designed by Walter Burley Griffin, who came up with his winning design in 1911. Built to prevent a 'civil war' between Melbourne and Sydney for 'Capital' status, Canberra is plonked literally in the middle of nowhere, in some of the driest land in Oz. Despite that, it's got a good feel to the place and is probably one of the least crowded cities I've ever been to.

The highlight of Canberra for me was the Australian War Museum, with its incredible exhibits on show giving the Imperial War Museum a run for its money. They've got the actual uniform worn by the infamous 'Red Baron' during WWI, including one of the very boots he wore when he was shot down. They've also got one of the most famous Lancaster bombers still in existence, G for George. It survived over 90 missions into enemy territory earning her crew the right to retire from front line service. I love to read about the amazing acts of selfless bravery our troops have undertaken. I don't know about you, but it really makes me appreciate the life I've got, and make the most of it whilst I can.

After another cracking home cooked meal by Phil, washed down with several more beers, I was soon saying farewell the next morning as I rode East to the coast at Bateman's Bay. This is a beautiful wee coastal town and I sat here for a half hour or so just watching the world pass me by in the sun. Wherever I am, I love to just sit and people watch for a bit. Seeing people all over the world just getting on with life, kind of connected me back to home as I thought of all my friends and family getting on with theirs whilst I was away on this trip. It's fairly unreal, here I was waltzing around the world on this great adventure, yet what I experienced is just everyday life for the people of that town, that country or continent! I wonder if those visiting Blighty on their trip get the same sense of wonder and excitement when they visit Peterhead, Birimingham or the like? Mind you, I get a sense of wonder when I visit Peterhead myself… a sense of, I wonder what the hell am I doing back here! (Sorry Peterhead)

I followed the Princess Highway North, before turning onto Grand Pacific Drive, which took me over the famous Sea Cliff Bridge. This is a glorious bit of engineering that whisks you out over the sea as you follow the contours of the rock face along the coast. It's only short, but I can say now that I've done it!

Soon enough I'd reached 'Bald Hill Lookout', a popular spot for bikers, hang gliders and tourist's alike. With its high altitude view point, it's the perfect place for hang gliders to launch off over the ocean below, soaring on the many thermals that abound the area. A local legend is Lawrence Hargrave, the father of suspended flight. Way back on the 12th November 1894, he lifted himself off Stanwell Park Beach, overlooked by 'Bald Hill Lookout', by suspending himself under four box kites! He also pioneered the world of aerofoils, noticing the effect a thicker leading edge had on the lift produced, thereby leading the way to today's aeroplane wings. It's a real shame as his work at the time just wasn't fully understood or noticed, so many that came after him, developed his work and took the credit.

Anyway, from here I rode through the Royal National Park, along it's beautifully twisted and forest lined roads, before popping out in the suburbs of Sydney! I couldn't believe that within minutes of one of the greatest cities on earth, you have a national park with such awesome roads. Yet another reason to move to this incredible country.

21.7 - Sydney

My plan for Sydney was fairly simple. A chap called Ferghal Donohoe had been in touch through the facebook page, and offered me a place to stay for a few days. With so many friends, new and old, all wanting to meet up in Sydney, it was going to be a hectic few days. I'd planned a couple of days with Ferghal, then a quick move North to Andrew Edwards place, where he was going to help me get the Beast crated and off to the shipping agents ready for Chile.

Bruce SMART

Keeping the theme alive, Ferghal literally had a beer in hand as I rolled onto his drive, and gave me a welcome akin to family. In an instant it felt like I'd known him and his family for years, the warmth of the Irish is a beautiful thing, and Ferg continues to keep in touch to this day, becoming a real good friend. Mate if you're reading this, you're a true legend and gentleman.

Over the next few days Ferghal introduced me to a mate of his Mike Harrison, another Aussie who was also following the trip. Between the two of them, I was made to feel like family and an old friend. Mike even took me for a tour of Botany Bay in his boat, where Captain Cook first landed back on the 29th April 1770.

We had a cracking day there before I had to belt off to be interviewed on a local radio station called www.rierageradio.com. Rob Milton, Tim Graham and Phil Harlum were a great bunch of lads who took a real interest in the trip, spending the entire show chatting about our stories and love of biking. A huge thanks to Ferghal and Mike for organising that, I owe you one big time lads.

On my last day with Ferghal, Cloudagh and his wee lad Riley, they took me up into town, early doors, to get some pics in front of the Opera House and Harbour Bridge. They did an incredible job with their site recommendations I think you'll agree, it's a truly beautiful place, thanks so much guys.

It was soon time to bid farewell and head North to Dee Why and Andrew Edwards place. Once again beer was waiting, and Andrew and his wife Susan made me feel right at home once more. It's amazing to think on this journey that I've met so many genuinely incredible people, who have all gone out of their way to make a complete stranger feel like one of the family. It's a humbling thing to experience and it has changed me for sure. I hope the new me manages to shine through and stay the distance now I'm back in the normality of life back home. It's all too easy to fall back into your old ways and your old way of thinking, but I'm fighting it each and every day.

Over the next few days Andrew and I got the Beast all crated up on the back of his truck, then dropped her off at the export yard, ready to be flown to Chile behind me.

For those interested, here are the details for this shipping leg:
I used 'Ship My Bike' (shipmybike.com.au) as the agents in Oz. The contact there is:
Josh Mikkelsen,
Email: josh@shipmybike.com.au
Tel: 0409 897 774

Drop Josh an email to tell him what you're after and he'll take care of the rest. A real gent to deal with, he makes the whole process incredibly painless. I still can't believe how easy it was to ship the bike, absolutely nothing went wrong? Completely unheard of normally in my experience!

It's not cheap, but then you are transporting your bike halfway around the world. The rates for air and sea are as follows, correct as of Jan 2014:

By sea, Sydney to Santiago:
Seafreight: AUD $1650 / bike assuming 3-4 cubic metres
Docs, handling and agency: $265
Pick up (metro area): $220 + GST
Approx 60-62 days transit time – plus 2-3 days each side for packing/unpacking etc
Custom crating: $800 + GST (unless you can source your own crate)
Insurance for total loss: approx. $350, dependant on value of goods
Weekly sailings

By air, Sydney to Santiago:
Airfrieght: AUD $13.40/Kg
Dangerous Goods fees, prep & certification: AUD $295
Flight daily

Bruce SMART

Although initially it looks like Sea freight is the cheaper option, once you take into account the cost of living for over 2months whilst you wait for your bike, together with the added 'costs' that are inevitable at sea ports, it's actually often cheaper to just fly. So that's what I did.

All crated the bike was 282kgs, meaning the final cost all in to get the bike on a plane and out of Oz was around £2,900. It flew on the Tuesday after I left, and due to the wonders of the international date line, arrived one hour earlier than it left? It then took a day to get unloaded, taken to the holding warehouse and processed, before the Qantas agents in Santiago were ready for me to collect her.

But back to Sydney:

After dropping the Beast off at the yard, I set about finishing the Indonesian Vid, episode 12, and getting it uploaded. I'd been finding it increasingly hard to keep up with the work load of late. Mostly it was my own fault, I'd leave the blogs until the end of each country or section, same with the vids, meaning I ended up with a huge workload at the end of most months. On top of that there was the Fast Bikes articles, as well as an increasing number of interested press who all wanted features on the project. Unfortunately there was no financial reward in any of it, but it all helped to get the word out, which in turn increased the prospect of charity donations and trip subsidiaries.

My last few days in Oz were spent with Andrew and Susan Edwards at their beautiful home in Dee Why. I'd arranged for a wee social gathering at 'The Lord Nelson' pub in downtown Sydney, where friends old and new could meet up for a jar and a natter. After catching the Manly Ferry into town, I'm more convinced than ever that nobody can possibly ever get stressed in Oz. Makes my daily commute to work seem like the journey to hell!

It was a cracking turn out with friends of old, Duncan Blackhall, Ian Blaiklock and Kieron Whitfield turning up (there was beer involved so that's a given), as well as new friends Katherine, Colin, Barry, Gillian, Ferghal, Mike, Andrew and Susan. A top night was had by all and a great way to bid farewell to this beautiful country.

I flew the next morning from Sydney to Santiago, but not before a quick tour of the beautiful surrounding areas like, Pittwater, Palm Beach (Home & Away Territory), Whale Beach, and Bigola Beach.

Andrew left me thoroughly depressed at the prospect of living back in London (friends & family excepted of course). Life in Australia strikes me as filling you with the mindset of 'anything is possible with hard work'. Yes it's expensive to live there, but there is loads of work, and if you're prepared to put the graft in, the rewards are there. People in Australia seem to have the right balance of life and work. They work to live their lives the way they want to live them. Not living to work as so many of us seem to do in the UK.

I've got to say another huge thank you to Andrew & Susan Edwards for their kindness and friendship. Thank you for sharing your home and for making me feel so welcome. It was great to see you guys again when you stopped over in Blighty after I got back too. I look forward to seeing you guys again one day soon.

It had been emotional folks, I absolutely loved Oz, but now it was time to go. A huge thank you to everyone who made this stage of the trip so special, thanks for taking the time to meet up, thanks for opening up your homes to me, and thanks for the support. It really does mean the world.

Next stop, South America.

CHAPTER 22
SOUTH AMERICA

Day 254 – Arrival in Santiago, Chile

Thanks to the wonders of international travel, I arrived in Santiago an hour before I left Sydney? Clearing immigration and customs was a synch, I was soon reunited with my baggage. As is my routine now, I quickly set about looking for somewhere to buy a pre-paid SIM card for my phone so I could keep you folks up-to-date with my travels. If I'm going to be in a country for more than a week, I like to have a local SIM card so I can access the t'interweb on the road. Wifi is all well and good, but when you really need the web, I've found it can be hard to find a Wifi signal. Once you get the local SIM, Wifi is everywhere. Sod's law.

Once again there was nowhere in the airport to get a SIM, so I went to the ATM to arm myself with the local currency, the Chilean Peso (about 930 pesos to the £1). It wouldn't take my card, bugger. Thankfully I still had some Ozzy dollars so got these changed and grabbed a taxi to the hostel I'd pre-booked, Santiago Backpackers (www.santiagobackpackers.com) Arriving in Santiago was weird as I was once again the odd one out. Having spent the best part of 6 weeks in Oz, where everything was strangely familiar yet new, I was once again in unchartered territory for me. The main language throughout the South & Central America's is Spanish, and my sum total amounts to "Dos cerveza por favor". But as ever, you get by and the local people take great delight in hearing my bungled 'Spanglish' attempts.

The hostel was a great place to base myself in the middle of the city for a few days. Fellow travellers surround you, from all over the world, and usually they speak English so the odd conversation is very welcome. The Beast wouldn't be ready to pick up until Monday so I had the weekend to chill, work on the next blog/vid and Fastbikes article, as well as fit in a wee bit of sightseeing around the city. I found that most major capital cities have a 'Free Walking Tour' available, and Santiago was no different.

Meeting up with the guide early Sunday morning, imagine my surprise when he turned out to be a Scottish lad called 'Johnny'. Not only that, but he also came from a wee village down the coast from where I grew up! It is indeed a small world folks. As we waited for the rest of the group to arrive, an elderly American couple approached the guide and enquired as to why there were so many police officers around the main square where we were standing. The poor old dear looked terrified so Johnny did his best to reassure her, saying that in all his travels, Santiago was by far the safest place he had ever been. Content and happy, the old girl returned to the sanctuary of her husband's arms and the two of them gazed at the beautiful sights around us.

Right at this point a local pisshead arrived and started hanging off Johnny and a few others, merrily trying to get pictures taken of himself and his unwilling new friends. Johnny did his best to humour the chap and get him away from everyone, but he was a determined lad. Eventually one of the group, who it turned out was a South African copper, had enough and pushed the guy away as he made a drunken lunge towards him. With that, our merry guest produced a flick knife and started waving it about like he was D'Artagnan from the Three Musketeers! Thankfully he was too drunk to know what was going on around him so the Springbok and myself easily 'disarmed' him and he had a nice wee sleep for the rest of the day.

I'll never forget the look of abstract terror on the faces of the old American couple, that was the last we saw of them! With the excitement over and done with we got on with the tour around the city. Santiago is a beautiful place, a real mix of the historical and new, intertwined in an emerging and vibrant cosmopolitan city. There is now a heavy influence on the arts and culture, the various universities providing an energetic and young audience to the bustling restaurant and café scene that is rapidly growing throughout the centre. Despite me not speaking any Spanish, the people I met were all too willing to try and talk, a mixture of their limited English, my 'Spanglish' and the wonders of international sing/shout language. We got by.

22.1 - Shipping

After 6 days in the city, the Beast was finally ready to be picked up. The shipping agents were great, a huge help and made the whole process flow by. Arriving at 1pm, I was on the bike and riding out by 4pm, heading out the city on the famous Pan American Highway.

The Qantas agents in Chile are:
Amsaero
www.amsaero.cl
Email: import-export@amsaero.cl

They were brilliant, they spoke enough English for us to get by, although I ended up asking one of the girls in the hostel I was staying at in Santiago, to translate for me. I met their agent at the International customs depot at the airport, and he walked me through everything that had to be done. All in all it cost me about £90 to get the bike through Chilean customs, all above board with receipts. I didn't even need to tip the agent, I offered but he refused, stating it's all part of the service!

22.2 - Hitting the Pan American Highway

The 'Pan-American Highway' is a series of roads that connect the very Southern tip of the American continent, Tierra Del Fuego in Chile, to Deadhorse at the very top of Alaska. I'd basically planned to follow this route all the way from Santiago up through South America and Central America, to Mexico City where I'd then head North to Texas via Montgomerey.

Heading up through Chile, the landscape is rugged as you skirt the Andes to the East, the Pacific Ocean to your South & West, and the Atacama Desert to the North. No wonder the Chilean people actually call themselves islanders. Within hours I was bang in the desert and the fuel stops became scarce. I'd been told that the max distance between fuel stops was about 260km in South America so didn't bother filling up my jerry cans. Nope. Wrong. I hit 286km before the engine ground to a halt and I was dry. In the middle of the Atacama Desert, the driest place on the planet where there are parts it has NEVER rained. In a strange land, with a language I couldn't speak. How hard could it be?

Luckily the Teapot God's were smiling once more. I'd started to walk along the road, leaving the Beast unaccompanied, with my two jerry cans in hand. I'd no other option, the land is fairly hilly around there so there was no way I could push the bike. It was baking hot, and within minutes of stopping, I was drowning in my leathers. The Garmin SatNav had said there was a gas station about 15 miles further along the road, so I figured I'd just have to walk there and hope someone stopped along the way to give me a ride.

The first few trucks and buses didn't even alter their course as I tried to flag them down, I swear they aim for you out here! Thankfully a mother and daughter pulled up in their Chelsea tractor to see if I was ok, and the young daughter spoke English. Happy Days. Unfortunately they were going the other way and told me the next petrol station was about 50km's away. My heart sank. At that point a truck came the other direction and thankfully stopped, as I stood in the middle of the road – 'Thou Shalt Not Pass' style. The daughter then translated for me to the driver, who kindly offered to give me a run to the petrol station, and what's more he would even run me back again as he was very worried about leaving the bike, and wanted to make sure I realised it probably wouldn't be there when we got back! I'd no other option so we hit the road. Thankfully the gas station was only about 5km down the road, so I was soon back with the Beast, and we were once again on our way North. Yet again the kindness and generosity of complete strangers saves the day.

By day 261 I was reaching the northern reaches of Chile. Protruding out the Atacama Desert, just off 'Route 5 the Pan Americana Norte' near the city of Antofagasta, you come across a peculiar sight. An 11m tall 'hand' sticks straight out the sandy floor, unlike anything I've ever seen before. Your eye is drawn to the sculpture as soon as it appears on the horizon, you just can't miss it. Built by Chilean sculptor Mario Irarrázabal back in 1992, the 'Mano Del Desierto' is a real 'must-do' for anyone traveling by, so I had to get a few pics before heading to the border with Peru.

It's a real 'must-do' in these parts and makes a great pic for the album. Unfortunately what you don't get told is that it's festooned in graffiti and used as a toilet by many who visit!

I arrived in the town of Arica, right near the border with Peru, late at night and found 'Hostelling International Doña Ines' where I got a bed for a couple of nights. This place had a great review on 'Hostel World' and it didn't disappoint. The owner Roberto is a brilliant character who makes you feel like one of the family as soon as you arrive. It's a real party house where anything and everything is possible, I thoroughly recommend it if you're in town.

Crossing over into Peru was easy, it cost nothing and was nice and straightforward. Border crossings in Southern America are great, they follow the standard process like every other border in the world where you go through passport control and then customs for the bike. The staff are friendly, everything appears official and not underhand in any way. Oh how it changes when you get to Central America, but more of that later.

22.3 - Peru

My plan for Peru had been to head to the town of Cusco so I could visit Machu Pichu, but unfortunately the tyre Gods had other ideas. I'd tried to get a fresh set of Bridgestone T30's when I left Oz, but as was becoming clear now, Bridgestone were doing absolutely nothing to help anymore, so this wasn't arranged. I've made a very good friend out of my contact with them, Steve has been nothing but supportive and a great mate since we met many moons ago, but Bridgestone themselves just didn't seem interested in the trip any more. It was such a waste as their tyres were stunning and, had they promoted it properly, they could have had unbeatable promo material if they'd bothered to use it. But that's by the by now.

The set I'd got in Darwin had done over 10,000Km around Australia and I was hoping the rear would last until I got to the Peru capital, Lima, but as I crossed the Peru border the rear was going off big time. The high temperatures and continuously straight roads were hammering the centre of the tyre after over 14,000Km's.

As I climbed into the Andes, on the way to Lake Titicaca, the road became just a dirt track, in fact it was more of a goat path. As I rode along the stones and sand, the breathtaking scenery enveloped as far as the eye could see. Mountains soared ahead, rich greenery swamped the low-lying land and I wondered how far this 'road' would be like this. I'd done a few km's by the time I had to make the decision to turn back, I just couldn't risk the rear tearing on the jagged rocks and me getting stranded out there in the middle of nowhere.

So I retraced my steps, along a fantastic stretch of road, the Highway 36 that leads North from the city of Tacna in Peru. It really is a great road, just a shame it's all the way out here!

Rejoining the Pan American I'd planned to ride to Cusco along the main highways, visit Machu Pichu and head to Lima to get a new tyre – hopefully. Unfortunately this didn't quite work out as the rear was going off really quickly and I doubted I'd be able to ride the 750 miles to Cusco, then the 500 miles to Lima. Reluctantly I made the decision to head straight to Lima, missing out Machu Pichu. I was gutted but I'll just have to go back at some point in the future, another one to add to the list of places I've missed or want to go back to. It took me a few days to reach Lima and I spent a few nights camping out in the desert again, the desert night skies are a truly amazing sight to behold.

Being in the middle of nowhere, hundreds of miles from any city or built up area, there's no light pollution and the sky comes alive. I've never seen the sky so alive since growing up in the North East of Scotland. I tried to take some pics but they just didn't come out, I really need to learn how to use a camera properly! To give you some idea of what the night sky is like down there, check out this incredible video on Vimeo – 'Ancients from Nicholas Buer'.

Reaching Lima I managed to find a sportsbike shop that had a new rear tyre in my size, so picked it up and found a local garage that could fit it to the rim. Job done.

Fresh boot on the rear, I was soon crossing into Ecuador on arguably one of the best roads I've ridden yet. Highway 35 leads from the border crossing with Peru in the South, all the way to the capital, Quito in the North. It is absolutely superb, pristine new tarmac, laid along the twistiest mountainous course, set amongst sheer stunning scenery. It reminded me a lot of Northern Spain or South East France. Truly superbly epic. Yep, THAT good.

The crap fuel in South America was taking it's toll on the Beast, her power was way down, at times she even felt like she'd stall at low revs. I stopped by 'Freedom Ecuador Bike Rental' in Quito as the owner had been in touch via the facebook page. They very kindly put me on to their mechanic, Diego, who worked his magic on the Beast and soon had her ship-shape once more.

22.4 – Columbia

I soon crossed in to Columbia, at arguably the easiest and most straight forward border crossing I'd encountered in South America. I must confess, I was expecting hassles at the Columbian border, but once again the media hype is exactly that. I can safely say that Columbia had by far the friendliest and most easy going people I'd encountered in South America. The first question I'd get asked all through Chile, Peru and Ecuador was, 'How much is the bike worth, how much money do you make to afford that'. It reminded me of Africa, without the threat of guns, and I must confess put me on guard a tad at times. But in Columbia, people would greet me with a smile, instead taking an interest in how I arrived in their country and where I was going. I even got proposed to at a petrol station by one of the female attendants! She was absolutely stunning, looking more like a Benny Hill 'secretary' than a fuel pump attendant in a micro short skirt and too-tight top. Shell, Esso, BP et al – take note!

There's a section of jungle between Columbia and Panama called the 'Darien Gap', with no roads linking the two. Attempts have been made in the past to build a road through the jungle, but the drug baron's who use the paths to smuggle their goods, soon put paid to all that. Or that's the story that's told at least.

So for now you have two options, air or sea. I soon arrived in Bogota where I was to fly the Beast across the Darien Gap, and once again David Wyborn of 'James Cargo' provided me with the contact info of a great shipping agent in Bogota.

22.5 - Columbia to Panama Shipping

I used the following at 'LynCargo.com'

Contact: Veronica Mosquera
Email: veronicam@lyncargo.com
Cost: £650 (not including fee's at Panama end)

Arriving at their offices in Bogota, I was escorted to the airport freight terminal by one of their agents and he walked me through the whole process. It took about 3 hours in total, the majority of the time is spent waiting for the various police and military checks of your bike and kit. On the face of it, they appear to take a fairly hardline approach to drugs smuggling here, it was probably the most stringent custom's check I'd had yet on the trip. Everybody (staff and guests) are bodily searched each and every time they enter or leave the freight warehouse area, bags are x-rayed and cameras scan your every move. It was also the most relaxed way of shipping the bike, in that it didn't need to be crated, or even empty of fuel. You simply ride the bike to the warehouse and disconnect the battery. They pop it onto a skid and it's wrapped in plastic wrap right where it stands. The wrapping is supposed to make it 'sterile' after the customs check, but the wrapping only goes about halfway down the bike, leaving it completely accessible from underneath? I didn't argue and all was well.

22.6 - Panama, Day 276

1 ½ hours after taking off from Bogota, I was landing in Panama City, and straight into little America. Subways, Burger Kings, all the familiar sights were here, and I indulged. I had to wait over the weekend as the bike wouldn't be ready for collection until Monday morning, so spent it in a great wee hostel bang in the middle of the city. It gave me a day to try and catch up on some 'work' as I was way behind as usual. As is customary in hostel life, beer was involved and I met some magic people from all over the world. It would've been great to stay a bit longer and explore the city with some of the folks at the hostel, but I just wanted to get on and get through Central America now. I was fatigued, really fatigued with life on the road now. I just wanted to be somewhere I could recognise, talk with people in my own tongue and feel secure and at home.

Monday morning arrived and I was soon at the freight depot of the airport, going through the standard process to get the Beast cleared and into Panama. It's fairly straight forward, but it'd certainly help to speak Spanish. As it was, I muddled my way through it all and was soon heading back to the hostel aboard my steed.

STATES
MEXICO
MEXICO
UNITED STATES
CUBA
HAITI
BELIZE JAMAICA
GUATEMALA
EL HONDURAS
SALVADOR NICARAGUA
COSTA RICA
PANAMA
COLOMBIA
COLOMBIA
ECUADOR
PERU

CHAPTER 23
CENTRAL AMERICA

I must admit, I was a bit apprehensive about a few stages of the forthcoming trip, mainly El Salvador and Mexico to be honest. I'd heard some real horror stories about these places, and the media is always full of the carnage being inflicted in parts of Mexico by the cartels. But as ever, I'm more than aware that what is reported via the media is purely what they, or others, want you to know. You really have to experience things yourself, with your own eyes and ears, to know the real story. It's exactly the same in the UK, our media are some of the worst offenders in my opinion. Many times I've dealt with incidents at work first hand, only to watch or read complete lies about them a short time later.

And so it was with Central America, at no time at all did I ever feel in danger from anyone, people were only ever polite and helpful. The borders are fairly archaic for the most part though, very like African ones. There are few signs telling you where to go, leaving you wandering around aimlessly in the heat, easy prey for the many eager 'helpers' who make a living out of charging tourists to walk them through the process. Don't get me wrong, if you can afford it and apply a modicum of common sense to the amount you give them, these folks can make the whole process fairly straight forward and short. Many of the officials receive backhanders from them so they jump the queues and the paperwork is generally just stamped without question.

For me it wasn't an option. As ever the budget was anorexic, and having been to 51 countries by now, I was fairly up to speed with what needs to be done. That all said, I absolutely hated some of the border crossings through Central America. You have to pay 'taxes' just to join a queue at times, and these are official! You get a receipt for the tax, it may only be $3, but if you haven't got the receipt when you get to the front of the queue, the official behind the counter makes you go back and pay it. These little 'taxes' crop up everywhere, it did my head in, as did the need to photocopy everything a multitude of times.

The officials had photocopiers sitting right behind them, but they'd still make you go away and get them done at one of the various stalls located around the border site. Sometimes I'd queue, whilst everyone else just pushed in, reach the front and be told I needed 4 copies of my driving licence. I'd go and queue up for these in the sweltering heat, return and queue up once again at the original kiosk, only to reach the front and be told I now needed 2 copies of my passport and copies of the exit stamp, then copies of the bike paperwork, it just did my head in how every border was different. If you're planning on crossing Central America by land, just make sure you've got plenty of photocopies of your doc's, and a bucket load of patience.

On a serious note, before you get to the border, make sure you get a big bottle of drinking water. You can find yourself standing in the heat for quite a while so you need to keep hydrated. The more hungry and dehydrated you get, the lower your tolerance and patience levels will become. You just have to try and relax, chill out and go with the flow. It'll all be done eventually.

23.1 – Costa Rica

A notable country for me was Costa Rica, as this is where I met Don Dicker. It's quite a name eh, I've got to admit I wasn't sure if he was pulling my leg or not, but the man is a true gent and a living legend.

Arriving at the border around mid-morning, I was just in time to see an impromptu blockade be setup right before my very eyes. Bollocks. 3hrs later I'd had enough so just rode up to the blockade and asked in my best phone voice if they'd let me through as I was late. To my surprise, they moved the trees out the way and I slid through. If you don't ask!

I crossed into Costa Rica about mid-morning and had just planned to ride straight through in one day to Nicaragua. I was just thinking about stopping to do a wee piece to camera for the vids, when instead decided to stop and fill up with fuel. Whilst there a couple of chaps introduced themselves as a couple of American bike lovers. Well that's an understatement actually. One of them, called Don Dicker, I kid you not, actually has over 300 bikes in his personal collection, back in his purpose built museum in California. Don used to race for Suzuki and then drove for Porsche, the man has a life which reads like a book. I hope one day he gets around to writing it.

With that, Don invited me to stay at his place up in the mountains and wouldn't take no for an answer. So I took him up on the kind offer, to be fair I didn't actually realise he wouldn't be there to begin with though! He had to go to the city for business and just gave me directions. The man was amazing, here's me a complete stranger literally off the street, and he was not only offering me somewhere to stay, but also letting me stay at his place whilst he wasn't there!

Following his directions, I turned off the main road and followed a dirt track high up into the mountains. Nearing the top I met Carlos, Don's gardener, who accompanied me on his quad and escorted me to the home atop the hill. It was like nothing I could have imagined, just absolutely breathtaking, Don had a beautiful place with the most amazing views out over the Pacific Ocean. What's more he had a pool with a poolside bar! Not quite the cheap hostels and wild camping of the norm, I could get used to this!

A few hours later Don arrived back home accompanied by two beautiful young women, Serena and Anita, the bloke was now my hero! No, not what you're all thinking. Serena lived there in town and Anita was her friend visiting to get away from the snow up in Canada. I was also introduced to another chap called 'Jamisun', an amazingly talented musician who was also visiting on holiday.

I spent the next couple of days enjoying life in this tropical paradise, surrounded by the most incredibly friendly and genuine people you could hope to meet. We had a great time over the next few days hanging out at the pool and a messy tequila filled night down in town, where 'Jamisun' was performing. The bloke is a stunning guitarist, check out his website at Jamisun.com There's a real social scene in Costa Rica, it's all about living life, enjoying yourself, music, beer, and one or two chemical enhancers. The place is party town central.

I had only planned to spend 2 nights at Don's then hit the road, but the tequila night and great company put pay to that. I'm getting old these days so hangovers hurt, a lot! An extra night at Don's saw me fit enough to carry on once more, so I said farewell to all my new friends and hit the road.

I was on a mission now, racing through the Central American countries at a rate of knots, eager to reach Mexico city and then the USA. At one crossing, I was absolutely dying in the heat, plus I'd picked up the local lurgy too so was sweating profusely in my leathers whilst feeling altogether very sorry for myself. The folks behind the counter were convinced I had yellow fever and demanded to see my yellow vaccination card. Thankfully I'd had these all done in the UK before leaving, so all was in hand. Be mindful of this though if you're travelling South/Central America.

There's nothing in particular that stood out for me in these Central American countries, the scenery was beautiful in places, but I run with the 'Wow' test now. If I see something that makes me go 'wow', then I stop and get a pic/vid. If not, I just keep moving on. I hit Central America at pace, with almost a burning desire to get North up to the USA. I could taste home now and the hunger for a lifestyle and surroundings I could assimilate to was intense. Most of the countries I'd cover in only a day, only stopping for fuel as I sped my way Northwards.

El Salvador was somewhere that took me by surprise, not at all the suspicious, dangerous and war torn place I was led to believe it would be. The border was straight forward, the officials polite and helpful, the people friendly and full of smiles. I instantly felt at ease in the place and enjoyed the 5hrs or so it took to ride through it.

23.2 - Day 287: Mexico

By this stage I thought I'd passed the majority of the 'iffy' stages of the trip. I knew parts of Mexico had a violent and dangerous reputation, but as ever I'd judge that for myself. I had to go through the country so what would be, would be.

The border from Guatemala was very straightforward, once you found the right one. You can't just follow a main road to the border though, oh no. Some crossings are purely for freight, others are for private vehicles, but unless you speak the lingo, good luck.

Arriving at the freight border I was directed back into a local town and soon found the right crossing. I queued at the immigration booth to get my passport stamped, then rode to the spanking new customs pavilion, queued to get my paperwork checked and signed, then queued to get all my bags searched and the bike thoroughly checked for relevant serial numbers etc. Nothing new there, but the officers then just waived me into the country. No stamp, no paperwork, nothing?

Having been through this before at the Malaysia/Thai border, I enquired with them about why I got no stamp. They told me that this wasn't the 'official' border into Mexico? No, that was another 150km further North, way inside the country. Common sense does not apply here folks, be warned.

I got the officer to point to where it was on google maps on my phone, then hit the road. A few hours later and after several police and army checkpoints, where they didn't actually check anything, instead just waved me on, I arrived at a huge checkpoint and saw the familiar sign for 'Aduane' – Customs in Spanish.

Approaching the counter I handed over all my paperwork and passport. The guy went through exactly the same process as they did at the previous border, then dropped the bombshell on me. In order to get into Mexico you have to pay a $35 immigration fee and $120 immigration deposit. On top of that you then have to pay a tax fee of about $50 for the bike and another $420 tax deposit! This tax fee depends on the age and type of vehicle, and it's non-negotiable. You can pay by cash or card, and you get it back once you and the vehicle leave Mexico. I can vouch for that as it has indeed be returned to me, minus the initial fee's.

The problem for me was that this pretty much wiped me out financially. After paying, I had exactly $52 left in my wallet and that was it. I'd nothing left in the bank and what's more, they didn't take US dollar down here in Southern Mexico as the exchange rate was so bad! I was nearly out of fuel, it was getting dark, I hadn't eaten in 2 days and was out of water.

Ask me if I was happy. No, I wasn't happy. Bollocks.

Thankfully I managed to persuade a guy at a petrol station to take dollars, but only after I'd filled up first then told him it was all I had. (Down there for dancing, wink wink). He had the last laugh though as he took $20 for $10 worth of fuel!

I rode as far as I could into the night then found somewhere to pitch the tent for the night. I was desperate, my mind was racing, what the hell was I going to do? Thankfully I still had my UK SIM card with me so quickly popped it into the phone and picked up a local cell signal. I sent out mercy texts to Nikki, my dad, Bridgestone and Delta, explaining my situation and hoping that one of them may get the message and help out if they could.

As ever, Nikki came to the rescue, bailing me out yet again on this trip. I'm indebted to her, literally, for her support throughout TeapotOne, and have a hell of a lot to do to make it up to her when I get home.

Delta came through too, depositing the last of their official sponsorship money, and my dad also kindly loaned me a few bob, so I was back in the game and ready to hit the road once more.

The only issue was that there weren't actually any ATM's anywhere around me?

Everyone I asked just pointed either South to Guatemala, or North to the first major city of Oaxaca, 200km away. There was nothing else for it, I'd just have to ride as far as I could and try every gas station to see if they'd take my card.

It's amazing the difference a day makes. Yesterday it felt like everything was against me, every road led to a brick wall. Today, the world was full of smiles, fresh air, roses and sunshine. The first place I tried took the card no bother, and what's more I could even use it to buy water and food from their store! I demolished a 2 litre bottle of water and the driest cheese sandwich on the planet. I didn't care, life was good once again.

By the end of the day I'd reached Oaxaca and found an ATM to arm myself with the local Pesos. After a good nights kip and shower at a motel, I hit the road the next day, destination Mexico City. Although I stuck to the main highway, the views at times were spectacular as often the road would climb high into the hills, becoming more like a twisty A or B road in the highlands of Scotland (with more sun admittedly).

By late afternoon I was well inside the Mexico City boundaries, but the place is absolutely massive. You can ride for miles and still not reach the centre! Eventually I found the hostel I'd pre-booked, bang in the centre of the city. Unfortunately, as has happened on a few occasions, despite advertising that they had parking available, when I got there this wasn't the case. Located down a pedestrian precinct, I'd have to leave the Beast out on the street for 3 days, that just wasn't happening. Despite the friendly faces and nature of all the people I'd so far met in Mexico, even they were telling me that the bike wouldn't last 20 minutes left alone in the street! They kindly let me use their wifi to find another suitable place, and I was soon checked-in to a cheap, but fairly decent motel a few miles away. This would be home for the next 3 days as I was to meet a Mexican bike mag and hopefully get the Beast serviced by Suzuki Mexico! How good was that!

'Motociclismo Mexico' (www.motociclismoonline.com.mx) is the Mexican equivalent of 'Fast Bikes Magazine' or 'MCN'. Their editor, Serafin Rebollo, had contacted me over a year ago to offer his help if I ever came to Mexico. After a few emails, he'd kindly offered to meet up and run a piece in his mag on the trip. What's more, he'd also contacted Suzuki Mexico and now they wanted to offer their help by giving the Beast a full service at their main dealership, 'Pro-Shop Suzuki' (proshopmexico.com). I couldn't believe my luck, Suzuki UK and Suzuki Japan hadn't shown the slightest interest in the trip, not offering a single bit of help throughout. In an instant my faith in the brand was sky high once more, at least in Mexico it was.

Serafin and another tester from the mag called Jonatan Torres, turned up at my motel the following morning to take me on a guided tour of the city. They were all too aware of the negative press Mexico receives globally so wanted to show me it's true colours. I'm so glad they did as the city is fantastic, full of history, culture, sights and sounds.

The Mexican people are incredibly friendly and helpful, they're also a really sociable bunch with every open space and park in the city full of families and couples, all mingling together without any problem. It was the complete opposite of how Mexico is portrayed to us in the West. Never once did I feel threatened or unsafe, even when way out of the cities. I found the people everywhere to be kind and helpful, it's a place I want to go back to and explore more, and one day I hope I will.

Mexican people are really sociable. If you go wandering around any town or city, particularly in the evenings or weekends, you'll see loads of folk congregating in the squares and parks, just spending time together.

Monday morning saw me dropping the Beast off at 'Pro Shop Suzuki' and instantly they went to work on her. Honestly, within about 5 minutes of arriving, they had her in the work shop and stripped down, oil changed and brake pads whisk off in a heartbeat. I'd also told them about the handling issues I'd been having since Japan – a mere 35,000 or so miles ago, so they said they'd take a look here too.

For the rest of the day Serafin, Jon and I continued the tour of the city whilst they tried to source some new Bridgestone BATTLAX T30 or BT-023 tyres for me. Unfortunately we drew a blank on them, but I was fairly sure I could make it to San Antonio, Texas on what was left of the rubber.

That evening the lads took me back to the shop to pick up the Beast, she was like new! Not only had they washed her and given her a full service, but they'd also found the source of the handling issues. I never quite got the exact details through translation, but it seems something was loose or broken in the front forks/headstock region. They were pointing at the steering dampener a lot too, but whatever they did, the bike felt like a Gixxer again as I rode her back to the hotel. Once more I had a smile on my face riding the Beast, I couldn't wait to hit the rode again. Everything felt new and tight, like a bike does when it comes back from a quality service. They'd replaced the throttle cable as it'd become stretched over the last 80,000 miles, and what a difference it made. The clutch cable too had been changed, the chain, front and rear pads, everything tightened and lubricated back to showroom issue. Thank you so much to everyone there at 'Pro-Shop Suzuki' and 'Suzuki Mexico' for all your help.

First thing the following morning I was packed up and met Serafin and Jon near the outskirts of town as we rode to the main 'Suzuki Mexico' plant. A group of bikers from both the 'Pro Shop' and 'Suzuki Mexico' had gathered to accompany me on my ride out of the city! We got some pics in front of the plant then hit the road North out the city. The folks rode with me for about 150km before we stopped for a typical Mexican brekkie and some more pics. It was great to meet everyone and reinforced what I'd learned about the great Mexican people and their hospitable, friendly nature. I can't thank all these folks enough, and a massive thank you goes to Serafin and Jon for arranging all of it. Gents, if I can ever help you guys out, and if you're ever in the UK, you know to just drop me a line. Cheers Gents, it was an absolute pleasure to meet you both and I look forward to seeing you again.

From Mexico City I just followed the main highway North to the city of Monterrey, where I stayed the night on it's outskirts before carrying on North to the border with the States. The temperature had really dropped by now, I was actually freezing and had to dig my fleece and winter gloves out! The R&G heated grips were banging on full power, piping heat into my hands. Bliss!

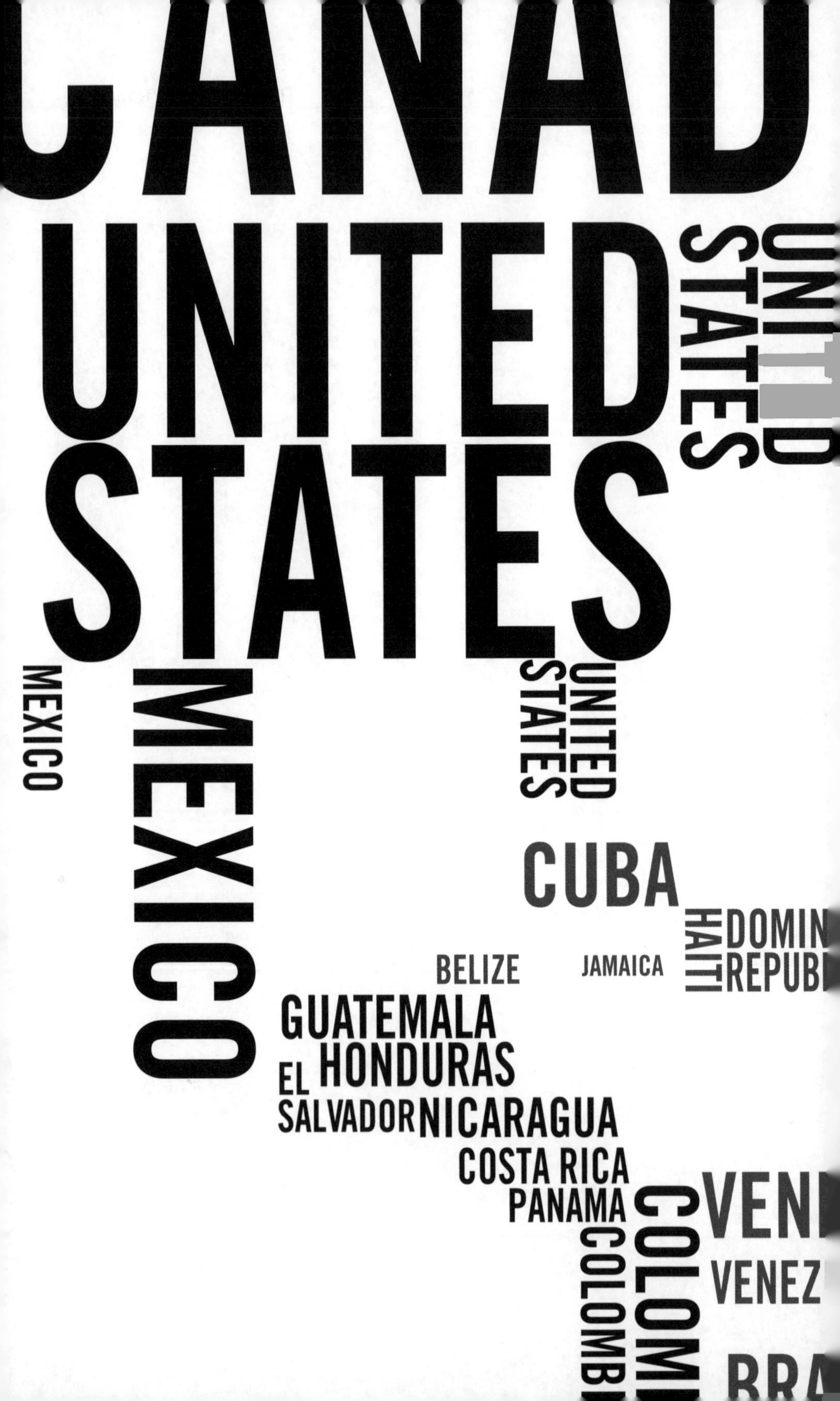

CANAD
UNITED STATES
UNITED STATES
MEXICO
MEXICO
UNITED STATES
CUBA
HAITI DOMIN REPUBL
BELIZE   JAMAICA
GUATEMALA
EL HONDURAS
SALVADOR NICARAGUA
COSTA RICA
PANAMA
VEN
COLOM
VENEZ
COLOMBI
BRA

CHAPTER 24
USA! USA! USA!
- 26th February 2014

For months and thousands of miles, I'd been dreaming of reaching the States. The familiarity, the variety, the friendliness and the unknowns, it hasn't failed to live up to my expectations.

The border into the States was fairly easy, but as ever in Mexico there are set borders for private and freight traffic. Naturally I got the wrong one so it took me a while to find the correct crossing. For your reference, follow the signs for 'Bridge 2'.

The process leaving Mexico was straightforward, no exit stamp in your passport, they just check it and that's it. Remember to stop at the 'Aduanne' kiosk though to get your tax permit for your bike cancelled, or you won't get your deposit back.

Crossing into Texas from Mexico at the 'Loredo-Columbia Solidarity International Bridge', I crossed the Rio Bravo on day 294 and was met by a cluster of stocky uniform clad officers, each bearing utility belts, combat trousers, bomber jackets and baseball caps, merrily chewing away on gum. With hearty smiles they welcomed me over, one had even heard about the trip as he was a biker. Great stuff!

Although relieved to finally be in the USA, I had the growing feeling that the trip was starting to come to an end.

24.1 - Getting the Beast into the USA

I've got to admit, the process of getting myself and the Beast into the USA was surprisingly easy. The folks at 'James Cargo' had forewarned me that I'd need to complete an EPA form 3520-1 (http://www.epa.gov/otaq/imports/documents/420b10027.pdf) prior to entering the country. This is essentially to temporarily import the bike into the States. It's a few simple forms that you should complete and send off about 6-8 weeks prior to your arrival, they'll then send you an exemption letter and that's that. I already had my electronic visa, (ESTA) so apart from a $7 fee, that was that. I was now in the U.S.A Hell Yeah!

The temperature had really plummeted over the last 2 days, more like back home in the North East of Scotland than Texas USA, and as I crossed into the States the snow began to fall. It was more sleet really, but I was bloody freezing. I'd every bit of warm clothing on my person. Fleece, extra socks, R&G heated grips, but I was still feeling it. I'm glad I gave myself about 6 weeks in the States before I headed up to Alaska through Canada. I reckon the temperature difference up there would have hurt me big time, after being used to the 20-40 degree heat and humidity I'd been experiencing since entering Russia almost a year prior.

Riding down a deserted road from the border point to the main interstate, my mind was wandering, dreaming of what lay ahead. The Garmin was telling me to take the next left, but there were two exits close together. Squinting through the glare, I suddenly realized it was the 1st one so quickly did my life-saver and moved into the slip road, braking hard. And then I was on the ground, sliding down the road on my left hand side. Bollocks.

Having spent over 2 months in the USA and Canada, I can say with some qualification that the roads have a fair amount of gravel and grit on them in places. It's probably just what's left over from the winter months, but it makes riding pretty treacherous in places, so beware peoples.

That's what happened here, I'd braked hard on top of some gravel that I hadn't noticed, which resulted in the front wheel just slipping to the side as I tried to lean into the corner. Bang, down we went. As I came to a stop in the middle of the road, I couldn't get up as the bike was on top of my left leg, from the thigh down. I could feel my boot was also stuck on something on the bike, further inhibiting my exit. Looking around quickly to see if I was in imminent danger of being run over, I was glad to see there was no other traffic about. After about a minute of squirming around, pushing and pulling, I eventually got my leg free and was back on my feet. Heaving the Beast upright again, I was gutted to see that the left footpeg had snapped off, and the left hand side was where the R&G fairing slider had had to be taken off when the dealership in Norway sheared off the bolt by over tightening it. The Beast now had even more scars and grazes, adding to her growing 'character' throughout the trip.

I decided I'd head to San Antonio, the next major city, to try and find a dealership there that hopefully could replace the footpeg and chuck a new set of boots on for me. It was only an hour or so away, but riding the bike with no left footpeg meant I had to either drag my boot along the road, or hold my leg up all the time. The first option just wasn't doable, so it was pain and agony for the next hour as cramp after cramp set in. As the cold ate into my soul, the adrenalin from the crash wore off and my ribs and shoulder began to announce their discomfort.

Arriving into San Antonio, the snow had begun to fall and the wind bit harshly into every crevice. There were groups of guys on street corners, blatantly waiting to either score or sell. Bail bonds, pawn shops and gunsmiths lined every street, 'where the hell had I arrived?!'

I soon found some accommodation in the form of a 'motel6' fairly near to the city centre. I later found out that they are the budget chain motel of America, not always located in the best parts of town, but generally available for around $30-$70 a night. Warm, tidy, clean and with generally good wifi, they were perfect for a weary traveller.

Booking in, the young lad behind the desk told me he'd given me a room on the ground floor, then told me to bring my bike into the room, it's what all the bikers did there apparently. If I didn't, the bike may not be there in the morning! We slept well that night.

Bruce SMART

A quick search online led me to 'Alamo Cycle Plex' so I headed there the following morning. A multi-franchise dealership, it's a huge building with an impressive array of vehicles outside. As I wandered in I was immediately met by a friendly hand shake and a hearty 'howdy'. I already loved Texas.

After quickly explaining what I was up to and what I needed, the young lads in the store went way out their way to assist, and I was soon speaking to the Service Manager, Tony Bayron. They had the tyres in store, but the footpeg would need to be ordered. Not only that, but Suzuki had undertaken a recall on my bike due to a faulty front brake issue. I'd been aware of this after I left, but being on the road there wasn't too much I could do about it. I'd even emailed, tweeted and facebook'd Suzuki to tell them I'd be in Japan, asking if it would be possible to get the work carried out there. As usual they didn't even grace me with a reply.

Unfortunately, if Alamo were to carry out any work on the bike, they were lawfully obliged to carry out the recall work too, which again would mean waiting for parts. So it looked like I would be in San Antonio for a while. Normally this wouldn't be too much of an issue, but the motoGP rider Colin Edwards Jnr had very kindly invited me to come and stay at his 'Texas Tornado Bootcamp' that weekend as he would be home from testing in Sepang. If I missed the weekend, then I'd miss the opportunity to meet one of the biggest and best characters in the sport.

Tony said he'd do what he could, so I spent an hour or so wandering around the store, then fell asleep in a comfy chair next to a TV. After what felt like minutes I was awoken to be told the bike would be ready first thing the following morning, no questions asked. To top it all off, they only made me pay for the tyres, having stripped a footpeg off a brand new bike straight out the crate. They'd need the evening to sort the brake issue, so I grabbed a room in a nearby motel before picking up my old friend the following morning. A huge thanks to Tony and his team at 'Alamo Cycle Plex'. They really did go way out of their way to help me out, exhibiting a level of service that is rare today. Thank you.

24.2 - Day 296: The Alamo

Now you can't come to San Antonio and not see the 'Alamo'. I must confess I didn't know too much about the place, apart from the saying, "Remember the Alamo" and the name of Davie Crockett. After parking up the bike and walking down the street towards the site, I was amazed at the tiny scale of the place. Essentially a mission in San Antonio, the 'Battle of the Alamo' took place from February 23rd to March 6th in 1836 during the Texas Revolution. To this day, all Texans are fiercely proud to be a 'Texan' and loudly proclaim that they are in fact a Republic, free to split from the United States at any time. I loved the pride the Texans have in their identity, as a Scot I can empathise with them. But let's not get into that debate eh.

Mexican President General Antonio López de Santa Anna led the revolt during the battle, with an army of a reputed 1,500 plus men. American commanders, James Bowie and William B. Travis, together with a garrison of about 300 men (once reinforcements arrived), held off the onslaught for nearly 13 days before they were overpowered, and every man of military age was slaughtered. There are countless tales of bravery, countless contradictions on both sides, but it's safe to say that a slaughter took place during that event, and a small band of brothers stood side by side to defend what they saw as theirs.

It's eerily serene now, you can walk all through the mission, see the marks left on the exterior walls from the battle, and imagine the horrors that went on throughout those grounds and beyond. Yet now it's a mark of pride for the American nation, almost a point of pilgrimage for many. Much like when I visited Auschwitz, I feel it's somewhere you have to experience for yourself to appreciate exactly what it's about. Worth a stop if you're in Texas for sure.

Leaving the Alamo I headed Northeast to the 'Circuit of the Americas' just outside the city of Austin, another 'tick' on my list of motoGP circuits around the world. My usual luck continued and I arrived about 20 minutes after the last tour of the day had ended. So as per most of the others, it was a quick pic and vid at the main sign and I was back on the road.

Bruce SMART

24.3 - Day 297: Texas Tornado

My mate Luigi had tweeted Colin Edwards to say I'd be rolling into town on my trip, and would you Adam'n'Eve it, he only went and replied, saying I should stop by his 'Texas Tornado Boot Camp'. So, I did! To be fair I knew Colin was out in Sepang for the final stages of testing that week, so didn't expect him to spend his first weekend back home with me, but I thought I'd stop by the camp and check it out anyway.

Pulling up the long drive to the ranch, straight away the air is filled with screaming engines, the smell of fuel and BBQ! Gotta love Texas. The first chap I met was one of the instructors, Steve Bodak, who gave me the warmest of Texan welcomes. Despite not knowing anything about my visit, he invited me in to the camp and I soon had a beer in hand whilst being introduced to everyone there. As luck would have it, Colin had apparently mentioned I may stop by to his family, and they were incredibly hospitable.

Whilst out on one of the circuits, I was chatting to some of the lads when I got a tap on the shoulder and was met by a guy in jeans, t-shirt, baseball cap and shades. He held out his hand and said, "You gotta be Bruce right". Holy crap, it was only Colin Edwards! I felt like a dizzy schoolgirl.

The man is every bit as down to earth as he appears on the telly. There's no airs or graces, he says what he thinks and is just one of the lads. I spent a long time chatting with his dad, Colin Snr, about my travels around the world as he too has done some travelling during his career in the oil industry. That night, we even got to celebrate 'Jnrs' 40th birthday with some of the best BBQ meat I've ever tasted.

The bikes are wee Yam's, with Bridgestone tyres – offroad on the front and road tyre at the rear, allowing the bikes to slide effortlessly, in turn giving the students more feel for how to handle the bike sliding under power.

I had to head off again the next day as the weather was closing in really fast, but I got to spend a couple more hours in the company of Colin, the fantastic array of instructors, and all the guests who were experiencing the camp themselves. It was a real pleasure to meet all the folks, thank you for making me feel so welcome.

If you've ever thought about doing the camp, I couldn't recommend it enough and I'm saving up for it one day. More info at texastornadobootcamp.com

Leaving the bootcamp, I headed West to LA. My best mate Chris and his wife Jessie were over visiting some friends so I thought I'd head over to fill in some time before I met my sponsor, Delta Energy Services, in Houston in a few weeks time.

The first few days across Texas were cold, seriously cold. My first night camping was torture as it plummeted well below zero. I awoke in the morning to frost and a thin covering of snow! The cold had killed all my batteries – the bike, GoPro's, Camera and phone all dead. After some pushing and heaving, I soon bump started the Beast and we were back in order. Thankfully I'd got a new USB charger in a Walmart recently, so could charge all the gadgets off the bike once on the move. I went through about 5 of these along the trip, they're great bits of kit but not very robust when used all the time.

The ride West was pretty boring to be honest, I just stuck to the interstates to eat up the miles. Arriving in LA I booked myself into the cheapest motel I could find online, right in the centre of it all. Motel 'Alta Cienega' is nothing special, clean rooms with a bathroom and a TV, nothing out the ordinary but very cheap by LA standards. Their claim to fame is that Jim 'The Doors' Morrison had stayed here when he first came to the city, and they've kept his room exactly as it was – apparently.

I spent a few days in LA with Chris and Jessie, meeting friends and generally just chilling out. Our mate Chutney was due to have his stag do in Miami in about a month's time, so Chris and I plotted his downfall, as well as sourcing a few items of suitable clothing. Remind me to never get married – oh hang on!

24.4 - Day 305: Getting my Kicks!

Heading back east again, grinding out the miles across this huge and vast country, the bike was an absolute pig to handle, shaking her head at the slightest hint of a bend, and dipping wildly under braking. I'd no idea what the back roads would be like around here, but with the Beast the way she was, to be honest I was happy to just sit on the motorways.

That was until I started to pick up the signs for Route 66, how could I not sample this folklore gem! My original plan had always been to do the east of the States before heading west along the top to Chicago. From there I'd ride the historic route 66 all the way to the West coast, before riding north along Highway 1 to Canada. Unfortunately budget constraints had meant I'd had to alter the route somewhat, so I wasn't sure if I'd get the opportunity to ride it again along the trip. Turning off the interstate, I was soon cruising along, listening to 'Kid Rock' and grinning from ear to ear.

Route 66, in the west at least, is just a long straight featureless stretch of road. It scythes through the desert, for the most part running alongside the major interstates, occasionally even integrating within them for short stretches. The road surface is fairly bumpy, even substantially potholed in places, but you're on route 66! Occasional ghost towns are scattered along the way, with each existing town clinging tightly to its '66' heritage with a plethora of gift shops, diners and memorabilia on offer.

I spent the night camped in the Mojave desert just south of Las Vegas. There are campsites everywhere in the States, with 'KOA' (Kamping of America) being a national chain located throughout the USA and Canada. The services available are top notch, but vary from camp to camp. For about $30 a night you can pitch your tent in a secure area, with laundry, shower and other facilities all close by. (www.koa.com)

24.5 - The Grand Canyon

My next target was to be the Grand Canyon, about 200 miles east. The ride there was great once I'd turned off the I40 onto route 64, just outside the wee town of Williams. Nipping along, I soon arrived at the toll road to the park, parked the bike up and walked on foot to the observation deck. The view that awaits is truly spectacular, nothing prepares you for the grandeur or raw awesomeness of the place. No picture or video does it justice, it's one of those places you simply have to see for yourself. It was packed with tourists, but waiting my turn I soon got my opportunity for some shots.

The Grand Canyon is some 280 miles long, about 1 mile at its deepest and ranges from 4 to 18 miles in width. Carved through the Arizona desert by the Colorado river over the last 17 million years, it's a must if you ever get to this part of the world. I can't recommend it highly enough.

Just outside the town of Winslow along the I40, in the middle of the Arizona desert, lies another natural phenomenon. The 'meteor Crater' is exactly that, the site of an asteroid collision with earth some 50,000 years ago. At almost a mile wide and over 500ft deep it can even be seen from space.

After a short stop over at the crater, I continued on to the town of Albuquerque to meet up with another chap who has been following the trip on facebook. George Evans is also an avid reader of 'Fast Bikes' and owns a beautiful Ducati Monster. He kindly took me on a tour of the local ancient Indian sites, the Pueblo 'Abo Ruins'. This is the site of an early Spanish mission located on one of the oldest Pueblo Indian villages, dating back to the 1300's. The Spanish set up the mission around 1630 in an attempt to 'civilise' the Indians, bringing them around to their Catholic faith. Eventually the Indians either converted or were forced to run from their homeland, but to this day the remains of the mission and village are now a national monument.

The Spanish built round holes within their missions to try & entice the local Pueblo Indians to come aboard their Catholic faith. The Indians could practice their own beliefs/faith in these pitts, as long as they took onboard the Catholic faith too. Eventually the Pueblo's were simply hounded out.

George very kindly even invited me to dinner at his folks place. The kindness festooned upon me by the biking community around the world is just incredible! George, I can't thank you enough mate, it was an absolute pleasure to meet you, Cait and your family.

24.6 - Day 311: Dallas to Houston

Leaving New Mexico I was soon back in Texas where I found the way to Amarillo, stopping for the obligatory picture. Next up was a quick stop over in Dallas to see my mates from Uni I'd not seen since their wedding back in 2000. Gordy & Suzanne had just moved to Dallas from Minnesota, but Gordy was already up to speed with the local watering holes and nightlife. It was good. Real 'Guuuuuuuuddddd'. I LOVE TEXAS!

Houston was my next port of call & I spent 4 days there with Delta (des-global.com). They'd very kindly supplied me with another suit as the original one was now in tatters, and not exactly a social hit due to being worn by a fat Scotsman in up to 51 degree heat every day for the last year and a half! 'Feridax U.K.' had also kindly supplied some new SIDI boots, SPADA gloves, and a new liner for my SHOEI XR-1100 lid. PIPEWERX had sent a new hanger for my can, so I was shining like new once more. Don't worry, it didn't last long.

Delta had kindly arranged for some media attention whilst there so I was interviewed by a local online magazine, and live by 'FOXNews' on their Saturday morning brekkie show!

After that it was off to the rodeo, but not just any old rodeo. Nope, this was the largest rodeo event in the world, 'Rodeo Houston'. I've got to say, it was a great laugh and I'd certainly go again. The actual rodeo events really grab hold of you, and before you know it you're hollering like 'Billy The Kidd' at the cowboys tackling 1000lb cows to the ground from their horses at full pelt! These lads have bollocks!

It's a true community event here. Texas kids rear these beasts & they're sold at the show, bought by huge multi-national oil companies & the like. The companies use it as a tax write-off & the money goes straight to the kids to pay for their College education.

What a great idea!

Leaving Houston I headed to New Orleans to meet up with some old mates and 'KriegaUSA' for a day or two. Mud and Kirsty where over from the UK and riding a Harley from Daytona to Las Vegas, so our paths crossed in New Orleans for one night only. First off had to be Bourbon St, which ended in a drunken mess once more. The place is a tourist trap but has to be done if you've never been to this city before. We certainly made a good attempt at drinking the place dry, a top night was had by all.

Next day I met a chap called Chris Bishop who had also been following on facebook, and is another avid Stateside 'Fast Bikes' reader. Chris kindly offered to show me around the real New Orleans, not just the tourist 'norm'. He & his family lost everything during the horrific flooding which followed hurricane 'Katrina' that struck a few years back. He took me to where his home once stood, talked about the communities that flourished there, how they pulled together and rebuilt. The man has a deep love and passion for his hometown, and it was a pleasure to spend a few hours in his company.

Chris also introduced me to the 'Po-Boy', a local speciality in New Orleans. Essentially a big sandwich, originally it was just the left over scraps in a baguette, eaten by the street workers & those in the poorest of society. Now it's a delicacy, available with all manner of fillings, trimmings and side dishes, it's absolutely beautiful.

Saying goodbye to Chris that afternoon, I was filled with adoration for the man and his family. To have faced adversity the way they had, lost practically everything in the face of nature at its most ferocious, survived the many months of despair that hit the city, and to then rebuild their lives within that same city they called home, this took a very special type of person. I found myself being not full of pity for them, or woe, but an enormous sense of life and everything it means to be alive. Invigorated, that's probably a better word for it actually, invigorated for having met him. Chris if you're reading this bud, I'll never be able to thank you enough, or put into words what it meant to experience your city with you. But thank you.

Bruce SMART

About 5 mins after leaving Chris I rode down a main street in New Orleans city centre, only a few blocks from Bourbon Street. Sitting at some traffic lights waiting for the green, I heard a familiar 'POP' then the unmistakeable smell of cordite in the air. That was a gunshot, right around the corner!

With that a tsunami of people surged down the sidewalk from the direction of the shot, some cowering for cover behind vehicles waiting in the traffic. The light turned green and I could ride forward, turning my head to catch a glimpse of a guy sitting in the road behind a bus. There were folks with him so I carried on down the street, finding out later that it was a drug deal gone wrong, the two assailants amongst the crowd who ran by me earlier. They'd actually run down the street behind me straight into a police officer who was running towards the sound of a gunshot. Thankfully they all carry over here and both suspects were dealt with and detained. I caught the whole thing on my GoPro too!

I spent my last night in New Orleans with a chap called Michael Walshaw who heads up Kriega USA. Kriega are a British company who specialise in soft luggage for motorcycles, and they'd very kindly provided all my bike luggage for the trip. I never wanted the traditional hard panniers, favouring instead the versatility that soft bags provide. They look great on the Gixxer, keep your kit dry and you can easily remove them when needed. Even to this day, some 100,000 miles later, I've still got the same bags they gave me to do the trip and I use them whenever I need to carry anything on the bike. In fact I use the rucksack each and every day!

A big thank you has to go to Michael and his beautiful wife Leia, for their fantastic hospitality in New Orleans. They looked after me for a few days, supplying me with beer and cracking hospitality. Kriega also very kindly replaced one of the luggage straps that had broken during one of my numerous 'falls' on the bike. Guys it was a pleasure to meet you, and I really do hope we meet again.

24.7 - Barber Motorsports Museum, Georgia & 'The Dragons Tail'

I was soon back on the road, heading through the state of Alabama ("Gump, Forrest Gump"). I even stopped by the port of Bayou La Batre, where Forrest Gump had his shrimp boat with Lt Dan!

Next destination was the fabulous 'Barber Motorsports Museum and Racetrack'. This place has the greatest collection of vintage & modern motorcycles and cars on the planet, with over 1,200 currently in the collection. It's a 'Santa's grotto' for any petrol head out there and I can't recommend a visit highly enough.

They also have their own racetrack around the museum on which they even hold trackdays. It's apparently one of the best tracks in the world as they incorporated all the best corners from the top circuits out there, amalgamating them into one, 'Super' circuit. I never got a chance to sample it but one day........ One day.

I'd arranged to meet another chap who'd been following the trip here at the museum, so after a few hours walking around, Jon Wilkens and I were making our way to his home near Buchanan, Georgia. Along the way we stopped off at the 'Talladega Superspeedway' – home to the film 'Talladega Nights', "Shake and bake baby". Generally the roads in the USA had been nothing special bike-wise, mostly long straight ribbons of tarmac, with very little in the way of bends to entertain you. That said, I'd mostly been on main roads, but even then there'd not been much in the way of forest or mountains that may conceal the twisties dreams are made of.

That all changed as I got into the 'Deep South', with Georgia, North and South Carolina all containing simply awesome roads through their mountains and woodland. John had been incredibly kind and got me a new front wheel for the bike, so we soon had that changed over once back at his man cave. This place was better equipped than some dealerships, complete with 'Fast Bikes' centrefolds adorning the walls. He's another avid Stateside reader, with editions going back many years still stacked up all over his beautiful house. The wheel had been buckled since the end of Russia, some 35,000 miles ago, no wonder the Beast had been handling like a pig, the buckle was huge, over 10mm travel!

The incredible TeapotOne fortune shined on me yet again as I arrived at Jon's place, the front bearings had almost completely gone, they probably wouldn't have even lasted another day they were that bad. But I needn't have worried as Jon works for a major bearing manufacturer, NSK, so this was no problem.

It never ceased to astound me how things just seemed to work themselves out on the road. I found that when an issue arose, as long as you didn't give up, a solution would eventually present itself in one form or another. I've been determined to live my life like that ever since, NEVER give up.

Jon and I, with the help of a few friends, spent the day fully servicing the Beast, Jon's mate Eric even gave her a wash as he couldn't stand seeing a bike that dirty. We were soon out on the bikes again, ripping up the local roads to check out our handy work, ensuring everything was shipshape before we headed to the famous 'Tail of the Dragon' at Deal's Gap in Tennessee. The roads around Jon's place were beautiful on the bike, made all the more enjoyable by the fact the Beast was no longer walloping into, around and out of every bend.

I've got to admit, I now rode like a newbie. I'm not saying I used to be Rossi, but I was never a slouch either. Since my crash in Japan I've just not had the same confidence in the bike's front end, tottering my way around bends like a newborn baby Bambi and braking erratically in all the wrong places. With the new straight wheel on the bike, it was like someone had taken me by the hand and was back, there by my side. I can't tell you the difference it made, the front actually felt like it would stick to the road and not just fly off to the side at any minute. That was right up until I braked, then all hell broke loose! Turns out the discs are also warped, causing a severe juddering any time the brakes are applied. Ach well, braking was for Harley riders anyway eh.

Jon and his wife Bonnie were the perfect hosts for a few days at their home, where I got to sample some fishing in their lake, walk around the woods, and even got to refresh some of my shooting skills on their own outdoor gun range! I loved this place, it was exactly how I pictured my own dream place. A big beautiful wooden home surrounded by hills and woodland, located bang in the middle of biking bliss. It makes living in London even more depressing now I'm back!

Soon it was time for Jon and I to hit the road north up to the famous 'Dragons Tail'. This place needs no introduction amongst biking' addicts, 318 curves in 11 miles, it's biking heaven and every bit as good as it's reputation. Without doubt, one of the greatest motorcycle roads in the world. In fact, you can't go wrong anywhere around US129, just about every road reveals tremendous sections of curves and twisties, carving their way around mountains, through woodland, and alongside waterways. Absolutely epic, every bit as good as the Black Forest in Germany, South East France or Northern Spain.

Arriving at the main shop and lodge at the base of the route, a similar frenzy of anticipation begins to envelope your very being. I remember feeling like this my first time at the Nurburgring, wanting to give it all I've got on the fabled Tarmac, but at the same time bricking it in case it all ended in tears. As Jon and I wandered around the gift shop, I spied a few stickers and badges that I'd claim as soon as I 'did' the Dragon, but not before.

The lodge also houses another infamous landmark, the 'Tree of Shame'. Essentially this is an existing tree in the middle of the car park area, on which any one who crashes whilst riding the Dragon must hang a part of their bike! It's like a totem pole of biking shame, festooned in a technicoloured nightmare-coat. I'm relieved to say I didn't add to it, this time.

As Jon led the way along this glorious stretch of road, instantly I knew why it possessed the reputation it has as one of the greatest biking roads in the world. It's like a roller coaster for bikers, full of turn after turn through beautiful countryside, whipping you up and down the mountains along ever changing gradients. Bike after bike make their way in both directions, the usual Harley's and Goldwings strangely 'kanked' right over, chrome beer-bellies scraping the ground as their pilots grin like madmen who've escaped from the asylum. Even writing this now I can't help but smile, it's pure, dead, brilliant!

Slowly I began to get my mojo back, but Jon sure spanked me on those amazing roads as he tore off ahead. I can't thank you enough for your kindness and generosity, it was a real pleasure to meet you. Thanks to Jon and his wife Bonnie for their hospitality at their beautiful home, I've now found where I want to live!

24.8 - Day 330: On to Daytona, Florida & Beyond

Now heading south, the next stop for me was Daytona Beach in Florida, where I was to meet up with family I'd not seen since a holiday when I was 5! My Great Uncle Bob, a true hero in my eyes, is a former US Marine and retired NYPD, the man is everything you'd expect a great man to be, and at 98 he's not ready to lie down yet. It was great to see him and his family again after so long, we chatted forever and caught up on the times gone by. All too soon it was time to say our farewells once again, my Uncle Bob's handshake was as strong as ever as we hugged goodbye.

After the delights of the mountains in the deep South, the roads in Florida are quite a contradiction. Flat, featureless and straight…… very, very straight. I rode to the tip of the American continent in Key West, via Orlando and the Everglades, got the obligatory snap-shot, then rode back up to Miami where I was to meet my mates for a stag do, organised to coincide with my visit. Happy Days.

Arriving in Miami, I headed to the hotel that was to be home for the next few days for my mate's Stag (bachelor party). On the way I passed 'Miami Ink' so had to stop and get some pics as I used to watch this show with my son when we went out to Spain to visit my folks during the holidays. I even met Yoji as I left the shop, but was too shy to stop him and ask for a pic, sorry!

Chutney (the groom) has been a great mate from my first days at Uni in Glasgow, some 20 years previously. We've all kept in touch, even though loads of the lads have now spread themselves all over the globe. One by one we've all fallen foul of the fairer sex, and now it was his turn. I'll not go into the details, but we dressed him in suitable attire for each day, and a sound job was done in ensuring he was incapable of speech for the majority of the weekend. Top job by all, and a massive thanks to Chris for organising the whole thing, good work Blackhead.

24.9 - Day 341: Heading North & New Adventures

Nikki was coming over Stateside for a few weeks so I'd planned to meet up with her in New York, then again for a few days up in Boston. She'd lived in the USA in a previous life so was over to visit old friends in Boston. Leaving Miami I had 2 days to cover 1,500 miles including a stop off in Washington DC to meet the staff of Born Free USA. That's a hard slog at the best of times, but after the weekend of debauchery I'd just had, I wasn't in a good place!

The ride north was horrendous. Halfway through the skies got mean and dark, the temperature plummeted, and then it rained. Not the fine mist stuff you can ride through no bother, this was the stuff that gets you wet in about a nano second flat. Visibility was practically zero, I was following the hazy lights ahead most of the time.

Trundling into DC, Born Free USA were supposed to have a photoshoot around the capital. Unfortunately due to the rain this had been cancelled, so I went all that way for a quick pic in an office. That's life though, it's nobody's fault, but I really wish I'd had time to explore D.C, there is so much I'd love to see there. Auch well, another place to add to the list for a return trip or two.

Drenched to the core and colder than I'd been in quite a while, I was back on the Beast heading north to New York. It's only about 4hrs ride normally, but the rain had now turned to snow, the temperature ever in a downward spiral. It took me almost 8hrs to cover the 300 odd miles to my mate Blackhead's place, and by the time I arrived I was bordering on hypothermia. But I was there.

I spent the next week in a beautiful place called Chappaqua, about 30 miles north of

Bruce SMART

Manhattan. Nikki had come out to see me, the first time we'd seen each other in over 7 months. I've got to admit, this last stint coming up through the America's had been tough and I was real glad to see her again. As I've said before, I had been feeling progressively worse as the trip progressed, and as it turns out I was developing a heart condition but didn't know it. I'd put the fatigue and general unwell feeling down to a culmination of 4 years hard work, and over 14 months of life on the road. It's been a bit of a relief to now find out there was an actual underlying medical issue.

I've not hidden how hard I found the African leg of this trip, in fact it actually broke me and I'm not too proud to say so. I was under prepared mentally for the rigours of Mauritania, the rawness and evil of human nature at its worst. The desert nearly claimed me, and the people of the country put me in harms way countless times. I said to myself that if I made it through, I'd make an honest woman of Nikki so the plan was put into action once I returned home. However, with Delta Energy Services coming forward with the opportunity to rekindle the trip, I left again wondering if she'd still be around when I got home. The incredible person she is, she backed me the whole way, always there to offer support and help whenever it's been needed. She's one in a million, I love her with all I am, and to cut a long story short, we got engaged in Central Park.

I'd spent the best part of over a year sat on my arse on a bike. So when my mate Chris asked if I could help him out in his garden I jumped at the chance to stretch the muscles. What a mistake! Chris wanted a new lawn around his house, meaning we'd need to rotavate the existing grass, rake it, weed it, put new topsoil down, seed it, and so on. After the first full day of rotavating, I was in bits.

We spent a few days tearing up the grounds around his home, trying to get as much prep work complete in readiness of my hopeful return in about 3 weeks time, just before I flew from New York to Ireland for the last stage of the trip.

But back to bikes. From NY I headed up to Boston to spend a few days with Nikki and some friends there. After fitting a new rear Bridgestone T30 tyre, I was back on the road heading West on route up to Alaska.

Along the way I stopped off at the famous Indianapolis Raceway, another motoGP circuit to tick off the list, then north through Chicago towards the border with Canada. The weather once again changed for the worse, it really is almost a living, breathing being here in the States. It's incredible to see in person, the skies literally change before your eyes, clouds turn from white fluffy 'puffs' to angry swathes of blackness that chase you mercilessly. Tornados were breaking out all across the middle of the USA, that's an unfathomably huge area!

I watched in awe one afternoon as I rode along the interstate, the skies to my South visibly being sucked into a huge vortex before my eyes. It reminded me of some of the skies I remember seeing on the old 'Flash Gordon' film! It didn't turn into a tornado there and then, but as the hail began to fall I reached the safety of a motel later that night farther north, the news relayed the stories of what I'd missed. Huge devastation to the South, snow and hailstorms, flooding, mass tornado outbreaks, it was like a disaster script!

Over the next day or so I was averaging between 400-700 miles a day, a mileage I'd need to keep up all the way to Alaska and back to New York if I was to hope to keep on schedule. I stopped off at the Indianapolis Speedway to get yet another pic and vid in front of a motoGP circuit, then fired on through Chicago and north towards the Canadian border as the temperature steadily plummeted.

UNITED STATES CANADA

CANADA

UNITED STATES UNITED STATES

MEXICO MEXICO UNITED STATES

CUBA DOMINICAN REPUBLIC
BELIZE JAMAICA HAITI
GUATEMALA
EL SALVADOR HONDURAS
NICARAGUA
COSTA RICA
PANAMA VENEZUELA
COLOMBIA VENEZUELA GUYANA
BRAZIL
ECUADOR COLOMBIA
PERU BR

CHAPTER 25

CANADA

DAY 357

The journey north across the border to Winnipeg in Canada was non-descript. Painfully non-descript. The area from the Great Lakes north of Chicago, West to the Rockies, is known as the 'Prairies'. They're flat and featureless, but in Canada they're even worse. Nothing. Absolutely nothing. I'd gone to Canada expecting mountains, forests, bears to be sitting at the roadside eating honey, moose meandering by rivers whilst Salmon frolic up the rapids. It shows it on the telly, it must be true. To an extent it is, just not in the Southern middle section from Winnipeg to Edmonton, about 1,000 miles of bugger all.

Along the way I bumped into another British biker, Ed Gold (www.edgold.co.uk) who was riding back to Alaska. Ed's an eccentric photographer and a diamond bloke, so we buddied up to try and null the boredom. He'd spent a tour out in Afghanistan with the Para's, photographing their day-to-day lives out there with a view to publishing a book. He's also lived in remote Argentina with the surviving Welsh colony there, documenting their lives in an incredible book called, 'Welsh Patagonia', and was now on his way up to Alaska to live with the Eskimo's for a bit! Just when you think you're all windswept and interesting, you meet someone who completely pisses all over your chips!

The ride West was hard. The monotonous miles of featureless straight road were made even more torturous by high winds, heavy rain and snow, and freezing temperatures. I'd never been this cold on the bike for so long before. It hit below -35oC with the windchill and I was in pain every second I was riding. My R&G heated grips have been awesome, but finally packed in just after I got into Canada, so I bought some handle bar muffs out of desperation. I'm now converted, I don't care if I looked like a tit, I could almost feel my fingers again.

After a quick oil and filter change in Edmonton, we were back on the bikes heading north, but the delay caused by the inclement weather now meant there was no way I'd reach 'Deadhorse' in Alaska in time for me to do the return journey back to NYC. I had to be at the shipping agents by the 15th May to get the Beast over to Dublin in time. Ed and I carried on riding towards Alaska, hoping that some miracle would happen and I'd be able to eat up the huge distance required to get to Fairbanks, but it wasn't to be.

The weather got even worse, the sleet turned to snow at times, the temperature dropping even further. It was just pain all the time, I could only ride for about 20 minutes before having to stop and put my hands on the Pipewerx exhaust until the feeling came back. So just after I started the famous 'Alaskan Highway' in Dawson Creek, I had to turn back South at Fort St John and begin my long trek back alone. Ed and I said our goodbyes and he carried on North to Anchorage, Alaska, where he was going to be living with the Inuits around Northern Alaska, documenting their lives in pictures. Keep an eye on his site www.edgold.co.uk, as the man is always heading off on amazing adventures, always on a shoe-string budget, always living wild or in people's sheds, always infatuated with a passion for his craft that is reflected in the quality of his work. I met Ed again once he returned to the UK after completing his job in Alaska, he even presented me with a copy of his new book about his time there with the Inuits. As usual it's breathtaking, I can only hope the man gets the recognition he truly deserves and I urge you to check his site out. I'm sure we'll meet again and I'd love to do a joint project with him some day. We'll see.

After turning off the Alaskan Highway just North of Fort St. John, I was on my own again riding the Don Phillips Highway, alongside the beautiful Peace River. Crossing from Alberta into British Columbia you are immediately surrounded by the Canada I'd expected. Beautiful majestic snow capped mountains, lush forests and rivers abound, amazing ribbons of tarmac meander their way through beautiful countryside. It was everything I'd expected.

The route 29 road from just north of Fort St John all the way to Chetwynd, is fantastic. It's got it all, very much like the Black Forest roads in Germany and parts of the Route Napoleon in South East France. With the new straight front wheel, I'd got my confidence back on the bike again so was happy to push her more into the bends, loving the freedom of movement you get on a bike when in full flow. There's wildlife all around up here, Elk are plentiful by the roadside, moose and bears abound – yet I saw neither. If I could do my time in Canada again, I'd forget about the middle and just go straight to BC, Yukon and into Alaska, USA. For me that's the 'Canada' I wanted to experience.

However time was against me so I made the most of the journey South to Vancouver, devouring the amazing 'Sea to Sky Highway' along route 99. This is another 'must-do' road and one to add to your bucket list. Awesome, no other words are needed. Except the speed, as after Whistler it becomes much more policed with a painfully low 50mph limit. Oh and another thing, Canadians CAN'T drive, so have your wits doubly about you here. The entire country reeks of weed too so you may be a tad more peckish as you ride.

I had a nights stop over in Vancouver to see 2 mates, Boastie & Kirsten, who'd emigrated here the month before I first left the UK, way back in 2012. As usual beer was the principle ingredient, as well as great chat. They hadn't changed a bit, both great people who are undeniably made for each other. Loving their time in Canada, both had embraced the lifestyle on offer and I hope they make a cracking life for themselves for the future years ahead.

Now Boastie is a proper old-school 'rugger-bugger' who could drink an Irish 'navvie' sober. The years hadn't softened this 'God-Given' talent so very soon I was enjoying his company in a variety of Vancouver's watering holes, catching up on the times gone by. He's a master story teller, in possession of a Brian Blessed-like 'GORDON'S ALIVE' voice that makes any topic hilarious and powerful. I miss the blokes company, I really do, and it was great to just fall back into the good times again, if only for a few hours.

Bruce SMART

The following morning, after saying my goodbyes to Boastie and K, I was far from bright and breezy but on the bike crossing the border back into the USA, down to Seattle then East along the I90. This is a motorway that basically runs coast to coast across the States. It's torture on a bike, but I had 3,000 miles to eat up in only a matter of days so it had to be done. I've got to admit though, for a few stretches through Montana and Wyoming, it's actually a pretty nice ride. Montana in particular is a stunning place, full of beautiful mountains and valleys, I'd love to explore the back roads here as I bet they're awesome on a bike. I will be back.

On the edge of the Badlands in South Dakota, you find the Mount Rushmore monument. I wanted to stop off here for a quick pic as it's somewhere I've wanted to see. The road whisking you gradually up into the mountains is a refreshing change from the monotony of the interstates, corners are introduced back into your life as you glide into the trees and hills.

Soaring around a switchback in the road, you're suddenly presented with Mount Rushmore itself, the faces of presidents surveying the land before them. It's a surreal experience to actually witness first hand, and one I'm glad I've done.

Next up for me was the long slog East to Niagara Falls. The deadline to freight the Beast from NYC to Dublin was drawing ever near, leaving me only a matter of days so the going would need to be long and brisk. Unfortunately the Beast pee'd herself outside Buffalo, basically she dumped all her coolant out as I was filling up with fuel. She'd done it once previously in Malaysia, and after checking all hoses and the radiator, I could see nothing wrong so just bled the system, filled it back up, and hit the road once more.

Soon enough I was looking out over the impressive falls, battling for a vantage point amongst the throngs of other tourists. The falls themselves are every bit what I was expecting, the thundering force of water endlessly crashing down the depths almost hypnotic to see firsthand.

Whilst there I was approached by another chap who'd been following the trip, I'm really sorry if you're reading this mate, I'm afraid I can't remember your name! But thanks very much for coming up to say hello, it really was brilliant to meet and chat with so many people all over the world who took the time to say hi.

I covered the 3,000 odd miles from Vancouver to New York (via Mount Rushmore and Niagara Falls) in 5 days, and rode the Beast to the shipping agents near JFK airport. Dropping her off, I was soon back at my mate Blackhead's place where we spent the next week or so finishing off his lawn. We had to rotavate, prepare & seed about half an acre, including shovelling 25 tonnes of top soil, before prepping and seeding. It was a bit of a shock to the system when I'd just sat on my arse for the last year! I also had the usual stuff to be getting on with like Fast Bikes article, vids, a few internet enquiries about the trip, and final arrangements for the shipping and homecoming. I met Chris' neighbours Pat & Sheryll again, who'd been avidly following the trip as well! It was great to meet them, both very genuine and welcoming people who are the life and soul of ANY party, and I can't wait to see you all again the next time I get Stateside.

And that was that, countries number 52 & 53

CHAPTER 26
IRELAND, ISLE of MAN TT, & HOME

The last section of the trip took me from Dublin in Ireland, up through the biking mecca that is Northern Ireland, across to the Isle of Man for the TT, then across to the mainland and down to London, ending the trip of my dreams back at the Cenotaph where I started way back on the 1st October 2012. What the future holds, I've no idea, but first things first...

26.1 - Day 383: Dublin, Ireland Country #54

I left the USA on the 25th May 2014 and arrived at 'God early' o'clock in Dublin the following day. After making my way into the city centre from the airport, I headed straight to O'Sheas Merchant Temple Bar pub, where I had a room booked above. Unfortunately it was still too early to get in, so I went for a wee wander.

I've been to Dublin a few times previously for the rugby, but never got much further than 'Temple Bar'. 5 days of nothing but Guinness plays havoc with your memory, and guts, so it was quite refreshing to just stroll through the streets in the early morning, breathing in the air and getting used to be being on home soil again – well almost.

Top of most folks lists when visiting Dublin is the Guinness Factory, so with a few hours to kill I made my way there, arriving just as they opened up, literally. If you've ever waited at the door of a pub for it to open, then you can visualise the look on the face of the girl who opened the storehouse door that day. Met by a bearded fat bloke who hadn't slept in 2 days, wearing clothes that he'd carried around the world for the last 14 months, I'm surprised she even let me in! But she did, and for that I'll always love her.

Bruce SMART

If you've never been to the Guinness Storehouse then it's well worth the trip, if only to see the home of this truly global brand. The place is enormous, the history and tradition surrounding it's existence equally as immense. Even if you don't like the 'black stuff', you can't help but be drawn in by the whole process of its production. It really is an art form, and once you've appreciated that, then there's even a bar on the roof that gives you a free pint!

Being Scottish I couldn't turn down free beer, even mid-morning, so suitably refreshed I wandered back to my pub and got checked in. That first day I managed to last until about 3pm before I just crashed out and slept until the following day. Waking early I got to work on the usual - episode 14 of the trip series, as well as the next Fast Bikes article, and started the USA blog too. Towards the end of my 4 day lay over, I met up with some folks who'd been following the trip as they kindly offered to show me some nightlife.

I bumped into Bernie O'Reilly & Anthony Jameson in the car park of the 12 Apostles in Australia. We'd had a long chat and they'd mentioned they lived in Dublin, so dropped me a line to meet up for a beer. Andy O'Hare had been following on facebook and it turns out we have a mutual friend in common, Micky Peers who I work with. Not only that, but Andy and Mick used to be in the RAF and were stationed together at RAF Buchan, up in the Northeast of Scotland. What's more, I used to play rugby for my local town of Peterhead, and we often played RAF Buchan, so would've played against Andy back in the day! Small world eh. Needless to say, we all had a top night, and it ended somewhat drunken, with Andy and I exploring the delights of Temple Bar. Irish hospitality is a joy to experience, but usually comes with a penance in the form of a 3 day hangover! Andy, Anthony and Bernie, it was an absolute pleasure to meet up with you all, thanks so much for taking the time to entertain a complete stranger. There's always an open door here when you're in these parts.

I awoke the following morning in an instant, sitting bolt upright, still in my clothes from the night before, thundering head and a mouth that felt like the beer monkey had not only crapped in it, but rolled around in there too! What's more, I was supposed to be at the shipping agents in half an hour to pick up the Beast, before riding to 'Cotter Motorcycles' for a service and new tyres, then head up to Cavan near the border with Northern Ireland. Not my best plan of action then, to get completely wazzucked the night before!

Thankfully I didn't have much to pack so was soon at the shipping yard, facing my first major obstacle of the day. The Beast had been completely boxed up in a solid wooden crate, and neither the yard nor I had any tools to open it. Normally I crate the bike in a metal basic frame, before it's wrapped in layers of clingfilm. Nice and light and easy to open, and as it normally flies, protection is not too much of an issue.

But, the shipping agents in New York had done a thorough job here, so armed with a hammer, I set about smacking the proverbial out of it to get at the Beast. An hour or so later and I was finally able to get at my tank bag where I keep my tools, then set about dismantling the rest of the crate. Unfortunately the battery had gone flat so I then had to push her up and down the courtyard in full leathers until she fired into life once more, and soon was on the way to 'Cotters Motorcycles' (www.cottermc.com), a few hours late and soaked in beer sweats.

Simon and Steve run the kind of dealership I love. Their enthusiasm and knowledge of the sport is awesome, their attention to customer care and satisfaction an attribute that is hard to find in today's biking market place. Despite me being more than a few hours late, they welcomed me in, armed me with a brew and got to work on the bike. Whilst there I also met Tony Toner, a whirlwind of a man and the chief 'who's who' in the Irish motorcycle world. Tony interviewed me for his mag, 'Bike buyers Guide' and we spent a good few hours just nattering away.

Tony is your typical Irishman, 2hrs in his company goes by in a blur of laughs, quips, stories and general pisstake. I came away from our chat with aching jaw muscles and tears of laughter in my eyes, he's a complete star and joy to be with. He very kindly invited the Beast & I over for the Irish Motorcycle Show in March 2015, so if you read this in time, come and say hi and I'll introduce you.

Before I knew it, it was after 6pm, the Beast was serviced and complete with a new set of excellent Bridgestone BATTLAX T30's. After a few pics with the lads, I fired North to meet up with an old friend in Cavan. A huge thanks to Simon and Steve at www.cottermc.com for their kindness, generosity, and excellent service. If I lived in Dublin they'd surely be the choice place for me to get my bikes serviced, 100% professional and great customer care. Top job lads.

26.2 - Cavan, Ireland

Do you remember Ferghal Donohoe, the Irish chap I stayed with when I first got to Sydney? I stayed with him, his wife Clodagh & their wee lad Riley for a few days and had a great craic. Wouldn't you know it, but he was only over in Ireland to watch the Northwest 100 and the TT. Unfortunately his dad had fallen ill, so he invited me to come and visit at his parental hometown of Cavan. Biker's the world over, true bikers, are a very special breed of people and their common traits of openness, friendliness and genuineness are a beautiful thing to experience. Countless times I've been bowled over how complete strangers have invited me into their lives, often becoming good friends in a very short space of time. Ferg is one of those folks, but enough blowing smoke up his arse!

Arriving in Cavan, I was soon sitting at his parental kitchen table, beer in one hand, steak in another. People seem to know me very well. After eventually getting his wee lad Riley off to bed, we popped down his local for a quick pint and a natter. 4am, we crawled up the hill and passed out!

The next morning we stopped by his brother Adrian's studio as he wanted to take a few pics of yours truly – I think some neighborhood kids needing scaring off? As you can see from the picture, if anyone can make me look half respectable, they've got a real talent, and Adrian sure does. Like his brother, it was an absolute pleasure to meet Adrian and share a few Guinness' with him the previous night.

Next we had a quick stop over at the local 'Castlemanor Care Home', where the lads' father, Paddy, was recuperating after a recent illness. I got a chance to meet the man, and can see why he has such a cracking family, it was a pleasure to meet you Sir.

26.3 - Day 387: Northern Ireland

After a wee chat with the residents, I said my farewells to everyone and hit the road north once more. Ballymoney in Northern Ireland was my next stop, the home of the legendary Dunlop family. On the way I rode some brilliant roads, the likes of those included in the Cookstown 100 and other Irish Road Racing. They're similar to the back roads I remember from the North East of Scotland, beautifully twisty in places, open and barren in others, but generally not the type of places you'd expect to see motorbikes topping out at 200 miles an hour!

Arriving in the wee town of Ballymoney, I quickly found 'Joeys Bar' down next to the railway station. It's a small unassuming place, a few benches outside and the sign above with Joey in his leathers and his famous yellow lid either side. Step inside and you're enveloped in a biking dynasty, newspaper clippings, photos, trophies, helmets, leathers, even bikes adorn the walls. Everywhere you look is dedicated to Joey and Robert, and all their incredible achievements. I got chatting to the lady behind the bar after buying a few of the pin badges for the lads back home. Straight away she began asking about the bike, why I had all the stickers and luggage, and why it was so battered! Telling her about my trip, her eyes lit up and in an instant she was on the phone telling people all about it. Soon enough a couple of other lads rocked up and I was telling them all about it. Like everywhere in the world, bikers are a brilliant bunch of folk, I never tire of their company, it's a wee clique of fellow obsessed maniacs, I'm right at home!

I found out later that that lady behind the bar was Linda, Joey's wife! A beautifully kind woman who made me feel very welcome in her bar. I look forward to going back one day.

26.4 – The Giants' Causeway

A short time later I was hiking down a path to the incredible Giant's Causeway on the northern coastline, somewhere I've always wanted to visit and it didn't disappoint. The natural formation of basalt rocks appear eerily man-made as they slide down the shore into the sea, step by step, row by row. There's a story that goes behind the formation, and it goes along something like this:

An Irish giant named Finn MacCool was challenged to a fight by a Scottish giant called Benandonner. Finn built the causeway across the seas to Scotland, but as he reached Scottish shores he spied Benandonner and realised he was much bigger than him. He fled back to Ireland but was followed later by Benandonner who followed Finn to his home. Finn's wife Oonagh disguised him as a baby, tucking him into a cot. When Benandonner saw the size of the baby in the cot, he fled in terror back to Scotland, believing that the father must be some super giant, destroying the causeway behind him.

The Giant's Causeway in Northern Ireland is an amazing thing to see in person. You could spend hours just wandering over the rocks, looking at all the different formations. (Maybe it was just the geologist in me?)

If you're ever in this neck of the woods, it's well worth a visit, and the roads to get there will bring a huge grin to your face too. After that I headed to Belfast for the weekend, where I'd be getting the ferry over to the Isle of Man in a few days time. But for now, beer once again was calling as I stayed with an old friend from Uni for the weekend.

I have to say, I loved my time in Ireland. It's a fantastic country with fantastic, welcoming, funny and friendly people. It's only across the water from our own shores here in Blighty, yet possesses some of the greatest roads you could ever wish to propel yourself down on two wheels and an engine! Get off your arse, get the ferry booked, and get over there, you seriously won't be disappointed. I'll certainly be heading that way as soon as I can, and will look at a regular tour there in the future. See you on the road folks, we'll get the craic!

26.5 - Day 389: The Isle of Man TT

Sunday arrived and I headed down to the Steam Packet port, boarding my ferry for the Isle of Man TT. My earliest recollection of bikes is seeing the TT on the telly many years ago, names and bikes I knew nothing about, yet in later years I discovered these people where the legends of old. Since passing my bike test the TT had been on my 'list' but I'd never bit the bullet and gone for it. What better time then than on my homeward leg of a trip of a lifetime.

I booked my ferry way back last August when I was in South Korea, it's mega easy, just find your chosen crossing at www.steam-packet.com and book it. You only pay a £40 deposit (this has now changed) and that's that until about a few months before your crossing, lovely job. All you need to do then is secure your accommodation, but unless you do it at least a year in advance, or know someone on the island, you'll probably be limited to camping.

The crossing itself is only a few hours and it was great to meet a few folks who'd been following the trip, thanks very much to all those who came over to say hi. Arriving at the port of Douglas, I rolled off onto the dock in a great queue of bikes, only to be met by a woman waiving her arms and shouting my name! I could get used to this.

Tracey Wheeler had been following the trip for a while and was setting off on her own adventure later that year to ride solo to Romania for charity.

After saying hello to Tracey, her other half Darren, and her mates, my Mrs Nikki wandered over in the rain. She'd arrived earlier that morning and would be staying with me until the 11th. Tracey very kindly gave Nikki a run up the road to the campsite on the back of her bike. Believe it or not, it's the first time she's been on the back of a road bike, I've never taken her out on the bike before!

Nikki had found St Georges Campsite (www.stgeorgesafc.co.uk), right on Glencrutchery Road, just minutes from the main grandstand and start/finish line. It's a great place to stay if you're camping, there's a bar and chip wagon on site – I could stop there really eh, and plenty of showers and toilets too. The main paddock is just over the football pitches, with the main beer tents and merchandise stalls all located there too. Only issue is if you

Bruce SMART

want to head into Douglas, the walk back up to the top of the hill at the end of the night will give you thighs like Bradley Wiggins!

I'd arrived too late to participate in the Simon Andrews tribute lap on Mad Sunday, which I was gutted about but it couldn't be helped. The man got a fantastic turn out and it was great to see so many people showing their respects to Simon and his family in our own way. Well done to all involved.

Monday arrived and it was time to watch the 1st race of the Supersports, so Nikki and I wandered down to the bottom of Bray Hill to take our first view of the TT action. Standing in amongst the crowd, you're right on the edge of the road, stone walls and solid buildings all around. You hear the fantastic Manx TT radio commentary announce the first rider is off, then the distant scream of inline four begins to envelope your very being. It gathers momentum like a herd of wailing banshee's as the speed hits fever pitch. The bikes literally fly down the incredibly steep Bray Hill, screaming passed you in a blink of an eye, the air almost 'popping' as their pressure wave hits you. In an instant they're gone and off into the distance up the hill. It's incredible to witness first hand, nothing can prepare you for the speed, the excitement, the nervous tension you feel as you realise that if they crash, you'll probably witness the end of a life here. That's the realities of this race in many places, but that's what makes it what it is.

Unfortunately, yet again the course claimed another soul in this very race. 65 year old Bob Price died instantly when he crashed on the third lap at Ballaugh Bridge. Sleep well brother.

That night a mate of mine was in town so we popped into Douglas to meet up for a few beers. Bob Collins needs no introduction to those in the industry, he's practically a living legend and a great lad too. We met through a mutual friend a few years ago and as he works down at FWR Tyres (www.fwr.co.uk) I've got to know him since. Mad as a box of frogs, with the kind of skill and expertise on a bike that should warrant his place on the BSB grid at the very least, Bob is a whirlwind of a character to be around, particularly when there's booze involved, but also a cracking bloke too.

As usual the weather plays a huge factor in the scheduling of the races during the TT race week. The Superstock TT had to be postponed to the following day, so we went to Ramsey to watch it from another viewpoint. Standing at Parliament Square you can see the bikes thundering into the town down the straight from Milntown. They brake incredibly hard, back ends sliding out at times, before slamming it right then left around the pubs, folks literally feet from them with pints in their hands, cheering aloud. It's an incredible atmosphere and spectacle, almost magical at times. Josh Brookes in particular seemed to lap this section up, visibly faster than most others through this section, his short circuit pedigree and basic ball size coming to the fore!

After the Superstock race we moved along to the Ramsey Hairpin for the next races, but unfortunately the rain came in and ended play for the day. Heading back to Douglas on the electric railway, the news came in of another rider lost on the course. All passings are sad, the loss of a life has a huge impact on all those involved. But the loss of Karl 'Bomber' Harris hit the racing world particularly hard. I never knew the man, but all those who did had nothing but kind and emphatic words to say of him. Karl lost his life during the 2nd lap of the Superstock race at Joey's Corner. Sleep well brother.

As the racers themselves say, 'Life goes on', and so it should. It's all part of road racing, it's what makes it the spectacle and addictive sport it is. If we sanitised these events, the way a sector of the media and a branch of the public who don't understand the sport want, then we'd lose not only a fantastic spectator sport, but also the riders themselves. Each of them, men and women, who come to ride the TT and other road races in Ireland know the risks involved. For some that adds to the thrill, for others it's what makes them tick.

Such is the nature of the beast, life and racing goes on, and we spent the next couple of days watching the races at various points along the 37.5 mile course. Of note for me was Governors, another cracking view point as the machines brake hard for the roundabout before diving into an incredibly tight right hand corner and accelerating hard away.

Bruce SMART

Senior race day on the Friday came quickly, and awakening that morning in the campsite you could feel something different in the air. I can't put it into words but the Senior felt different to every other day I was there. There's an excitement, apprehension and tension in the air as soon as you wake up, the buzz is palatable.

Nikki and I headed up to the 'Bungalow' to watch the Senior TT. You hear the bikes from miles away as they round the Gooseneck and begin the mountain climb, the appearance of the helicopter on the horizon betraying their imminent arrival. As they scream over the Veranda, they soon sweep around Graham Memorial and passed you at the Bungalow, knees scraping before they accelerate hard down Hailwood Rise towards Brandywell. Absolutely awesome, the crowd is full of grinning maniacs everywhere you glance!

With Michael Dunlop practically annihilating everyone else throughout the week, Nikki and I booked our tickets to watch the new film 'Road' about this inspirational road racing family. All I can say is, if you've not yet seen it, do everything you can to experience this epic film, an emotional roller coaster that'll have you breathing hard at times. In fact when the lights came up in Douglas, there wasn't a dry eye in the house, people just sat in their chairs for a few seconds, trying to take in the cinematic masterpiece they'd just sat through. I loved it, 5/5.

26.6 - Day 396: Marco Simoncelli Tribute Ride

I also had the opportunity to attend the Marco Simoncelli tribute lap the Sunday following the TT. Organised by a great chap called Craig Brinkley, the whole event was to remember Sic, but also to raise funds for his foundation through donations. I'd never ridden the TT course before, and this year the mountain section had been left one-way for the duration of the TT, allowing ample time to sample this biking mecca. After joining everyone for the tribute lap and a spot of lunch at Creg-Ny-Baa, I soon went off to have a go by myself for a few laps. Ab-So-Lutely magic, epic, superb, and any other superlative you can throw in there. Until you actually ride the course, you just can't appreciate how technical some parts are, especially at almost 200mph! And bumpy too! Even at a sedate 50mph (the posted speed limit in sections) you're still being bucked about your seat by some of the undulations along the way. How these riders do it with an average speed of up to 132mph is almost beyond comprehension. Then we come to the mountain section. Holy Jehovah, that is a stretch of tarmac that any biker in the world would fall in love with.

So that was that, TT 2014 all over and done with. It'd been something I'd wanted to see and experience first hand since I was a kid watching the heroes of old tackle the course. If I had the talent and cash I'd even love to try my hand at it one day, but for now I'll settle for simply experiencing it with the annual pilgrimages who flock here year on year. It really is something special, something unique and something that should never be tamed, watered down or interfered with. For those who want to go but have as yet never done it, do it, just do it folks. If you've ever had the inclination to visit for the TT, just get your ferry booked and do it. I'll see you there one day.

Our ferry back to Liverpool wasn't until the 11th so Nikki and I had a few days to explore a bit more around the island. Taking the steam train down to Castletown, we just wandered through this beautiful wee village, stopping in the various shops and grabbing a few brews along the way. As luck would have it, we were able to get a place on an earlier ferry on the 10th so were soon packed up and sailing back to the mainland.

I've got to say a huge thank you to everyone who came up for a chat during the TT. It was great to hear how you'd all been following the trip and I'm glad you've all enjoyed following the trip as much as me. Many of you told me of your own dreams to one day travel on a bike, and I meant it when I said, 'just do it'. The hardest part really is just setting off, after that you're just riding your bike and dealing with whatever comes your way. (By the way, to whoever kindly stole my Kriega tank bag at the campsite, you're no biker. You're a C&^k.)

CHAPTER 27

ENGLAND, HEADING HOME

Back on the mainland, Nikki and I once again went our separate ways, although this time only for a few days. I headed to Coventry where I'd be visiting the HQ of my sponsor 'Delta Energy Services'. I'd last been there when I restarted the trip back in May 2013, so it was weird to now be back there having almost finished it. The feelings were really starting to gather now, a mixture of relief and satisfaction that I'd done it, but also slight remorse that this dream would soon end and the realities of day-to-day life would soon be once again upon me.

I simply couldn't have done it without Delta's support. After the 1st attempt it was going to take me a few years to save up enough to go again, their sponsorship and subsequent support allowed me to go again immediately. Their support along the way, and drive to secure further finances, kept me on the road and allowed me to live out my dream and keep a promise. For that I'll always be thankful to Bob and Martin for everything they've done.

They'd very kindly put me up in a hotel for my last night on the trip, and Bob, Luigi and a few lads met me for dinner and a few beers that evening. I've got to admit, I was a bit numb to it all, not quite ready to admit this was the end of a dream, not quite ready to stop rolling on from day to day. I'd missed my Mrs, family and friends whilst on the road, I'd missed the normality of everyday life as I used to know it. But there was no escaping the fact I'd changed since leaving all that time ago, I wasn't the person I was when I left, but even after all this time alone with my thoughts, I'd still no idea who I actually was?

Bruce SMART

Martin, Lee and Kev from Delta, as well as Luigi from Bridgestone all met me at the hotel the morning of the 12th. We rode the back roads to Silverstone, meeting up with Rootsy, the editor of Fast Bikes Magazine, and a load of others who'd kindly taken the time to join me for the run home. My old flat mate from Uni, Walshy, even rocked up on a wee hired 50cc moped. He'd only just passed his CBT, specifically so he could join me for the ride home, it was brilliant to see the wee bugger again.

We set off as planned at 11am and took the back roads south to Aylesbury, all the while trying to keep the speed sedate so Walshy could keep up. Unfortunately by the time we hit the fuel stop in Aylesbury, he was nowhere to be seen, so after a brief wait, we hit the road to London along the A41.

This is the road I ride everyday into work from Nikki's place to Central London. These roads were the paths to the mundane, the boring lifeless day-to-day life I worked so hard to escape from. Yet here I was full circle, ending my days of living the dream along the very same roads, and it made me wonder if it was all actually a dream? Had I just done this, had I actually just ridden my bike around the world, seeing sights you only ever see in books, met folks you only ever read about, lived an adventure as good as the rest?

Soon we were in the grind that is central London traffic, and the task of keeping around 15 bikes together was proving near impossible. Eventually it just became every rider for themselves as we filtered, jumped, and pushed our way through. Soon enough, we were riding up Whitehall from Parliament Square, the Cenotaph standing tall and proud before me. As I pulled up in front of this beautiful monument, it still hadn't quite hit me that this was it. Across the road I saw Nikki and my son Ellis, as well as a host of other friends who'd taken the time to come along. Hugging them each hello, I was home and it felt great, but it didn't feel like home anymore? Anyhow, to the bar we went! My mate Walshy eventually arrived on his moped about 30minutes after everyone else and got a bigger round of applause than I did! Great work bud, you're a legend.

So that's that then. 442 days, 73,987 miles through 54 countries, and so far it had raised around £10,000 for my selected charities. It was nowhere near my target of £70,000 but my plan is to donate a percentage of the profits from each sale of the book and DVD, so hopefully this total will go up even more.

I started back at work on the 21st July, instantly it felt like I'd never been away. I've never hidden the fact that I'm not happy in my job, but bills need paying and that's just life. Already the restrictions started, you can't say this, can't go here, shouldn't do this and that. I'm just not the same person I was, perhaps I've been out of 'real' life for too long, but I know there's so much more out there now.

So what next? In the immediate future I have to repay a lot of people. I've got credit cards and overdrafts to clear, favours and goodwill to replenish. Now there's a wedding to organise and pay for, as well as the prospect of buying and setting up a home together with Nikki.

Unfortunately it turns out I developed a heart condition whilst away and so have a few health issues that need sorting out quite sharpish. Hopefully it's nothing serious, but the majority of 2015 is going to be written off work wise as I'm put on restricted duties. I've no overriding urge to bugger off on another huge global trip again yet, but there are certainly places I never got to that will need exploring one day.

One thing is for sure though, being away I've realised what we have right here on our doorstep in the UK and Europe for biking. We have most of the best biking roads in the world, some of the most spectacular scenery and places to visit, and fantastic and welcoming communities. I've got a real urge to explore so much more of what is on offer around me now, to just get on my bike and go exploring for a few days or a week or so. Literally anyone can do that, so I've got a few plans up my sleeve and will let you know all about it at a later date.

I can't thank everyone for all their help along the way, I hope I thanked you in person at the very least. So this is a general 'Thank you very much' to all of you out there, to those who helped me get this up and running all those years ago, those who helped me at the side of the road, opened up their homes and lives to me, got involved through the social media, and those who even came up to me in the street to say hello. You're all what makes life so good, bikers or not, don't ever lose that. Thank you.

Take it easy, enjoy whatever you're doing, but remember,

LIVE your life!

Me

My Dad, Me & Mum - the inspiration for the whole trip

From left clockwise: Woody 'helping' at one of the many events we attended; Nikki guarding the cash box & running the London marathon dressed as a teabag!; Turner adopting his favourite role; The initial route; The Beast being wrapped; All done & ready for the off! Si Clare who designed the TeapotOne logo & typeset;

APPENDIX
THE TRIP IN PICS

From top left: Ready for the off; full police escort from the Cenotaph; wet already at Dover; Normandy beaches in France; Omaha Beach; the US graves atop Omaha Beach; quick cuppa; first of the motoGP circuits - Assen;

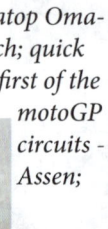

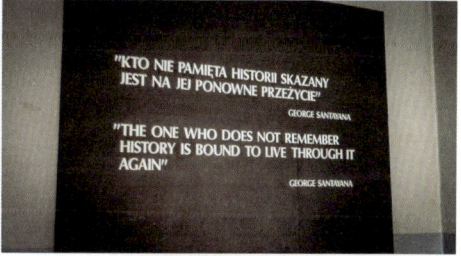

From top left: Germany - Nurburgring & Sachsenring; Auschwitz - 'Works Sets You Free', the guard hut on the parade square where SS guards watched prisoners freeze to death, "The One Who Does Not Remember History Is Bound To Live Through It Again"; Salzburg - home of Mozart, most beautiful McDonalds in the world, the bridge of love; Brno - another pic in front of a motoGP circuit sign, as close as I could get!

From top left: Beautiful Austria; Lake Garda, Italy; Misano Marco Simoncelli Circuit; Got to love Italian place names; Central Spain; Jerez circuit; Gibraltar, 5th Rosia Battery where Nelson's body was brought ashore after the Battle of Trafalgar; Me with Mr Gibraltar, Mr Solomon Levy M.B.E, former Mayor of Gibraltar.

From top left row: Hassan II Mosque, Casablanca, Morocco; Casablance Waterfront, Morocco; Stone City Walls of Marrakesh, Morocco; The beautiful Atlas Mountains, Morocco; (inset) You really don't want to have an off here - Atlas Mountains, Morocco; Ait Benhaddou is an ancient Ksar on the edge of the Sahara, Morocco; Camping in the Sahara, Western Sahara; The Sahara Desert, Western Sahara; Wild Camel, Mauritania; (inset)1st sub-frame break, Mauritania; Robert, he saved my life, Senegal.

From top-right clockwise: Back at the Cenotaph for round 2; Raymondo (google 'Wandering Waltons') at Squires Cafe; Fireblade forum www.1000rr.co.uk lads let me join them for the Scotland leg; John O'Groats, Scotland; Getting wet in Glencoe, Scotland; Lands End, England. Next stop, Fokestone & over the Channel - again!

From top-left clockwise: Bridge between Sweden & Norway, near Halden; Harbour port in Stavanger, Norway; Meeting Ole Bang from Delta's Norway office; The Legendary Trollstigen, or 'Troll's Road'; Norway is just stunning; Camping on the road; (inset) 5-star living; Beautiful Fjords around Brekkestranda

Top-left clockwise: Top of the Trollstigen; The famous hump-back bridge along the Atlantic Road, Norway; Me & Emil Larsen, Norway; The Arctic Circle Raceway; Karina, Tom & Andreas, Norway; Some stunning views, Norway; Nordkapp, top of Europe.

Top-left clockwise: Sights of Helsinki with Scott; (inset-Cranes nest everywhere from Estonia Southward); Joey Dunlop's memorial in Tallinn, Estonia; Hungarian 'border'; Transfagarasan Highway, Romania; 'The Golden Gate' Kyiv, Ukraine.

From top left: Ukraine into Russia; St Basil's Cathedral, Moscow; famous GUM department store, Moscow; inside GUM; meeting Vladimir Zdorov - editor of Motorpebio, biggest bike mag in Russia; the Kremlin, Moscow; (inset) traditional Russian food - salted vegetables washed down with vodka;

top-left: Beast goes for a check-up; Ali Albetkov was my guide in Moscow; Biker spirit alive & well as I snap the subframe again; Camping wild; The Cherapanov Family in Novosibirsk, Russia; Max, me, & Gennady; The Syuyumbike Tower, Kazan;

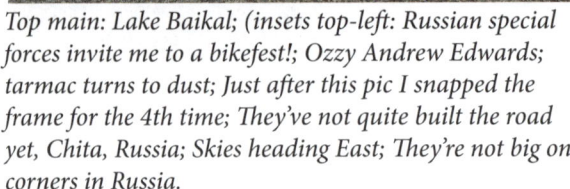

Top main: Lake Baikal; (insets top-left: Russian special forces invite me to a bikefest!; Ozzy Andrew Edwards; tarmac turns to dust; Just after this pic I snapped the frame for the 4th time; They've not quite built the road yet, Chita, Russia; Skies heading East; They're not big on corners in Russia.

Top main: Hard going in parts of Russia; Top-left: Camping rough in the Zilov-gap; inset-right: North to Magadan or East to Vladivostok?; 1058 miles until next turn! Bottom main: Beautiful view over Vladivostok; inset-top: Carlos & Phil, top lads I met in the hostel in Vladivostok; inset-right: the Beast waits at the dock as I head to South Korea.

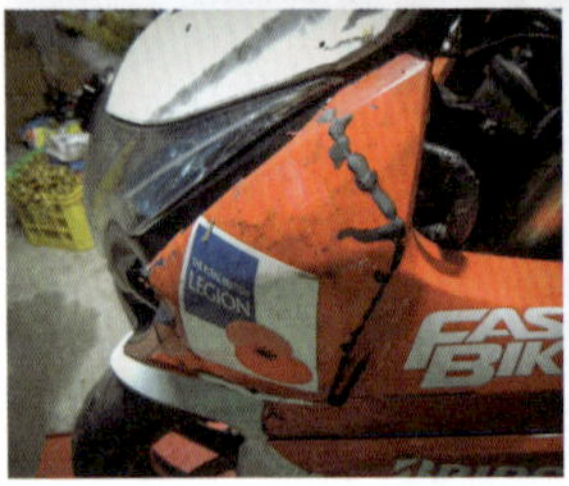

Top main: Mount Osorezan, Japan; (Inset-left: Work is needed; Inset-right: Hiroshima, Japan); above: the brilliant Pete Wilkinson fixes my mess, cheers mate; below: a few pics from the rest of my time in Japan, awesome place & great folks.

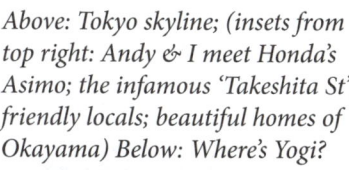

Above: Tokyo skyline; (insets from top right: Andy & I meet Honda's Asimo; the infamous 'Takeshita St'; friendly locals; beautiful homes of Okayama) Below: Where's Yogi?

This page: Thailand; Opposite page: Thailand, Malaysia, Laos

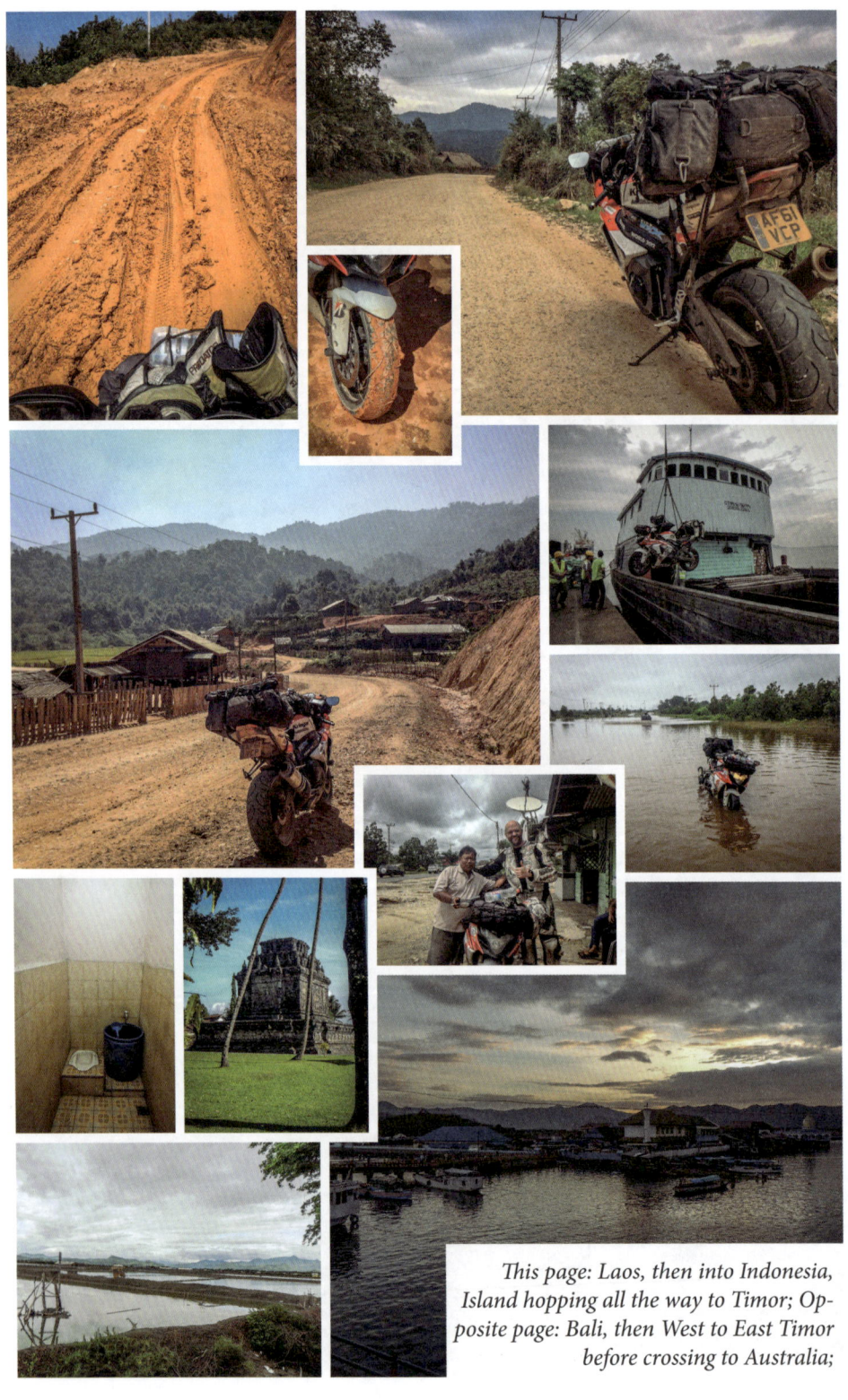

This page: Laos, then into Indonesia, Island hopping all the way to Timor; Opposite page: Bali, then West to East Timor before crossing to Australia;

This page: Following the Pan-American Highway North from Chile, through Peru, Ecuador & Columbia, before crossing the Darien Gap to Panama & Costa Rica:

Opp-page: Australia;

The amazing Mexico, completely opposite of what it's portrayed in the media. The people are incredibly warm & friendly, the country a mix of modern & traditional. Go & see!

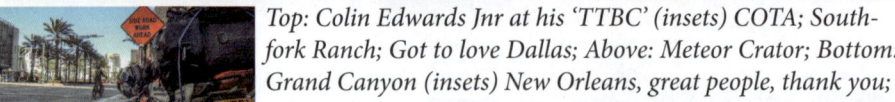

Top: Colin Edwards Jnr at his 'TTBC' (insets) COTA; Southfork Ranch; Got to love Dallas; Above: Meteor Crator; Bottom: Grand Canyon (insets) New Orleans, great people, thank you;

Top: my sponsor, des-global.com in Houston; Barber Motorsports Museum; Jon & Bonnie Wilkens invited me to stay in Georgia, Jon even serviced the Beast before taking me to the 'Tail of the Dragon', awesome.

It was a rapid ride down to Key West, Florida before heading to NYC & Boston to see Nikki & get engaged! Then it was North to Canada, where the temp hit -38oC with windchill!

Above top-left & right insets: British Columbia, the 'real' Canada; Above left & right: View of Vancouver Bay, Boastie & Kirsten; Left: 'Empty Sky' 911 Memorial, NYC; Below: View of Manhattan skyline; Left inset: Niagra Falls, Right inset: Mount Rushmore.

Opposite page Top: Giant's Causeway, N.Ireland; (insets top-left: Guinness factory, Dublin; top-right: 'Cotters Motorcycles', Dublin, Quality customer service; bottom-left: Joey's Bar, Ballymoney, N.Ireland, bottom-right: Ferry to Isle of Man, Belfast, N.Ireland.) Bottom: Start/finish of TT course, Douglas; (insets top-left: Creg-Ny-Baa; Joey's Memorial on the 'Mountain'; The hustle of the start line;) (insets bottom-left: Mountain course; William Dunlop at 'the bungalow'; Bruce Anstey;) This page top: Views of Castletown, Isle of Man; This page bottom: Outside Delta's UK HQ (inset: the Delta team); Meeting mates at Silverstone for the final ride home; After 442 days, 74K miles & 54 countries I finally get back to the start line, Cenotaph, UK. Thanks to everyone for all your support. Job done!

the quality quarterly
dedicated to
motorcycle travel

available worldwide or online
www.overlandmag.com